CW01510965

Bearing Light: Flame Relays and the Struggle for the Olympic Movement

In recent decades, five to ten times as many persons have turned out for the Olympic flame relay as have watched Olympic sports contests live. *Bearing Light: Flame Relays and the Struggle for the Olympic Movement*, the first anthropological analysis of the contemporary torch relay, exposes and interprets the transformation of the ritual across a 25-year period, from Los Angeles 1984 through the IOC's 2009 announcement that, in the aftermath of the politically contentious Beijing performance, there will be no more global relays. This volume offers a rare case study of continuity and change in a leading transnational and trans-cultural ritual form.

Through data publicly revealed for the first time, the reader is carried fully backstage and into the conflicts and negotiations among Olympic organizing committees, the Greek Olympic movement, national governments, and transnational actors like the IOC, commercial sponsors, and operations management firms. Readers will come to know the leading flame relay authorities and practitioners, gaining a deeper understanding of the Olympic managerial revolution with its characteristic 'world's best practice' language. Analysis of the transnational flow of Olympic operations management offers important corrections to much existing globalization theory by demonstrating both how powerful and how culturally and politically parochial world's best practices can turn out to be. The dialectic between the cultural performance genres of ritual and spectacle provides a further intellectual architecture for these studies posing the question of whether the Olympic Movement will be able to survive the successes of the Olympic Sports Industry.

This book was previously published as a special issue of *Sport in Society*.

John J. MacAloon is Professor and Academic Associate Dean in the Social Sciences Graduate Division and Professor in The College at The University of Chicago. His anthropological and historical studies of the modern Olympic Movement and Olympic Games have earned a global reputation. He was an executive member of the International Olympic Committee 2000 Reform Commission and has advised many Olympic bid and organizing committees and National Olympic Committees.

Bearing Light: Flame Relays and the Struggle for the Olympic Movement

Edited by
John J. MacAloon

Routledge
Taylor & Francis Group

LONDON AND NEW YORK

First published 2013
by Routledge
2 Park Square, Milton Park, Abingdon, Oxon, OX14 4RN

Simultaneously published in the USA and Canada
by Routledge
711 Third Avenue, New York, NY 10017

Routledge is an imprint of the Taylor & Francis Group, an informa business

© 2013 Taylor & Francis

This book is a reproduction of *Sport in Society*, vol. 15, issue 5. The Publisher requests to those authors who may be citing this book to state, also, the bibliographical details of the special issue on which the book was based.

All rights reserved. No part of this book may be reprinted or reproduced or utilised in any form or by any electronic, mechanical, or other means, now known or hereafter invented, including photocopying and recording, or in any information storage or retrieval system, without permission in writing from the publishers.

Trademark notice: Product or corporate names may be trademarks or registered trademarks, and are used only for identification and explanation without intent to infringe.

British Library Cataloguing in Publication Data
A catalogue record for this book is available from the British Library

ISBN13: 978-0-415-44832-1

Typeset in Times New Roman
by Taylor & Francis Books

Publisher's Note
The publisher would like to make readers aware that the chapters in this book may be referred to as articles as they are identical to the articles published in the special issue. The publisher accepts responsibility for any inconsistencies that may have arisen in the course of preparing this volume for print.

Printed and bound in Great Britain by the MPG Books Group

Contents

SPORT IN THE GLOBAL SOCIETY – CONTEMPORARY PERSPECTIVES

Series Editor: Boria Majumdar

BEARING LIGHT: FLAME RELAYS AND THE STRUGGLE FOR THE OLYMPIC MOVEMENT

Sport in the Global Society – Contemporary Perspectives
Series Editor: Boria Majumdar

The social, cultural (including media) and political study of sport is an expanding area of scholarship and related research. While this area has been well served by the *Sport in the Global Society* series, the surge in quality scholarship over the last few years has necessitated the creation of *Sport in the Global Society: Contemporary Perspectives*. The series will publish the work of leading scholars in fields as diverse as sociology, cultural studies, media studies, gender studies, cultural geography and history, political science and political economy. If the social and cultural study of sport is to receive the scholarly attention and readership it warrants, a cross-disciplinary series dedicated to taking sport beyond the narrow confines of physical education and sport science academic domains is necessary. *Sport in the Global Society: Contemporary Perspectives* will answer this need.

Titles in the Series

Forty Years of Sport and Social Change, 1968-2008
"To Remember is to Resist"
Edited by Russell Field and Bruce Kidd

Global Perspectives on Football in Africa
Visualising the Game
Edited by Susann Baller,
Giorgio Miescher and Raffaele Poli

Global Sport Business
Community Impacts of Commercial
Sport
Edited by Hans Westerbeek

Governance, Citizenship and the New
European Football Championships
The European Spectacle
Edited by Wolfram Manzenreiter and
Georg Spitaler

Indigenous People, Race Relations and
Australian Sport
Edited by Christopher J. Hallinan and
Barry Judd

Olympic Reform Ten Years Later
Edited by Heather Dichter and
Bruce Kidd

Perspectives on Sport and Music
Edited by Anthony Bateman

Reflections on Process Sociology and
Sport
'Walking the Line'
Joseph Maguire

Soccer in the Middle East
Edited by Issam Khalidi and Alon Raab

South Africa and the Global Game
Football, Apartheid and Beyond
Edited by Peter Alegi and
Chris Bolsmann

Sport – Race, Ethnicity and Identity
Building Global Understanding
Edited by Daryl Adair

Sport and the Community
Edited by Allan Edwards and
David Hassan

Sport, Culture and Identity in the State of
Israel
Edited by Yair Galily and
Amir Ben-Porat

Sport in Australian National Identity
Kicking Goals
Tony Ward

Sport in the City
Cultural Connections
Edited by Michael Sam and
John E. Hughson

Sport, Memory and Nationhood in Japan
Remembering the Glory Days
Edited by Andreas Niehaus and
Christian Tagsold

The Changing Face of Cricket
From Imperial to Global Game
Edited by Dominic Malcolm,
Jon Gemmell and Nalin Mehta

The Consumption and Representation of
Lifestyle Sports
Edited by Belinda Wheaton

The Containment of Soccer in Australia
Fencing Off the World Game
Edited by Christopher J. Hallinan and
John E. Hughson

The History of Motor Sport
A Case Study Analysis
Edited by David Hassan

The Making of Sporting Cultures
John E. Hughson

Routledge Online Studies on the Olympic and Paralympic Games Series

Routledge Online Studies on the *Olympic* and *Paralympic Games* (ROSO) is a unique learning resource, publishing scholarly and multidisciplinary research on the Games.

Aimed at academics, researchers, lecturers, students, authors, educators, athletes, coaches, journalists, Olympic and Paralympic centres, policy-makers, professionals and anyone with an interest in the Games, it aims to stimulate the production of new knowledge and facilitate dialogue and connections across disciplines.

ROSO contains over 1000 journal articles and book chapters, including handbooks and major reference works dating back to the 1960s on themes including: the media, education, gender, politics, governance, management, law, business, ethics, legacies, the environment, disability studies, athletic performance and history. ROSO's Managing Editor, Dr Vassil Girginov of Brunel University, UK, has curated the site thematically to enable users to search their areas of interest effortlessly.

Routledge has also commissioned over 40 new journal special issues across disciplines on Olympic and Paralympic Studies that will be unveiled on this innovative platform and published as books.

http://www.routledgeonlinestudies.com/

Titles in the Series

Citation Information

The chapters in this book were originally published in *Sport in Society*, volume 15, issue 5 (June 2012). When citing this material, please use the original page numbering for each article, as follows:

Chapter 1
Introduction: the Olympic Flame Relay. Local knowledges of a global ritual form
John J. MacAloon
Sport in Society, volume 15, issue 5 (June 2012) pp. 575-594

Chapter 2
This flame, our eyes: Greek/American/IOC relations, 1984–2002, an ethnographic memoir
John J. MacAloon
Sport in Society, volume 15, issue 5 (June 2012) pp. 595-635

Chapter 3
Olympic Flame Relay operations under a 'world's best practices' regime: a conversation with Steven McCarthy
John J. MacAloon
Sport in Society, volume 15, issue 5 (June 2012) pp. 636-673

Chapter 4
'My programme became very strict': a conversation with Athanassios Kritsinelis
John J. MacAloon
Sport in Society, volume 15, issue 5 (June 2012) pp. 674-699

Chapter 5
The 2004 International Relay: a Greek around the world with the Olympic Flame
Pinelopi B. Amelidou
Sport in Society, volume 15, issue 5 (June 2012) pp. 700-712

Chapter 6
Struggling to celebrate: management of the 2004 Olympic Flame Relay segment in Greece
Spiros Spiropoulos
Sport in Society, volume 15, issue 5 (June 2012) pp. 713-727

Chapter 7

American media, intercultural stories and the 2004 Olympic flame ceremonies
Marianthi Bumbaris Thanopoulos
Sport in Society, volume 15, issue 5 (June 2012) pp. 728-743

Chapter 8

Hybridity and subversion: the Olympic flame in India
Boria Majumdar and Nalin Mehta
Sport in Society, volume 15, issue 5 (June 2012) pp. 744-759

Introduction: the Olympic Flame Relay. Local knowledges of a global ritual form

John J. MacAloon

Social Sciences Division, The University of Chicago, Chicago, IL, USA

This article introduces and contextualizes an anthropological study of the Olympic Flame Relay across 25 years, from Los Angeles 1984 through the aftermath of Beijing, punctuated by the announcement by the International Olympic Committee Executive Board in March 2009, that there would be no more global relays. This extended ethnological research offers a rare case study of continuity and change in a leading transnational and transcultural ritual form. It also further exposes the managerial revolution, with its characteristic language of 'world's best practice,' that has succeeded the commercial revolution in international Olympic affairs. Analysis of the transnational flow of Olympic operations management offers important corrections to much existing globalization theory, demonstrating both how powerful and how culturally and politically parochial world's best practices can turn out to be. Finally, this extended case study offers a further development of the author's theoretical work on complex cultural performance systems, in particular the dialectic between the performative genres of ritual and spectacle that indexes the wider Olympic Movement's struggle to preserve itself from the successes of the Olympic sports industry.

Mise-en-scène

On 4 August 2008, during the International Olympic Committee (IOC) Session in Beijing, senior IOC member Richard Pound forcefully asserted that the global flame relay for the Beijing Games should never have taken place.[1] 'This came very close to being a disaster. The risks were obvious and should have been assessed more carefully. The result is that there was a crisis affecting the Games.' Only the diversion of attention caused by the Sichuan earthquake saved the Beijing Games, according to Pound, because after the international torch relay, 'many countries ... were in full boycott mode'. Pound demanded to know from the IOC leadership, how this global flame relay had ever been approved and its risks so poorly assessed.[2]

Among its several purposes, this volume offers a thorough answer to Pound's question. It will not be a simple answer. Even if the specific events of the 14 March 2009 uprising in Lhasa and the Chinese government's ensuing crackdown could ever have been anticipated, the IOC was already contractually, administratively and organizationally committed with certain international partners to a structure of Olympic Flame Relay (OFR) practices that had come into being across the 25 year period analysed in this volume.[3] In the first years of the twenty-first century, these behaviours became normalized as 'world's best practice' in the newly dominant managerial discourse of the IOC administration and in its instructions to Olympic Organizing Committees (OCOGs). Among other merits, this OFR model was believed to insure complete ritual security against all externalities.

Discrete events depend upon predetermined contexts; here, a structure of OFR practices that will be exposed for the first time in these pages, including the crucial backstage roles of transnational operations contractors and commercial sponsors whom neither Mr. Pound nor President Jacques Rogge mentioned in their public debate about the Beijing relay.

Contemporary globalization theory has overwhelmingly focused on political economy and especially multinational corporations, but even within these domains, it has paid scant attention to the field of operational management. In Olympic studies, we now have a substantial scholarship on the commercialization and the new organizational sociology of the Olympics,[4] but we have barely begun to analyse the transnational labour flows increasingly characteristic of Olympic Games production at all levels. These scholarly shortcomings are to a large extent a methodological artefact, in my judgment, and the ethnographic studies in this volume aim to help alleviate them.

In Beijing, Dick Pound's challenge was not a simple *post facto* response to the attacks on the 2008 OFR (Figure 1) in major cities around the world by pro-Tibet and human rights protesters against Chinese government policies. Indeed, as early as the 2003 IOC Session in Prague, the report of the Olympic Games Study Commission (OGSC) that Pound chaired contained an explicit recommendation that international torch relays not be permitted and that relays instead be confined to host countries of the Games. 'The Commission had noted the high costs of an international relay, the more complicated logistics, the political risks and the minimal benefits to be derived from "cameo" events in various countries.'[5] The OGSC's report was passed unanimously by the Session and, therefore, should have had the force of law in Olympic governance. Nevertheless, the IOC Executive Board under President Jacques Rogge and with the support of the IOC administration, most notably the Olympic Games Department and its Executive Director Gilbert Felli, subsequently permitted an international flame relay for Beijing. Either they chose to ignore the Session's 2003 action or else judged that the acceptance of the Beijing bid in 2000, a bid explicitly mandating an international relay, 'grandfathered' Beijing's plans against the Session's later resolution.[6] Pound complained directly to Rogge in a July 2008 memo that the latter rationale had no basis in the *Olympic Charter*. The Rogge administration itself had already announced that no global relays would be permitted for the Olympic Winter Games, and in the Beijing Session debate, Rogge countered that even the domestic relay for Torino had been briefly attacked (see Figure 2).[7]

Organizational and factional tensions among the IOC members and between the membership and the IOC's professional administrators were therefore deeply implicated in creating the context in which the contingent events of Beijing were occasioned and received by key stakeholders.[8] For social scientists, *histoire événementielle* is of interest chiefly as a means to shed light on such organizational and cultural structures and transformations of them, structures that in turn help to generate future events. In this volume, close analyses of the OFRs for Beijing 2008, Athens 2004, Atlanta 1996 and Los Angeles 1984, supplemented with fieldwork materials from Torino 2006, Sydney 2000, Lillehammer 1994, Barcelona 1992 and Seoul 1988, are deployed to this end. The OFR has long been an object of truly global awareness. These studies of its globalization as a ritual practice over the past quarter-century offer an opportunity not only to bring backstage operational practices into ethnographic light but also to help globalization theory overcome its admittedly inadequate treatment of indigenizing cultural forms and phenomena in deference to exogenously measurable political economic ones.[9]

Figure 1.   In the ancient Olympic stadium, the priestess delivers the 2008 Olympic flame to the first torchbearer on the relay to Beijing. Source: IOA.

Greeks, Americans and the 'world's best practice' model

The apparent success of the first global OFR for Athens 2004 – regional multinational relays having been held for Berlin 1936, London 1948, Tokyo 1964, Munich 1972 and Sydney 2000 – emboldened both the Chinese authorities and IOC administrators (who actually saw the 2004 relay firsthand only during its brief passage through their own

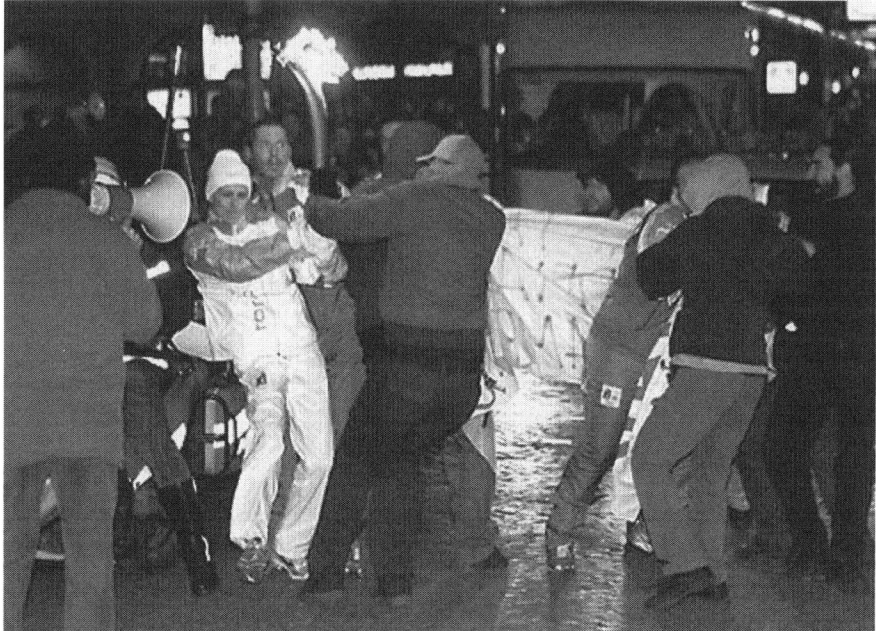

Figure 2.   Anti-globalization protestors attempt to seize the Olympic flame in Torino 2006. Source: TOROC.

cities). In fact, as the papers and most especially the extended interviews with Athanassios Kritisnelis and Steven McCarthy, the two most important figures in contemporary OFR history, will herein reveal, the 2004 OFR was an epic backstage struggle in both the planning and the execution phases. The protagonists were long-time guardians of Greek public and Hellenic Olympic Committee (HOC) official flame relay traditions and the transnational corporate agencies, commercial and operational, that were now able with IOC administrative support to present themselves as progressive providers of 'world's best practices' for all relays, regardless of their national cultural locations or potential intersections with local politics and transnational social movements.

In the end, the Athens Olympic Organizing Committee (ATHOC) leadership, with IOC encouragement, largely acceded to this new model, citing the competencies of non-Greek operators necessary to pull off their ambitious global OFR plan. This innovation was intended to reinforce in a spectacular way Greece's special importance in the Olympic Movement, while serving Greek pride and ambitions on a global stage. Because the project was so large, it was also very expensive. Therefore, corporate sponsors who had been pressuring the IOC and the Greek authorities for privileged access to the Athens flame relay would eventually be welcomed in at the 'presenting partner' level by ATHOC for both the global and domestic segments. Old-timers who had been through the flame relay battles of the past, wherein Greeks prided themselves as the sole bulwark against others' (notably American and IOC) commercial depredations against the purity of the Olympic flame, were shocked at the rapidity and thoroughness with which Coca-Cola and Samsung were allowed to insert themselves into the Greek OFR process.

As will be richly documented in these pages, Greek traditionalists within ATHOC were neutered or swept aside, including, in a crude and tragic way, the internationally cherished doyen and senior 'priest' of contemporary OFR ritual. The 2004 global relay did indeed create magical encounters, moments of utterly moving conjuncture of the symbolic values of the Olympic flame and the ideology of Olympism with local histories of global significance, including in the human rights field. At the same time, the Athens relay was marked by a daily battle against sponsor activation teams, particularly Samsung's, violating the rules of ritual protocol and good taste, threatening to trivialize the whole phenomenon. The operations management contractor – the US-based firm Além International, in this case– was again placed in the contradictory position of being the chief on-the-ground defender of the rules of sponsor engagement and ritual integrity, while simultaneously being tasked by the OCOG and the IOC with insuring sponsor satisfaction with returns on investments that paid for hiring the operating company in the first place. This fundamental contradiction has grown to be the central fact of contemporary OFR organizational life.

During the Greek domestic segments of the 2004 relay, the general euphoria was mixed with confusion and consternation on the part of older Greek publics confronted with the introduction of certain elements from the new 'world standard' model (or 'the American model', as Greek critics persisted in calling it). A caravan of up to 20 vehicles, rolling sponsor platforms full of cheerleaders and blaring pop music, uniformed sponsor promotion teams trying to 'rev up' the crowds, continuous motorcycle security, the permanent presence of an ungainly media truck blocking the public's view of the flame, torchbearers of all ages and states of fitness to accommodate a huge percentage of sponsor-selected flame bearers, the sale of torches to torchbearers, giant video boards at celebration sites: none of these things had ever been seen in Greece in the 66 years flame relays had been passing through its streets and country roads.

However, nothing would be more inaccurate than to suggest some monolithic 'Greek' reaction to these locally novel OFR practices imported into Greece from supposedly global practice. As already noted, there were extreme contradictions of interpretation and judgement within the ATHOC leadership itself, and attitudes also varied among younger cadres of educated and professional Greeks whom ATHOC, under Gianna Angelopoulou-Daskalaki, prided itself in recruiting largely outside of the normal Greek clientelism of family political affiliation. As a more mediatized and cosmopolitan cohort – moreover, one frequently seeking permanent employment in the transnational sport and event management industries, a possibility unknown to their elders – these young people might be expected to evaluate events from a different interpretive baseline. This is why I have thought it imperative to include in this volume the voices of three academically trained Greek and Greek–American professional participant observers on the 2004 OFR. Pinelopi Amelidou literally grew up in the HOC, and she analyses the global relay from her perspective as one of only five Greeks who travelled the world with this flame.[10] An employee of a main ATHOC domestic sponsor, she was 'on loan' to Além International Management Inc., the contracted global OFR operator, and she also carried the flame in Maroussi on the final day of the domestic relay. Spiros Spiropoulos analyses the Greek relay from his insider's standpoint as an advance and events team member of the ATHOC torch relay department, and he also carried the flame as nearly all staff are mandated to do in the newly standard model. Marianthi Bumbaris Thanopoulos worked on the relay as both an independent and NBC-contracted video producer, and she provides an account of American and Greek media practices with respect to the flame-lighting ceremonies in Olympia and in the Athens atmosphere as the flame approached for the Opening Ceremonies.

The Athens 2004 OFR itself can never be understood or properly evaluated without contextualizing it first of all in a history of tension between the IOC and the HOC over 'ownership' of the OFR during the Samaranch presidency, and second in the specific social dramas of relations between Greek authorities and publics and the American leaderships of the Atlanta 1996 and Los Angeles 1984 Olympic Games. Greek public opinion had been so inflamed by the loss by Athens to Atlanta of the rights to host the Centennial Olympic Games that there was a very real question as to whether Atlanta could even get an Olympic flame at all. The eventual success of the 1996 OFR in Greece was one of the most remarkable stories of intercultural diplomacy in recent Olympic history. In achieving it, the Atlanta Olympic Organizing Committee (ACOG) took as its absolute anti-model the 1984 Los Angeles OFR in which the actions of that American Organizing Committee under Peter Ueberroth created an intercultural imbroglio and a risk of public violence even greater than what would occur a quarter of a century later for Beijing. On the domestic side, the ACOG OFR team transformed certain innovations from Los Angeles and Barcelona relays into what would emerge as the 'world's best practice' model for the subsequent relays in Sydney, Salt Lake City, Athens and Torino, a model now enshrined as canonical in the IOC's OFR technical manual that is imposed on all OCOGs.[11] This story is told for the first time anywhere in the next chapter and is elaborated in the extended interviews with Kritsinelis and McCarthy that follow it.

Hidden actors, operational scripts, public protests

The IOC has rarely seemed as bereft of leadership or options as it did during the Beijing OFR demonstrations in major cities of several continents, and the historical and anthropological context exposed in these pages makes it possible to better understand this incapacity. For their own marketing and client-relations purposes, Coca-Cola and Samsung had pushed hard for a Beijing global relay in the first place[12] and, despite IOC administrators' early misgivings, the sponsors had won the day.[13] Indeed, Coca-Cola cared so much about the issue that it had secretly extracted from the Rogge administration a right of first refusal for all future relay sponsorships for the duration of the company's latest master contract with the IOC, a fact published here for the first time.[14] The OFR 'presenting partners' had made elaborate plans for their client torchbearers and 'activation strategies' for their sponsorships in many cities on the 2008 global relay, matters of contractual guarantee by BOCOG and the IOC. Even after the March events in Tibet, the sponsors were loath to compromise these arrangements, and they pressed the IOC and BOCOG to persevere. In global cities where impending protests led to radical OFR route alterations and security measures, sponsor torchbearer programmes were severely disrupted. Other activation practices went ahead, however, leading to the bizarre – some would say obscene – spectacle, as in London and Paris, of open vehicles full of Coke and Samsung cheerleaders passing through crowds of screaming and weeping pro-Tibet demonstrators whose boldest members were gearing up to break through the police to try to seize the flame and disrupt the relay (see Figure 3).

The newly standard or world's best practice model specifies that flame and flame bearer security inside a narrow envelope is the responsibility of OCOG/contractor supplied security personnel.[15] These 'accompanying runners' wear official OFR running togs, regularly assist flame bearers with lighting and extinguishing torches, and are intended to be indistinguishable from other relay personnel. In the 1996, 2000, 2002, 2004 and 2006 (Anglo-Saxon or European) relays, these security figures did indeed largely 'pass' for ordinary ritual personnel among casual observers. Even where they were in fact foreign nationals, there was little to demarcate them from surrounding host city or OCOG demographics. However, BOCOG and the Chinese government were not about to let their

Figure 3.   Sponsor platform full of cheerleaders moving incongruously through London crowds, many waiting for the flame to protest China's human rights policies. Source: Sam Hoffman.

international operations contractor Maxxam Ltd. – an Australian firm – supply the security runners. As a result, Chinese military police did the duty (see Figure 4).

In cities such as Paris, San Francisco and London, cultural conventions of racial typology made these flame guardians immediately identifiable as 'Chinese', and their general demeanour and uniform age, gender, height, weight and hairstyle made it clear they were security men. As a consequence, a whole new public polemic erupted, driven by the political context. How could British, or American, or French, or Indian or Japanese authorities have possibly permitted Chinese military police to operate within the national boundaries of these sovereign democracies, much less at a time when these same personnel were involved in the Chinese government's repression of Tibetans, Uighurs and Han human rights activists? On their parts, Chinese authorities were shocked by these polemics, for was not BOCOG simply and honestly following the IOC-sanctioned standard model of OFR practice? When the 2004 global Athens relay visited Beijing, the Chinese had made no objection to the security runners being American contractors. So how could this development on the 2008 global relay be the result of anything but nefarious, un-Olympic anti-China plotting? (After the London protests and polemics, the Chinese security runners in Paris all wore identical dark sunglasses, presumably to hide their epicanthic eye folds, an 'adjustment' that, of course, absolutely backfired).

In the newly standard OFR model, security outside the torchbearer envelope is completely the responsibility of local authorities. As Steve McCarthy explains in his interview with me, negotiations with local law enforcement are the most vexed aspect of the operators' work, even within one national relay context or on a politically untroubled global relay such as Athens'. In 2008, once the protests started, the intercultural clashes between the Chinese government/BOCOG, the host NOCs, and national and local

Figure 4. Chinese security men tightly surrounding the Olympic flame in the streets of London during 2008 pro-Tibet demonstrations. Source: BOCOG.

government and law enforcement in the global cities visited became insurmountable within the terms of this world's best practices model. The Chinese authorities tried to insist that local authorities maintain the original relay plans while suppressing all anti-China dissent in each city or, at the very least, keeping it miles away from the relay and its media coverage. This, in the dominant Chinese understanding, was each city's contracted 'Olympic duty'.[16] Obviously in the democracies visited, total suppression of peaceful dissent and protest was inconceivable, undesirable and impossible, and China's demands were typically dismissed as the parochial fantasies of an authoritarian 'dictatorship', having nothing at all 'Olympic' about them. In one narrow sense, the standard model did prevail, in that the ultimate outcome in each city was indeed dictated by the national and local political and police authorities. In another sense, the model was shattered in that the Olympic bodies – IOC, NOCs, the OCOG – ended up with little or no influence, much less any authority over the eventual outcomes, as the case study of Delhi by Boria Majumdar and Nalin Mehta in this volume makes perfectly plain.

These outcomes varied tremendously in the different cities, and this alone would make for a revealing comparative study of national cultures of dissent and policing and of the real processes of globalization (as opposed to the more simplistic theoretical models in which 'globalization' and 'homogenization' are treated as equivalent terms). At one end of spectrum were cities like Muscat, where the flame passed with no threat of political protest, no public disturbance and no special security requirements.[17] There was a range of outcomes in the democracies. In San Francisco, publics were led to believe that Chinese demands for a route through unpopulated territory had been rejected and that the relay would progress on the planned route, where demonstrators were massing. Instead, the route was secretly changed at the last second to another course through the urban core, open to the public, but giving protestors no time to relocate en masse until the local relay was nearly over.[18] In Delhi, by contrast, the relay was completely closed to the public behind an overwhelming security presence, and pro-Tibetan forces conducted their own 'peace and human rights relay' on a parallel ritual route. Thanks to their extraordinarily resourceful fieldwork and network of contacts, Majumdar and Mehta are able to offer in these pages a backstage case study of both the protest ritual and the completely restricted official relay in Delhi. Finally, at the other end of the spectrum, was China herself.

In most Chinese locales, there was no real OFR, only a devastating simulacrum performed by the state security forces and a BOCOG unable to resist. Planned relay routes were pared to a minimum, torchbearers often ran only a few metres, ordinary citizens were not allowed to approach much less to congregate along the route, resident foreigners were kept away, and busloads of carefully selected and screened enthusiasts were deposited and then picked up and deposited again down the road to cheer for the benefit of the official cameras. Each night the BOCOG website reproduced these images as evidence to the world (and to the largely benighted IOC) of a completely normal and happy OFR, proceeding according to plan through the various regions and minority communities of China.[19] Doubtless, Chinese authorities truly feared Tibetan and Uighur actors seeking a world stage for their grievances, and surely many of those Chinese citizens who carried the flame or actually managed to see the relay were sincerely enthused by it. But from the standpoint of Olympic ideology and ritual practice, this was a travesty reminiscent perhaps of something from the old USSR.[20]

The ritual core

Money and power follow meaning and cannot lead until they have acquired meaning for themselves. The developing interests of commercial sponsors and political actors in the OFR over the past quarter-century are incomprehensible without first grasping the symbolic core of the ritual. Its special genius lies in its simplicity. It is a literal *rite de passage*. Ritually light a fire in one significant place; relay it hand to hand across great distances; deliver it in another significant place before a huge crowd awaiting its arrival; extinguish it completely at the end of the festivities. The OFR is the ritual journey of a fragile symbolic object with an obvious and ever-present drama to it: can a single, little flame be kept alive across all that distance? And it is a quintessentially human drama: fire is both a primal and a universal human symbol; there is no culture known that does not make use in some way or another of its representational values. And this is a powerful social drama: only the collaboration of many thousands of persons will permit the flame to reach its goal intact, and each relayer's contribution adds in a pure Durkheimian way to the collective effervescence and social solidarity of the whole.[21]

The OFR is a ritual, not a sports event; it directly addresses and reproduces the values of Olympism by inverting their performative representations in the games of the Games. The OFR is a contest to keep the flame alive through the eager collaboration not the formal competition of human beings. In the paradigm exposed by Claude Lévi-Strauss, the ritual displays the human identity and equality normally hidden under social difference – all flame bearers strip off socially marked clothing for identical running togs; the contribution of each is equally necessary to the progress of the flame – whereas, the forthcoming sports events will each end with a differentiation and ranking of contestants who looked petty much the same as they toed the starting line.[22] As nearly every flame bearer I've interviewed will insist, carrying the Olympic flame is an athletic endeavour and accomplishment, not because the pace is quick and the distance overwhelming – though for the disabled and elderly who carry these days, they can be – but because of the tremendous responsibility and the pressure of focused attention upon you. You cannot falter! While *Citius, Altius, Fortius* is the motto for Olympic sport, for the OFR it would be something like Carefully, Slowly, Joyously. And while some Olympic athletes do carry the flame now, the overwhelming majority of flame bearers are ordinary human beings with normal human bodies and so represent common humanity in precisely the opposite way than the Olympians do. Flame bearers, moreover, do not need to be tested for performance-enhancing drugs.

For audiences too, the OFR is in key respects a counter-Olympic ritual today, a fact that contributes to so regularly turning passive spectators into emotive congregants out on the relay. Attending the Olympic Games is now beyond the reach of most citizens, even in the host country. It requires expensive outlays for travel, hotels and sustenance, while tickets are costly and, for ordinary persons who could never afford officially offered packages, obtainable only through complicated computer lotteries. In fact for 'premium events' – the opening ceremonies, key sports finals – only a token percentage of tickets are available, at any price, to the general public at all. Most tickets not already reserved for the 'Olympic Family' have been contractually allocated to sponsors, media partners and global VIPs. Ordinary citizens not already deterred by all this will have to take their legal and fiscal chances with scalpers. To witness the OFR, by contrast, all one has to do is get in one's car and drive to where the flame is passing, and these days OCOGs pride themselves in bringing the flame within a hundred or two hundred miles of a very large percentage of the host nation's population.[23] The OFR is free and unticketed; it is a public event in public space, and its whole design and conduct is predicated on open accessibility. The OFR also emphasizes through the relative absence of elites the connection between Olympism, symbolically condensed in the Olympic flame, and ordinary citizens and local contexts. Though matters are different at centres and boundaries, throughout most of the relay, high Olympic officials, celebrities and national and international media are scarcely present, in contrast to their high visibility at the Olympic Games themselves. The only uniformed officials witnesses see are the anonymous OFR operators and local police.

All Olympic performances emphasize the non-verbal and paralinguistic semiotics of the human body over verbal symbolic codes. This is, of course, key to the transcultural and transnational demography of attention to the Olympic Games. The ritual silence of the core performance of the OFR is normally broken only by cheering from the crowds.

The focus on the flame is thus further heightened. Still more importantly, the general absence of spoken or written texts offering any official exegesis and the relative paucity of media commentary – most of it after the fact – make the Olympic flame a particularly open signifier. It not only permits, it invites differential meaning-making, whether on the personal or cultural levels. No one tells you, except in the most abstract and generic ways, what the Olympic flame is supposed to mean, and therefore you are freer to make it mean for yourself and your group according to your own cultural codes.

For example, I've seen many Catholics and Orthodox spontaneously cross themselves as they carry the flame or as it passes them by on the road. I've interviewed dozens of Christians who have been startled and moved by the flame appearing just over the heads of those standing in front of them on the street corner, instantly identifying it with the Pentecostal tongue of flame in their religion. In Japan and Korea, flames have sometimes been divided into three, to pursue separate relay routes before being reunified for the opening ceremonies, thus embodying tripartite East Asian cosmology of the unified complementarity of Heaven, Earth and Humanity. On the Seoul 1988 relay, foreigners could not understand why the torch was so smoky. Some problem with Korean technology and manufacture? Not at all. Smoke is mist and cloud and Buddhist temple incense, deep cultural, religious and art historical motifs representing the opening of the three cosmic realms to one another. (A smoky flame also had the practical benefit of allowing bystanders waiting down the road to more dramatically anticipate its arrival.)[24] In Greece, the Promethean and classical references of the flame lighting by temple priestesses at Ancient Olympia and the iconic echoes of vase paintings in the relay itself are among the signals of the modern ideology of *ellenismos* in its continuous and structuring tension with *romeismos* – Orthodox priests are there to bless at every turn these neo-pagan representations – in Greek historical and political consciousness.[25] On its two 'normal' visits to Delhi, the OFR has been received in precisely the local style for indigenous processions of Hindu temple deities through the streets. Many other instances of the indigenization of the generic global forms of the OFR are presented in this volume that is focused on analysing the transformations of these forms in the particular political projects of a variety of state, commercial and civil society actors. Nearly all of this has proved invisible, however, to those – IOC authorities and academics alike – who have relied solely on press reports and officially sponsored videos and promotional texts for their information. These are precisely the kinds of voices tending to equate globalization with homogenization, instead of grasping how transnational cultural forms such as those of the OFR become more widely available as means for reproducing or indeed creating cultural difference.

The OFR now attracts five to ten times as many face-to-face spectators as do the Olympic sports contests. (More precise numbers are difficult to derive.) If the general public has been completely unaware of this fact, the IOC did not recognize it either until very recently. This remarkable demography of attention cannot be understood without grasping the symbolic forms and semiotic practices that compose the ritual performance.

The dialectic between ritual and spectacle

If performative simplicity and abstract symbolic coherence are hallmarks of compelling transcultural ritual forms, these features are precisely antithetical to the ethos of the cultural performance genre of spectacle. In previous work, I have theoretically modelled the relationship between spectacle and ritual in the complex, ramified Olympic performance system.[26] This volume offers an extended case study of the pragmatics of the dialectic between ritual and spectacle with its logic of 'more and bigger is always better'. I say dialectic, because as these pages will show, many of the chief agents of OFR spectacularization are themselves ritual adepts and devotees no less passionate than any other. As my interview with him in this volume makes clear, figures like Steven McCarthy, the chief architect of the new standard model, have been sincerely driven to create longer relays with many more torchbearers extending to more global cities throughout the world precisely to draw larger and more diverse populations into this extraordinary ritual experience. These actual persons are anything but the cartoon character agents of managerial capitalism and commercialist exploitation imagined in so much 'cultural studies' work on Olympic phenomena.

At the same time, many of the practical techniques enabling or accompanying the project of increasing the reach of the OFR are proving toxic to the ritual experience itself. Bigger relays are more expensive relays, leaving OCOGs at the mercy of the eager corporations, notably Coca-Cola and Samsung in the period under study here. And in return for their money, these presenting partners expect to be able to present themselves ever more intensively. The ensuing articles will demonstrate the severe difficulties OCOGs and contracted OFR operators have been having under the 'world's best practices model' of restraining the 'activation' (self-marketing) behaviours of sponsors, even where such limits have been contractually stipulated. Multi-vehicle pre-processions of sponsor platforms full of cheerleaders (cheerleaders!) and blaring pop music; small armies of garishly dressed young people handing out sponsor emblems, flags and trinkets; sponsor sideshows and dedicated media boards at celebration and relay rest sites; insistence on caravan side-visits to dealerships and the insertion of speeches by sponsor executives into the official programme; and, of course, the endless effort to sneak sponsor logos closer to the Olympic flame and its bearers: these are just a few of the tasteless affronts to ritual decorum brought on by reframing the OFR spatially, temporally and performatively as a spectacle. If you are waiting by the side of the road or in your village square to honour and experience the Olympic flame, in the new standard model, you will have no choice but to first endure all of this cloying hoopla. Indeed, if you are awaiting the flame's arrival to ritually protest against the host nation's human rights policies, you will endure this insipid nonsense just as well. Today, you can have the ritual experience only after the spectacle has had its chance at you.

To add one further sponsor practice in this Introduction to the many that will be discussed in detail in this volume, the multiplication of torchbearers in the recent mega-relays has certainly increased the number and range of persons who have performed and enjoyed this moving ritual experience. But there is a shadow story here too. The absolute number and percentage of torchbearers selected privately by corporate sponsors and media partners grew exponentially between 1984 and 2004. Indeed, sponsors value this privilege more than anything else, and the details are closely guarded secrets in their contracts with the IOC and the OCOGs, never openly discussed, and indeed concealed behind public programmes in which a sponsor such as Coca-Cola invites ordinary people to nominate torchbearers from their communities. Moreover, sponsors and their advertising agents are rarely comfortable with the 'open signifier' character of the Olympic flame. In their publicity, their trinkets, their speeches to torchbearers and their justifications to shareholders, sponsors interpret the meanings of the Olympic flame in ways that seek to tie together, at least superficially, 'our brand and the Olympic brand,' as they like to say with encouragement from the IOC Marketing Department. It is highly doubtful that many participants beyond the sponsor cadres themselves pay much attention to the content of all of this. But it surely does distract people's focus, however transiently, from the Olympic flame itself.

Operations managers of the new OFR model have been strongly committed to increasing media coverage of the event, as the rather paltry broadcast and print reporting of prior relays, even in some host nations, have seemed to them incomprehensible and regrettable. Certain innovations have been most positive, such as having a dedicated video shooting crew on the relay team to forward footage nightly to local media and back to OCOG headquarters (where relay B-roll has emerged as a central motivating tool for staff under the frenzied pressure of the approaching Games). But adding a camera platform to a large truck and placing it into the caravan directly in front of the flame bearer so that local, national and OCOG media can have the best imaginable shooting position has proved a step too far in privileging visual spectacle and its artefacts over ritual experience. This media truck now completely blocks the flame from being seen at all by the assembled crowds until it is exactly in front of them. There is no longer any possibility of seeing the flame itself approach over a real distance, a traditionally central part of the ritual experience. The surprise and disappointment of a ritual assembly that is now generally permitted only a fleeting glance as the flame goes by has been intense. Unless they look to the side, the flame bearers themselves, as they perform their ritual action, cannot see any vista or even the proximate route ahead, but only stolid cameramen and equipment banks in the darkened truck that completely blocks their forward visual field. To be sure, flame bearers treasure the close-in, professional photographs and in some cases videos of their ritual performances they can now order (at a fee). But this fact by itself cannot compensate for the attack on the pubic nature of the ritual and its core meanings represented by this media convenience.

Souvenir torchbearer photographs are not the only or even the most controversial of commodifications of the ritual experience in the world's best practices model. No OCOGs are more cash-strapped than American ones, and once expensive mega-relays appeared – each one seeking, in the logic of the spectacle, to be longer and larger than all previous relays – these OCOGs resolved to generate additional revenue from the OFR. As will be analysed in the next chapter, with its selling of the rights to carry the flame for $3000 a kilometre, the Los Angeles 1984 committee created a huge international conflict that nearly led to bloodshed at Ancient Olympia. For 1996, the Atlanta Organizing Committee knew better than to try that again, and in a diplomatic triumph actually managed to overcome the legacy of 1984 with the Greek public and authorities. But for its domestic relay, ACOG introduced the practice of selling the torch to its bearer. The disruptions to ritual logic and egalitarian decorum this controversial practice has produced will be closely analysed in other papers in this volume.

The Olympic torch is a classic instance of what Durkheim called 'the contagion of the sacred'. Anyone who has seen an Olympic relay knows very well how, after the flame has moved on, people gather around torchbearers and ask to 'just touch' the torch. Everyone wishes to have a photograph with it for themselves, and generous torchbearers in the afterglow of their experience often stay by the side of the road for an hour letting everyone who wants to hold it do so. But these days, torchbearers have to be careful too to preserve from theft this ritual object for which they have paid several hundred dollars, as there is now a vigorous market for Olympic torches on eBay and dedicated Olympic memorabilia sites. The remarkable linguistic transformation of the 'Olympic Flame Relay' into the 'Olympic Torch Relay' in Western popular, media, and even official Olympic speech – despite the fact that the torch is not relayed, the flame is – has coincided with this new commodification of the ritual object.[27] At the same time, it must not be forgotten that there would be little market for Olympic torches were they not ritual objects in the first place.

The public sphere character and openness so important to the core ritual meanings and atmosphere of the OFR are placed under threat in other ways by the standard model of relay practice that has developed over the past quarter-century. Bigger relays have meant much larger operational staffs and a caravan of many more and more richly appointed vehicles to move them about (with additional automotive and apparel sponsors necessitated). Today, the flame can seem a fragile captive within the belly of a giant vehicular snake that moves it along. With the media van proceeding it, each flame bearer is closely followed by the command car and immediately thereafter a giant motor home (or van bus for the narrower streets of Europe) carrying visiting VIPs. (These vehicles block spectators' views of the departing flame nearly as completely as the media truck did of the approaching flame.) OCOGs can reward their own friends and allies and powerful persons they wish to cultivate by assigning torchbearer slots to them or their children, but riding for some miles with the flame from the privileged vantage point of the VIP minibus is an experience deeply appreciated as well. (As this researcher can attest.) And should IOC and NOC officials ever venture near the relay, as many including the present author seek for them to do, there is now a means of properly accommodating them.[28] After this vehicle, at least a dozen other vans, buses, ambulances, sedans, police cars, even fire trucks, now follow. All this is justified by operators as required by today's 'more complex' relays, and it is certainly true that under such conditions, maintaining staff physical and mental health necessitates every convenience, as will be detailed in the following chapters. However, the net effect is once again to insert a new consciousness of imposing official organization between the Olympic flame and its ritual public.

As has already been mentioned in connection with the Beijing OFR and will be closely analysed in these pages, greatly increased security presences and practices have proved most controversial among the innovations of the new standard model. Of course, the IOC, OCOGs, NOCs and local authorities must be concerned with security of the Olympic flame and with public safety, but several key operations innovators come from security backgrounds and have been accused of serious overreach in this domain. For example, the practice of having the flame continuously flanked by security men on motorcycles, with others always jogging behind the torchbearer, however helpful this may be for crowd control, spectator viewing and torch maintenance, has been criticized as disrupting not only Olympism's message of détente and peace, but the entire history of practical relations between the Olympic flame and its publics. Indeed, these routines have been criticized even among proponents of the 'world's best practice' model as being too 'American', though Australian, Greek and most recently Canadian OCOGs have chosen not to abandon them, but rather to significantly decrease the number of accompanying 'motos' and security runners.

Steps such as these are what Steve McCarthy and other proponents of the standard model refer to as 'adjustments' of global best practices to local circumstances. For the 2010 Vancouver OFR, which by nearly all accounts was a great success and which, in comparison with Beijing, seemingly brought the ritual process back to 'normal,' a number of other adjustments were made besides rendering security less visible. The Vancouver Organizing Committee (VANOC) did not contract out relay operations to a transnational firm such as Além or Maxxam, but kept management in house, while directly employing Vidar Eilertsen, the Norwegian OFR veteran and former Além collaborator, as chief of operations. (Além itself independently managed and programmed for Coca-Cola torchbearers.)[29] With the Royal Bank of Canada, a non-consumer products firm, as the second major sponsor, the marketing activation wars typical of the Coke/Samsung 'collaboration' in other relays were significantly reduced. Efforts were also made to keep the sponsor caravan more low-key and further out ahead of the flame relay itself, to better conform to Canadian tolerance levels for overt commercialization. But other controversial features of the new standard model, such as the media truck, remained unchallenged. On the operations side, the possibilities of 'glocalization,' to use Roland Robertson's term, were, for Vancouver, still being organized within the parameters of the 'world's best practices' model.[30] On the meaning side, the OFR once again managed to attract the direct attention of millions of persons, some number of whom interpreted and experienced it ways that moved them deeply.

In other words, the dialectical struggle between spectacle and ritual in the contemporary OFR fully remains. VANOC chief John Furlong, who firmly believed that 'the relay was the secret to delivering Canada's Games,' demanded a route that 'would be 45,000 kilometres – the longest in Olympic history – and last every second of 106 days. But the truth is, having the longest route was never what got the team excited – rather it was the idea of bringing the torch close to so many people,' including 12,000 torchbearers (nearly five times the number of athletes in the Games).[31] Here we recognize again how spectacle and ritual can functionally recruit for one another, even while being antagonistic to one another as cultural performance genres. I had already made this theoretical point when my ethnographic study of the OFR began in earnest, and I have subsequently elaborated it with evidence from the Olympic opening, closing and victory ceremonies.[32] This volume presents in detail the micro-pragmatics of the dialectic in the case of the OFR.

London 2012 has given no sign that the OFR will not continue to be a central site of the struggle between the Olympic Movement and the Olympic sports industry, the latter embodied by the often ambivalent and ambidextrous agents of managerial rationality and commercial promotion. The special character of cultural performance and the ritual power of the OFR in particular may enable the ritual to maintain its core integrity for a long time to come. But, like the Olympic Movement in general, the OFR is now clearly confronted with the iron law of Max Weber that all charismatic phenomena inevitably die by their own administrative and economic rationalization.

Notes

[1] Previous work by anthropologists on the Olympic Flame Relay has been limited to singular performances. See MacAloon and Kang, *'Uri Nara'* on the Seoul OFR and Klausen et al., *Fakkel-Stafetten*, the latter a wonderful monograph on Lillehammer that sadly remains untranslated from the original Norwegian.

[2] Wilson, 'IOC member rips "disaster" of global torch relay'.

[3] Other contributors to this volume, IOC official and especially managerial speech, and popular discourse as well now generally refer in English to the 'Olympic Torch Relay'. I myself persist in the older usage 'Olympic Flame Relay' as being not only closer to the ancient Greek prototype (*lampadedromia*) and to modern Greek ritual practice, but also as an anthropological statement and intervention. First of all, the empirical fact is that the flame, not the torch is what is relayed. (Calgary 1988 was the only recent exception.) Second, the flame is the sacred thing for ritual adepts and partisans, not the torch, though once used in the relay, the latter certainly is transformed through 'the contagiousness of the sacred' (Durkheim, *The Elementary Forms of the Religious Life*). Third, the linguistic shift to 'torch relay' from 'flame relay' historically coincides with and marks the incipient commodification of the ritual critically analysed in this volume. Torches today are offered for sale to torchbearers and are resold on eBay and among memorabilia collectors. There is a market in torches; there is no market in flames. An essential ritual practice is that the Olympic flame is completely extinguished at every Olympic Closing Ceremony and does not reappear save at Ancient Olympia to inaugurate the rites of separation for the next Games

(Van Gennep, *Les Rites de passage*; Turner, *The Ritual Process*). Since the flame cannot be unitized under these conditions, it cannot be priced for a market, the core definition of commodification. Corporate sponsors compete to be 'presenting partners' and suppliers for the relay as a whole. But, they are not sold rights to the flame itself. Indeed, as we shall see, sponsors are today in a perpetual struggle with relay officials as to how near their corporate marks will be allowed to approach the flame. In French, the other official language of the Olympic Movement, the linguistic drift to *relai de flambeau* is less egregious. While *flambeau* means torch, it remains cognate with *flamme*, or 'flame'. In Korea, the performance is called *song-hwa pong-song*, roughly glossed as 'sacred fire reverently dedicated and delivered'. No mention is made of torches.

4   See, for example Barney, Wenn, and Martyn, *Selling the Five Rings;* Chappelet and Kübler-Mabbott, *The International Olympic Committee and the Olympic System*; MacAloon, 'Scandal and Governance'.

5   Richard Pound, personal communication, September, 2008.

6   The present author played a modest role in these Beijing flame relay plans. While it was probably always the case that Beijing organizers, with their 'everything is bigger in China' ethos, would have planned a global relay to outdo Athens 2004, I had several conversations on the subject in 1998–1999 with He Zhenliang, IOC member in China and the godfather of the Beijing bid (Liang, *He Zhenliang and China's Olympic Dream*). I reminded him that the Silk Road was the appropriate historical path/metonymy for the Chinese relay, and that China could complete what Tokyo had gestured at with its 1964 relay. (The original idea for a Silk Road relay from Greece to East Asia apparently belonged to Carl Diem, the chief inventor of the modern OFR, suggested by him for the never-to-be-held 1940 Tokyo Olympics. Borgers, *Olympic Torch Relays*, 30; Dietrich Quanz and Karl Lennartz, personal communications, 1991.)

Mr. He took the idea back to BOBICO, the Beijing bid committee, and by the time I arrived for consultations in February 2000, it was firmly installed in the Chinese bid. Meeting with a group of mid-level international relations and marketing managers, I was asked 'Which Silk Road route should we take? There are many Silk Roads'. I replied that you take the route with the most IOC votes. It took them a moment to understand my meaning: you tell voting IOC members in the Middle East and Central, South and Southeast Asia that if Beijing wins the rights to the 2008 Games, they and their countries will host the OFR. This is a matter of considerable importance for nations with no hope of ever hosting the Olympic Games themselves, as well as a valued opportunity for dramatic, public cameos by the IOC members and other local Olympic officials. The next day, my existing schedule was cancelled and I found myself ushered into a room with the bid's top leadership, including Beijing Mayor Luo, Secretary General Wang Wei, and Foreign Ministry officials. I was asked to repeat my advice, and a roster of voting IOC members in 'Silk Road' countries was drawn up. I was later told that a Beijing delegation was sent out to those countries only a few days after this meeting. While there is no way to know how many votes in Beijing's eventual landslide might have been influenced by OFR considerations, the route presented during BOBICO's final presentation to the IOC in Moscow did indeed 'chase the votes'. (That presentation also included the surprise plan to take the flame to the top of Mount Everest, a resolution that made my jaw drop and instantly implicated both the logic of the spectacle and political issues of Chinese hegemony in Tibet.)

7   A number of IOC members, of course, had a vested interest in the Olympic flame visiting their home countries, because it offered public 'star turns' for themselves. I shall not take up these IOC governance issues in any detail here. Suffice it to say that there is ample precedent for these constitutional problems. Certain of the recommendations of the IOC 2000 Reform Commission, passed by the 1999 IOC special Session, were subsequently ignored by the IOC Executive. See MacAloon, 'Scandal and Governance'. For a historical and public administration overview of Olympic governance, see Chappelet and Kübler-Mabbott, *The International Olympic Committee and the Olympic System*.

In Torino, cadres of protesters even physically impeded the relay and endeavoured to snatch the flame away from torchbearers (see Figure 2). These unprecedented actions against the OFR were carried out by a small group of anarchists angered at local development projects having nothing directly to do with the Games. In the most publicized incident in the northern town of Trento, four of those who briefly seized the torch from athletics Olympian Eleonara Berlanda were arrested. (Two received jail sentences of three and four months and fines of €5000.) But the press also reported a total of 36 less dramatic protests along the route, demonstrations whose rhetoric encompassed anti-globalization sentiment especially targeting the relay sponsor Coca-Cola. One relay segment through the Susa Valley was eventually cancelled, Coke and Samsung having already decided that their vehicles would not dare to accompany the flame through the Susa. (Infoshopnews, 'Four Anarchists Arrested'; Associated Press, 'Torch Relay Hits Protest'.) For Rogge's mention of Torino in the Beijing debate, see Wilson, 'IOC member rips "disaster" of Global Torch Relay'.

[8] Richard Pound contested for the IOC presidency in 2000 and with three other candidates lost out to Jacques Rogge. For Pound's own account of his defeat, see *Inside the Olympics*, 265–70. Absent from this text is acknowledgement of his intemperate post-election letter to sponsors suggesting that their interests would be compromised by Rogge, a letter quickly leaked to journalists. In response, Rogge publicly revealed that Pound's law firm had for years been secretly compensated for his services as IOC television rights negotiator, a scandal in an organization whose members serve as volunteers. Pound went on to make a critical contribution to world sport as president and chief animator of the World Anti-Doping Association and remains the most outspoken and reflective critic and leader of the loyal opposition to the Rogge regime within the IOC. See his major policy analysis, 'The Future of the Olympic Movement'.

[9] See, for example, the discussion in Sassen's classic *The Global City*, 347–49. Also, see Robertson, *Globalization*; Robertson and Guilianotti, *Globalization and Sport*.

[10] The late Byron Amelides, her father, was a long-time HOC employee who was instrumental in my being able to do the fieldwork on the Barcelona OFR reported herein. Together with Nikos Nissiotis, this book is dedicated to his memory.

[11] International Olympic Committee, 'Technical Manual on Olympic Torch Relay, June 2007'. The IOC describes its Technical Manuals as documents that contain 'key educational information on a specific subject (Games function or theme) ... functional requirements, constituent perspective, planning information, current practices. Technical Manuals are also annexes to the Host City Contract, and therefore contain contractual requirements' (6). Technical Manuals are not public documents, and I am grateful to Gilbert Felli who, in deference to my decades of anthropological and diplomatic work on the OFR, provided me a copy and permission to cite its contents in a general way.

[12] Popular and much academic discourse suggests that global corporations sponsor the Olympics to sell more soft drinks, bottled water, DVD players and televisions. As a general truism, it is impossible to argue, but the assertion is uninformed and simplistic when it comes to proximate sponsor agendas with particular Olympic programmes. The experience of carrying the Olympic flame is for most torchbearers unforgettable and for many a lifetime highlight. Coke, Samsung and national suppliers have learned how much favour and loyalty they can command from targeted business prospects, governmental officials, financial allies, celebrities and high-achieving employees throughout the world in return for supplying them (or their designated relatives) with the opportunity to carry the Olympic Flame, particularly in their own countries, places of work and even home neighbourhoods. A global relay contractually offers Coke and Samsung the torchbearer slots to court and reward elites in many countries where these companies do or wish to do business.

As the ensuing papers will show, there are other sponsor benefits, such as influencing the relay route to stop for celebrations at company offices and dealerships. But it is the torchbearer programme that matters most to them. OFR sponsors try to keep these activities and particularly the number of the torchbearer slots they control out of public view, often masking them with much smaller programmes of public-nominated 'community hero' torchbearers. Even IOC and National Olympic Committee (NOC) officials have been surprised at how far things had gone on recent relays. Marc Maes coordinated the 2004 Athens relay stops in Belgium and wrote a commissioned IOC report on behalf of the European NOCs who hosted relay visits. The unpublished report complained vigorously of how many torchbearer slots were reserved for the sponsors and how few were given to the NOCs, 'even for our great Olympians' in 2004 (personal communication, February, 2007). IOC Olympic Games executive director Gilbert Felli was taken aback when I informed him in 2006 of our research findings that 60% or more of the torchbearers on sections of the Athens relay were sponsor selected. Perhaps as a consequence, BOCOG published well in advance the percentages of citizen, Olympic Family, and sponsor torchbearers for its relay, with the last category substantially reduced, in percentage terms, over previous relays.

[13] Interviews in Lausanne in 2006 revealed some IOC anxiety about sponsor presence on the global Beijing relay that seemed to centre on Coca-Cola's special symbolic appeal as a target for

anti-globalization protesters, a lingering effect of Torino. Indeed, some in the IOC administration were imagining a 'solution' whereby Coke would be the lead sponsor presence during the relay within China – the Chinese market being imagined as Coke's biggest object of desire – while the less volatile Samsung would be presenting partner for the global relay segment. It was ironic, then, for me to discover in a subsequent meeting in Beijing with BOCOG OFR director Zhang Ming and her team that the Chinese were actively trying to find a way 'against IOC pressure' to avoid a Coca-Cola relay presence within China! BOCOG at that time wanted permission for five national sponsors to replace what Coke would contribute, but 'the IOC says that's too many' (doubtless reflecting certain verities of the IOC-endorsed 'world's best practice' model). Neither BOCOG nor its OFR-operating consultants Maxxam – the Australian company Di Henry opened as a copy-cat for Sydney 2000 of Steven McCarthy's American-based Além International – expressed any concern to us about Coke and Samsung 'presenting' the global portion of the Beijing relay. I am unable to report on the ensuing negotiations among the IOC, BOCOG and the sponsors. In the end, Coke and Samsung won pretty much the same initial arrangements on the international Beijing OFR as they had for Athens.

14   This intelligence about the latest Coca-Cola/IOC contract was provided to me by Michael Payne, former IOC marketing director, in an interview in his Lausanne offices in November 2006. Vancouver suggests that Samsung has been unsuccessful in its attempts to acquire a similar right of first refusal for flame relay 'presenting partnership' in its latest contract with the IOC. (To say the least, these contracts are not public documents.)

15   These security arrangements are detailed in my interview with Steven McCarthy who was the chief originator of them in the OFR context. The security envelope around the torchbearer expands or contracts, accordion-style, depending upon crowd and road conditions, but generally is bounded by the media truck in front, motorcyclists on the sides and the command car in the rear, with the torchbearer and one or more accompanying security runners in the middle. In city contexts, it is a space of around 100–200 square metres. Incidentally, this same envelope is mandated in the standard model to be free of all sponsor marks or signage. Only Olympic marks should appear within it, by analogy with the commercial signage-free Olympic venues at the Games. Durkheim classically defined 'the sacred' as persons, spaces and things, 'set apart and forbidden' (*The Elementary Forms of the Religious Life*). It is intriguing that in contemporary OFR practice, the sacred space is defined by the presence of the Olympic flame, the torchbearer, and a few ritual personnel, and the forbidding of both ordinary persons ('spectators') and identifiable sponsor marks. As will be made plain in these pages, the 'game' for sponsors becomes slipping from the spectacle and festival spaces into the ritual space through means ranging from sponsor-selected torchbearers to vehicle windscreens unavoidable in media pictures.

16   The accomplished American Olympic journalist Alan Abrahamson was a scheduled torchbearer in San Francisco and provided on his blog ('Behind the Scenes With the Torch') a participant's account of this chaotic strategy of accommodating public safety, dissent and relay responsibility in an American context.

17   Fenner, 'The 2008 Flame Relay in Oman'.

18   Political demonstrations of any sort are proscribed within Olympic Games venues as a matter of contract with Olympic host cities and governments. The Chinese authorities failed to see how the OFR route did not comprise an Olympic 'venue' and therefore why the same strictures were not being applied. The authorities in several OFR cities responded that the envelope around the flame was indeed to be kept politically neutral, while non-violent citizens just outside it we free to express themselves. The Chinese countered that the shouts and chants of these demonstrators did indeed penetrate the sacred space, just as their signage appeared in the background of media coverage of the flame. Therefore, Olympic rules were being violated to harm China.

When the PRC authorities saw that their protests would be in vain as the OFR global relay continued, they turned to encouraging pro-China demonstrators to come forward and to counter with their own chanting and placards. This led authorities in some cities to fear violent conflict between the two groups of demonstrators.

19   The reader can review this photo archive by going to www.gettyimages.com and searching 'Olympic Torch Relay'. It will be noted how rarely crowds that appear to have spontaneously gathered are pictured, as opposed to carefully organized and choreographed ones. By contrast, the captions to many of the photos posted to the BOCOG website for world distribution repetitively and formulaically insisted that 'tens of thousands of people were gathered on the streets and roads to watch the torch relay'.

[20] See Lane, *The Rites of Rulers*. This capsule account is based on off-the-record conversations with insiders on the China OFR, none of whom have been willing in public to deviate from the official story of a normal, happy relay throughout China. The reality of the 2008 relay in China is still today being treated as a state secret. By comparing the rosters of torchbearers and officiants in the 1986 Asian Games and the 1988 Olympic Games flame relays in Korea, Kang Shin-pyo and I were able to show how sensitive an indicator of domestic political change the OFR can be. (MacAloon and Kang, 'Uri Nara'.) Should similar data ever become available for Beijing, it would surely repay a similar study.

[21] For the classic arguments underlying this analysis, see: Durkheim, *The Elementary Forms of the Religious Life*; van Gennep, *The Rites of Passage*; Turner, *The Ritual Process*.

[22] Lévi-Strauss, *The Savage Mind*, 30–3.

[23] Furlong, *Patriot Hearts*, 154.

[24] See MacAloon and Kang, 'Uri Nara'.

[25] MacAloon, *This Great Symbol*; Herzfeld, *Ours Once More*.

[26] MacAloon, 'Olympic Games and the Theory of Spectacle in Modern Societies', and 'The Theory of Spectacle: Reviewing Olympic Ethnography'.

[27] See Note 2. Increased vigilance is now required on the part of OFR officials and security teams to prevent organized as well as spontaneous attempts to steal Olympic torches.

[28] MacAloon, 'Scandal and Governance: Inside and Outside the IOC 2000 Commission'.

[29] Cheryl Cagle, personal communication, Copenhagen, October, 2009.

[30] Robertson, *Globalization*; Robertson and Guilianotti, *Globalization and Sport*. For my own theory of 'empty forms and indigenous meanings,' related to Robertson's notion of 'glocalization', see MacAloon, 'The Theory of Spectacle'.

[31] Furlong, *Patriot Hearts*, 152–4, 163–75. Mr. Furlong's memoir is not unexpectedly glowing and self-congratulatory, as is typical of the genre. But its sections on the OFR give accurate and compelling indication of the role the ritual has come to play over the past quarter-century in the imaginations and motivations of top OCOG leaders. A.D. Frazier, the Atlanta CFO who played the main role in raising nearly $1 billion in corporate monies for those Games, has repeatedly told me that the only moments in which he was sure the effort was worth it were when he was out on the Olympic Flame Relay. By comparison with recent Summer Olympics, there were 13,200 flame bearers for Atlanta, a figure about 30% higher than the number of athletes in those Games. It is significant that for all the other differences between Winter and Summer Games today, their OFRs have grown equal in scale and importance.

[32] MacAloon, 'Olympic Games and the Theory of Spectacle'; 'The Theory of Spectacle'; 'Genre and Risk in Olympic Ceremonies.' In the continuing development of my theory of complex, ramified, multi-genre performance systems, this extended case study of the OFR is meant to directly respond to the legitimate demand of proponents of the 'strong programme' in the sociology of culture for precise specification of the social actors, contexts, and conflicts responsible for the development, reproduction, and transformation of those symbolic forms of greatest interest to cultural anthropologists. Against practitioners of 'weak programme', that is to say reductionist sociology, these papers are intended to demonstrate the necessity and the pay off of getting ethnographically backstage in order to avoid the superficially 'critical' reasoning from decontextualized texts that is in my opinion chiefly responsible for giving 'cultural studies' of sport such a poor scholarly reputation.

References

Abrahamson, Alan. 'Behind the Scenes With the Torch'. April 9, 2008. http://blogs.nbcsports.com/home/archives/2008/04/jasmine-and-I-are-standing.html (accessed August, 2009).

Associated Press. 'Torch Relay Hits Protest'. February 5, 2006.

Barney, Robert, Stephen Wenn, and Scott Martyn. *Selling the Five Rings*. Salt Lake City: University of Utah Press, 2004.

Borgers, Walter. *Olympic Torch Relays*. Berlin: Agon Sportsverlag, 1996.

Chappelet, Jean-Loup, and Brenda Kübler-Mabbott. *The International Olympic Committee and the Olympic System: Governance in World Sport*. London: Routledge, 2008.

Durkheim, Emile. *The Elementary Forms of the Religious Life*. Trans. Karen Fields. New York: Free Press, [1912] 1995.

Fenner, Sofia. 'The 2008 Flame Relay in Oman'. Unpublished paper, Department of Political Science, University of Chicago 2009.

Furlong, John. *Patriot Hearts: Inside an Olympics that Changed a Country*. Vancouver: Douglas and McIntyre, 2011.

Herzfeld, Michael. *Ours One More: Folklore in the Making of Modern Greece*. Austin, TX: University of Texas Press, 1982.

Infoshopnews. 'Four Anarchists Arrested in Scuffle Over Olympic Torch'. January 26, 2006.

International Olympic Committee. 'Technical Manual on Olympic Torch Relay'. Lausanne, June 2007.

Klausen, Arne M., Ellen K. Aslaksen, Odd Are Berkaak, Ingrid Rudie, Eduardo Archetti, and Roel Puijk. *Fakkel-Stafetten: En Olympisk Ouverture*. Oslo: Ad Notam Gyldendal, 1995.

Lane, Christel. *The Rites of Rulers*. Cambridge: Cambridge University Press, 1981.

Lévi-Strauss, Claude. *The Savage Mind*. Chicago: University of Chicago Press, 1966.

Liang, Lijuan. *He Zhenliang and China's Olympic Dream*. Beijing: Foreign Languages Press, 2007.

MacAloon, John J. 'Genre and Risk in Olympic Ceremonies'. In *Ritual als provoziertes risiko*, edited by Renate Schlesier and Ulrike Zellman, 31–52. Wurzburg: Konigshausen & Neumann, 2009.

MacAloon, John J. 'Scandal and Governance: Inside and Outside the IOC 2000 Commission'. *Sport in Society* 14, no. 3 (2011): 292–308.

MacAloon, John J. *This Great Symbol: Pierre de Coubertin and the Origins of the Modern Olympic Games*. 2nd ed. London: Routledge, 2008.

MacAloon, John J. 'The Theory of Spectacle: Reviewing Olympic Ethnography'. In *National Identity and Global Sports Events*, edited by Alan Tomlinson and Christopher Young, 15–40. Albany: State University of New York Press, 2006.

MacAloon, John J. 'Olympic Games and the Theory of Spectacle in Modern Societies'. In *Rite, Drama, Festival, Spectacle: Rehearsals Toward a Theory of Cultural Performance*, edited by J. MacAloon, 241–80. Philadelphia: Human Issues Press, 1984.

MacAloon, John J., and Kang Shin-pyo. '*Uri Nara*: Korean Nationalism, the Seoul Olympics, and Contemporary Anthropology'. In *Toward One World Beyond All Boundaries: The Seoul Olympic Anniversary Conference*, edited by Koh Byong-ik, 117–59, Vol 1. Seoul: Poong Nam Publishers, 1990.

Pound, Richard. *Inside the Olympics*. Toronto: John Wiley & Sons, 2004.

Pound, Richard 'The Future of the Olympic Movement'. Paper presented at the International Symposium for Olympic Research, Central Institute of Physical Education, Beijing, August 9, 2008.

Robertson, Roland. *Globalization: Social Theory and Global Culture*. New York: Sage, 1992.

Robertson, Roland and Giulianotti, Richard, eds. *Globalization and Sport*. London: Blackwell, 2009.

Sassen, Saskia. *The Global City*., 2nd ed. Princeton: Princeton University Press, 2001.

Turner, Victor. *The Ritual Process*. New York: Aldine Transaction, 1969.

Van Gennep, Arnold. *The Rites of Passage*. Trans. Monika Vizedom and Gabrielle Caffee. Chicago: University of Chicago Press, [1909] 1960.

Wilson, Steven. 'IOC Member Rips "Disaster" Of Global Torch Relay'. Associated Press, August 5, 2008.

This flame, our eyes: Greek/American/IOC relations, 1984–2002, an ethnographic memoir

John J. MacAloon

Social Sciences Division, The University of Chicago, Chicago, USA

This article presents an ethnographically based analysis of Olympic flame relay (OFR) relations among the Hellenic Olympic authorities and the Greek public sphere, three American Olympic organizing committees (Los Angeles 1984, Atlanta 1996, and Salt Lake City 2002), and the International Olympic Committee (IOC) across a 20-year period. It provides the first scholarly analysis of the controversies created by the Los Angeles Olympic Organizing Committee that nearly led to violence at Ancient Olympia during the flame-lighting ceremonies for those games. It explains how the Atlanta Committee for the Olympic Games managed to overcome this poisonous history through intensive intercultural diplomacy and to secure an Olympic flame for Atlanta. The structures and events analysed herein transformed the OFR in a variety of ways – from the IOC's attempts to increase its ownership stake in the ritual, to increased corporate sponsor interest in it, to the OFR's emergence as a potential weapon of international political protest – setting the stage for OFR struggles to come in the early years of this century.

Mise en scène

My hundreds of kilometres of travel in Korea with the flame relays for the 1986 Asian and 1988 Olympic Games had taught me the hard way what a physical, emotional, and moral ordeal these rituals are for their personnel.[1] In late February 1996, I was in Tucson, Arizona at the home of a friend, training for the upcoming journey to Greece as a member of the Atlanta Olympic Organizing Committee (ACOG) delegation to fetch the Olympic flame. A call unexpectedly came in from Charlie Battle, the ACOG international relations chief, and the following exchange ensued.

- John, don't think, just react to what I'm about to tell you …. Hillary Clinton is coming to Ancient Olympia for the flame-lighting ceremony.
- Charlie, this is bad news for us.
- Billy thinks so too. He's ranting that if she goes, he'll just stay home.

William Porter 'Billy' Payne was chairman and CEO of ACOG. A former college football player and suburban Atlanta real estate lawyer, he had conceived in a personal epiphany the outlandish idea of bringing the Olympic Games to his city. Then, through tireless lobbying work with a small group of friends – the 'Atlanta Nine', including Charlie Battle and eventual flame relay chief Ginger Watkins – bankrolled in significant part by his own funds, Payne actually succeeded against all odds in defeating Athens, Toronto, Melbourne, Manchester, and Belgrade for the rights to host the Centennial Olympic Games.[2] Payne was a conservative Republican[3] with political antipathy for the

Clintons, but I knew the main source of his pique lay elsewhere. Payne lived in continual anxiety about being forced from his own stage by one establishment or another. The old wealth of Atlanta had plotted to replace him as ACOG CEO with someone more accomplished. Now, the US First Lady was going to horn in on his great moment at the birthplace of the Olympic Games. The liturgy required that he share the stage with US President Bill Clinton at the Olympic opening ceremonies, but this ritual intrusion by the White House into the Olympic flame relay (OFR) would seem to him gratuitous and a personal affront.

My immediate reaction – that Mrs Clinton's presence at Olympia would be unfortunate for ACOG – had nothing to do with concern for Billy Payne's ego, or with Hillary Clinton's intentions. I already knew from her visit to the Lillehammer Winter Games how sincerely interested she was in the Olympic Movement and its youth development agenda. Mrs Clinton surely would want to see the Olympic flame-lighting ceremony, particularly since her daughter Chelsea would be travelling with her. After hanging up with Charlie, I made some calls that confirmed the political context of her trip. The Clinton Administration had been under pressure by the Greek–American lobby for its perceived tilt towards Turkey, and Mrs Clinton's trip featured an elaborate visit to Istanbul, where she had close friends. Archbishop Iakovos, the Greek Orthodox metropolitan in the USA, was one of those who suggested the Olympia visit to the White House as a diplomatic counterweight. The flame-lighting ceremony at Ancient Olympia is not only a key Olympic ritual, it has become a central, if sometimes conflicted performance of modern Greek national consciousness that therefore attracts a huge national television audience. Hence, it was rightly judged by the Greek–American lobby as a setting with sufficient *gravitas* to communicate forceful messages. But how much did the White House understand about this very particular *gravitas*?

This was the first thing that worried me, as I became the only person on the US side of this diplomatic conversation who had ever seen the ritual live, much less who had studied it carefully from backstage. Olympia would be no less a diplomatic minefield because it was the US First Lady and not the US President attending, or because it was formally a Hellenic Olympic Committee (HOC) not a Greek state occasion. This civil society 'cover' might serve US diplomatic convenience, but it would not reach far in Greece where Olympic governance has only nominal independence from the State. For example, the leadership of the HOC automatically changed with the political party in power, except that the change was delayed in Olympic years. Mrs Clinton's entourage would arrive with the Panhellenic Socialist Party (PASOK) in power, but with the HOC and the ceremony under control of a rump New Democracy (NEA) leadership. Long experience with Washington in Olympic affairs made me doubt its appreciation of the challenges of placing Mrs Clinton in the middle of this vexed political/ritual condominium.[4] For its part, ACOG had come to understand and to sort out its proper place within the push/pull of the Greek political parties. The announcement of Mrs Clinton's impending arrival would start the machinations and negotiations all over again.

Second, I certainly did not expect her handlers to grasp the abiding legacy of Greek antagonism to the USA that situated itself very specifically in the Olympic flame-lighting ceremony. Awareness of the outrage created in Greece by the flame relay for Los Angeles 1984 had been thoroughly suppressed in the USA. I had worked for four years laying groundwork and ACOG had laboured assiduously in Greece for two years to overcome this noxious heritage that, together with Greece's abiding rancour over Athens having lost to Atlanta the rights to the Centennial Games, had at one time made it seem unlikely that an Olympic flame could be obtained for ACOG at all. Now all this dedicated work could be swept away.

Finally, for all of its global symbolic cachet, the Olympia ritual is an intimate and fragile one, utterly dependent on the backstage care and expertise of two or three persons whom I had enabled the ACOG leadership to get to know and with whom a mutual confidence had begun to be established. I had been around US Secret Service security details and White House entourages enough to understand how large they would be in this instance and how thoroughly they could disrupt and overwhelm the traditional arrangements at Olympia. I shuddered to imagine the new demands, even commands that would be issued by foreigners to Athanassios (Nassos) Kritsinelis and his team of ritual directors, who usually had enough trouble with meddling Greek International Olympic Committee (IOC) members and HOC and Greek Sports Ministry 'luminaries'. After the ceremony, the White House would fly away and ACOG would be left with any fallout. We still had the relay through Greece, extended to honour the Centennial, and the handover ceremony in Athens, likewise elaborated by the Greeks to further salve the Atlanta wound to Greek national pride. If a national Greek television audience were upset by ritual changes or diplomatic gaffes during the Olympia flame-lighting ritual occasioned by the massive White House presence, the ACOG delegation would pay a very hard price throughout Greece in the coming weeks.

As matters eventuated, none of these forebodings about Hillary Clinton's presence in Olympia was realized. Despite long odds, her performance added a great deal in the end to overcoming the hard legacy of Greek/American OFR relations and to smoothing ACOG's way on the relay through Greece. But it took enormous additional labour and some intercultural serendipity to ensure that my initial reaction from Tucson would turn out to be all wrong.

Greek failure as American/IOC perfidy

While the reasons are always complex why an Olympic bid succeeds or fails, in the contest to host the 1996 Olympic Games, the Athens bid under the distillery magnate Spyros Metaxas largely defeated itself through its own arrogance. The open theme of the bid was 'Give Greece back the Games, and we will put things right again', a scarcely disguised attack on the governance and commercial innovations of the Juan Antonio Samaranch regime at the IOC. IOC members who fancied themselves progressives were not pleased. Second, the bid rooted itself in a conservative *ellenismos*, the domestic ideology asserting that modern Greece is directly connected to the Ancient Greek world that gave art, science, philosophy, and democracy to humanity at large. Controversial enough within its own *oikos*, this world view was a tough sell, at the end of the twentieth century, to IOC voters from India, China, the Middle East, West Africa, and other regions with their own claims on globally significant cultural patrimony. (Atlanta's key theme was racial collaboration in the home of the Civil Rights Movement.) Finally, Athens 1996 refused to engage the transnational expertise that IOC leaders had come to regard as essential to producing a successful Olympic Games in the contemporary environment.[5] This know-it-all, go-it-alone ethos particularly frightened those IOC and International Federation (IF) officers and administrators who would have to spend six years of their lives in and out of Athens should that bid prevail.[6]

That Athens lost their bid was thus not surprising to insiders. Yet, the announcement of victory for Atlanta on 19 September 1990 in Tokyo, still took me aback, first of all because I had expected Toronto to win, and second because the dim prospects for an Atlanta flame lighting and relay in Greece were instantly apparent. On top of the bad memories from 1984, there would now be a fierce backlash among the Greek public who were not expecting to lose the rights to the Centennial Games and who would take the defeat as a national scandal. That backlash was not slow in coming, and to defend themselves against it, the Athens bid committee and the Hellenic Olympic establishment, including its two IOC members, did nothing to temper, indeed quietly encouraged a public discourse that blamed the IOC for 'selling out Greece to Coca-Cola and CNN'. The notion that CNN had any positive influence over the IOC was quite absurd, given Ted Turner's efforts to develop an 'alternative Olympics' with his Goodwill Games. Coca-Cola Hellenic Bottling had been a big donor to the Athens bid, just as Australian Coca-Cola had supported the Melbourne bid.[7] That was the company's established strategy; it would never have been so foolish as to support only its headquarters city, Atlanta. But the facts were powerless against a Greek conspiracy narrative that so well fit the circumstances. Other than Atlanta-based multinational corporations, there was nothing else of global significance in the city to explain its victory to distant and lily-white audiences, and the blanket of commercial dirty dealing in contempt of Olympic ideals could be thrown simultaneously over the Samaranch IOC and 'the Americans'.

In 1992, the Barcelona Olympic Organizing Committee (COOB) and the city's Office of Cultural Affairs invited me to join their OFR delegation to Greece, and HOC ceremonies chief Nassos Kritsinelis asked me to accompany him on the relay from Olympia to Athens and at the handover ceremony.[8] I was most grateful for this opportunity to continue my general ethnography of the OFR, but my specific intent in accepting these invitations was to try to evaluate, on the ground, just how difficult things were going to be four years hence for Atlanta. The answer was not long in coming during this 1992 fieldwork.

My friends in the village of Ancient Olympia, even long-time critics of the Hellenic Olympic establishment, were themselves full of the Coca-Cola/CNN narrative. At the flame ignition ceremony, I overheard many Greeks complaining that 'the next time should have been for ourselves'. Throughout the relay to Athens, ordinary citizens regularly approached Kritsinelis and other HOC staff to attack the IOC and the Olympic establishment for 'selling out Greece'. Older women in particular would thrust themselves at the relay command car to shout imprecations at its occupants. I heard one phrase repeated so regularly that I asked its meaning. 'They are saying that if we don't take care of this flame, we should go blind. They are putting a curse on us'. Among the tens of thousands at the handover ceremony in the Panathenaic Stadium, there were protest placards and shouts of anger at Atlanta and the IOC. Many explicitly linked the torturous and nearly tragic events of 1984 (detailed below) with the situation eight years later, because of their shared causation by IOC/American ignorance and cupidity. It was very easy to imagine how tumultuous these same Greek crowds would be if the foreigners receiving the Olympic flame in front of them were American instead of Catalan and Spanish. I left Greece seriously doubting that an Olympic flame could be obtained for Atlanta at all. It haunted me to imagine that the Greek OFR ceremonies might have to be distorted and maimed again in 1996, intentionally this time instead of spontaneously as in 1984, in order for 'the Americans' and 'the IOC' to pry any kind of flame at all from its Greek ritual guardians.[9]

Surprising Atlanta

After finishing my work on the Catalan Olympic Games, as a member of an international research team assembled by Miguel de Moragas, founder of the extraordinary Olympic Studies Centre at the Autonomous University of Barcelona, I turned my attentions fully to the problem of the Atlanta OFR. I was extremely fearful that ACOG's inexperienced leadership would be completely ignorant of the historical and intercultural context of Greek/American/IOC flame relay relations and the monumental challenges that history would present. Any advice ACOG received from the IOC on this matter would surely be unhelpful. Despite, or perhaps because of the events of 1984, Juan Antonio Samaranch had kept a measured distance from the HOC, and was chiefly concerned with reminding the Greeks that the IOC not they 'owned' the Olympic flame. The prestigious IOC member in Greece Nikolaos Nissiotis, who commanded Samaranch's ear and thus was the only real mediator between the IOC and the HOC, had tragically died in a car crash on the road between Olympia and Athens on 18 August 1986. In Lausanne itself, Samaranch's commercial revolution was only just beginning to generate a managerial professionaliza-tion of IOC affairs. In the run-up to Atlanta, the sole IOC office taking any regular interest in the OFR was the Marketing Department and in particular its chief Michael Payne. Yet commercial sponsor interest in the OFR was a main source of the struggle between Greek and American intercultural imaginaries. Payne, who had never been in Greece for the flame ceremonies and whose job was to sell sponsorships, liked to argue that the flame relay had always had sponsors and, therefore, that Greek complaints were a tempest in a teapot. If asked, he would simply advise ACOG to be tough with the Hellenic Olympic establishment.[10] Finally, the ACOG leadership had already become well known in Olympic circles for its studied insularity and scepticism towards 'outside' experts, even the few like me who were not seeking employment.[11] Other than Charlie Battle, I as yet knew none of the ACOG principals and doubted they would be very welcoming to some 'Olympics professor from Chicago'.

In fact, when I appeared in her office, Ginger Watkins was perfectly gracious. As ACOG managing director of marketing communications, she had been given the OFR as part of her portfolio, following a historically revealing organizational pattern set by Los Angeles and Barcelona. (In Seoul, the OFR was the responsibility of the Culture and Ceremonies Department, as one would expect in a Korean cultural context.) My calling card in Atlanta was a domestic flame relay plan incorporating historic American journeys (e.g., Native American migration and pilgrimage routes, Lewis and Clark, the Pony Express, Cape Canaveral, the Selma March). This concept was eventually incorporated into the 1996 relay across America, in tandem with the newly standard marketing formula of bringing the flame within 200 miles of 90% of the host nation's total population.

What I really hoped to ascertain in these first meetings was how aware ACOG was of the major test of intercultural diplomacy they would be facing in Greece. ACOG leaders were, of course, perfectly conscious of the general resentment against them for defeating Athens, as well as of the Coca-Cola/CNN canard that trivialized their own achievements. The key issue would instead be whether ACOG could come to properly grasp the entire history of the 1984 OFR imbroglio created by Los Angeles, or whether the committee leadership would be taken in by the complete whitewashing of the whole affair in the most readily available 'independent' book on the organization of the LA Games,[12] by the more thorough but tendentious presentation of it in the LA '84 Official Report,[13] or still worse by Peter Ueberroth's vengeful and self-serving account of the controversy in his own memoir.[14]

While Watkins herself was not yet up to speed on these international relations issues when we first met, she had just made two very critical OFR hires. Hilary Hanson, a talented and energetic young public relations and marketing specialist who had been hired as flame relay director, immediately proved open to learning everything she could about the OFR.[15] Rennie Truitt, an experienced political advance man, had been charged with preparing a briefing paper for ACOG on all relevant aspects of the OFR. The focus of his report would be on producing a domestic relay intended to be even longer than the LAOOC's, taking advantage of its experience while avoiding its serious operational problems in the areas of route advance and torch bearer scheduling that Truitt would eventually (and brilliantly) take charge of for ACOG.[16] At the same time, he did not neglect the dangerous international relations fiasco with Greece that Ueberroth and Samaranch had created in 1984. At a long dinner in Chicago, I found Truitt already quite informed about it and both eager to learn and capable of understanding things from the Greek point of view. His final background paper strongly counselled ACOG to take the Los Angeles Olympic Organizing Committee (LAOOC) as its absolute anti-model when it came to OFR relations with the HOC and Greek public opinion while not counting on, indeed being actively cautious about any IOC 'assistance' in the matter. It was not long before all of the relevant ACOG officers – Payne, Battle, Watkins, and subsequently Andrew Young and AD Frazier[17] – as well the senior flame relay leadership team fully understood what a nearly tragic situation LA '84 had created in Greece, and that this legacy and not just the Atlanta's own wound to Hellenic national pride would have to be acknowledged, confronted, and overcome.

The flame's dark hour

In the view of the IOC marketer Michael Payne, 'It was Peter Ueberroth who took the torch relay to a whole new level. Ueberroth understood the potential of the torch to spark national interest and pride, uniting people behind the Olympic Games'.[18] In my judgement, this opinion is ethnocentric and parochial, as it ignores, for example, the extraordinary 'levels' of the OFRs for Tokyo 1964 and Mexico City 1968, the first relaying the flame from Olympia through Asia along the southern Silk Road, the second retracing Columbus's journey to the new world and the route of the Mexican conquest.[19] But there is no question that in 1984, Ueberroth brought the 'more is better' ethos of the spectacle[20] to the OFR in intensified ways: first of all, by mandating a transcontinental relay with the largest number of actually relayed miles ever (an initially planned 16,000, and in the event over 9000, requiring 82 days); and second, by commercializing and monetizing the relay in order to pay for this new scale of things, while actually generating significant revenue.[21]

In Ueberroth's characteristic way of thinking, 'Since this was a high-cost, high-risk project, our *first priority* was to line up another sponsor'.[22] For the first time in its history, the OFR would have not only corporate suppliers but also a commercial sponsor, identified as such and given advertising rights well beyond small logos on ritual gear. 'The U.S. telecommunications giant AT&T ... needed to reconstruct its national image after a federal judge had ruled that it should be broken up'.[23] Ueberroth also sold AT&T on the natural congruence of its business with the flame relay as a form of mass communication and as 'a means [for the company] to retain a national, united image during its restructuring process'.[24] On 29 September 1982, characteristically without any specific consultation with the IOC, much less with the HOC, Ueberroth 'announced AT&T as the official sponsor of the 1984 Olympic torch relay'.[25] In the end, AT&T provided not only a substantial sponsorship fee covering all costs, but also technical value-in-kind, as well as hundreds of 'cadre runners', staffers, and support personnel across the transcontinental route. In effect, the LAOOC subcontracted to its main corporate sponsor most of the operations management and staffing of its flame relay.[26]

The LAOOC also hit upon the idea of selling the rights to carry the Olympic flame for $3000 a kilometre to any individual or organization that could produce the funds.

This utterly unprecedented notion was, like the rest of Ueberroth's torch relay plan, unanimously opposed by the LAOOC directors and senior management, but Ueberroth stubbornly insisted and pushed the plan through.[27] In his post-Games memoir, Ueberroth attributed the original idea to David Wolper, the Hollywood impresario who had helped organize LA's Olympic bid and who would direct the opening ceremonies. While Wolper wanted to place the funds raised from selling torchbearer slots into the LAOOC's general account, Ueberroth insisted that from the beginning he saw that this 'wasn't the hook I was looking for' to win American public support for the relay and through it for the LA Games. Instead the funds should 'stay in the communities' through being donated to one of four charities for the sole purpose of 'youth sport development'.[28] These national philanthropies would take the lead in marketing what came to be called by the LAOOC the 'Youth Legacy Kilometers' (YLKs).

Strong reactions to these plans arose immediately, as they became known within the international Olympic establishment in the Spring of 1983. To Ueberroth's recollection, 'Both IOC President Juan Antonio Samaranch and IOC Director Monique Berlioux expressed concern about apparent commercialization of the relay, but changed their minds when they learned that not one penny would go to the LAOOC or to eligible Olympic athletes: The money would stay in the communities and help kids become better acquainted with Olympic sports programs. Samaranch and Berlioux considered this positive, long-range support for the Olympic Movement'.[29] I have been unable to locate anything in the IOC archives to confirm or disconfirm Ueberroth's account of this purported change of heart on the part of the IOC's two top leaders. It is clear, however, that their failure to ever publicly question the LAOOC's OFR plans made the IOC seem fully complicitous in the eyes of Greek public and journalistic opinion, once the issue became the object of national and international polemics.

Both the Greek IOC members Nikos Filaretos and Nikolaos Nissiotis did strongly object to the commercialization and monetization of the Olympic flame, when they first heard of the LAOOC's plans at the IOC's March 1983 Session in Delhi. Completely misreading IOC styles of governance with respect to reports by OCOGs at IOC Sessions, as well as Samaranch's command over the opinions of the independent members, Ueberroth allowed himself to be convinced that 'the Greeks, as part of the IOC membership, signed off on the project before the end of the session', simply because no vote was taken against it.[30] In fact, though they would in the end depart radically from one another in their practical actions, neither Nissiotis nor Filaretos ever 'signed off on the project' in the sense of endorsing in any way the LAOOC plans to have the relay corporately sponsored and to sell the rights to carry the flame.[31] Nor could they have, as leaders of the Hellenic Olympic movement known to, closely scrutinized by, and answerable to Greek public opinion in ways the Los Angelenos could scarcely imagine, given the public invisibility and marginality of IOC members and NOC officials in the USA. The LAOOC leaders were businessmen looking for a backstage 'deal' with Hellenic 'bosses' and repeatedly making the mistake, through the coming months, of believing they had such a deal after some private meeting, only to discover that the controversies had persisted and indeed grown in that court of Greek public opinion that the HOC, Greek IOC members, and government authorities were necessarily committed and responsible to satisfy. The general reaction of Ueberroth and his colleagues was to conceive of their Greek interlocutors as incompetent, political, deceptive, and possibly dishonest (as Ueberroth did not shrink in his memoir from characterizing Filaretos[32]).

As the final act of the private phase of OFR planning, the HOC and the LAOOC signed on 22 June 1983, the standard agreement for the former to provide to the latter, as to all previous OCOGs, the Olympia kindling ceremony, the relay to Athens, and the handover ceremony. By Ueberroth's own admission, this contract dealt exclusively with administrative matters – scheduling, equipment, housing, budgetary responsibilities – and did not mention what he euphemistically called in his memoir 'the scope of our relay'. The HOC, for its part, understood itself to be signing a purely technical document, as was its duty, and nothing further. But on the grounds that the two Greek IOC members had prior knowledge from the IOC Session (where they had protested), Ueberroth decided that 'the Greeks' had 'clearly understood our [total] plan' and were therefore agreeing to it all in this document. 'I figured the Greek issue was resolved'.[33]

Uneducated and naive about international Olympic and Hellenic history and institutions, and tone deaf to the nature of ritual,[34] Ueberroth and the LAOOC thus utterly failed to anticipate the perfect storm of outrage in Greece, when the 'American' plan to 'commercialize the Olympic flame' became publicly known there following the simultaneous press conferences the LAOOC held on 28 July 1983 in New York and Los Angeles to announce its OFR to the world.[35] In Greece, the Olympic flame is not only an iconic representation of contemporary Greece's international claims and aspirations, it had grown to become itself a master symbol of Greek national sovereignty through its deep embodiment of the foundational ideological tensions between *ellenismos* and *romeiismos* in modern Greek nationalism.[36] To appear to attack the integrity of the Olympic flame was thus widely perceived in Greece as an attack on Hellenic national dignity itself. And these were Americans doing it, not yet a decade after the fall of the Greek Military Junta that had been supported by Richard Nixon and the USA government in the name of anti-communism (as Bill Clinton would explicitly admit in his 1999 official apology in Athens, an event for which Hillary Clinton's 1996 Olympia visit and speech would set the stage). The 1983–1984 Greek/American flame relay imbroglio was also occurring in the midst of a ferocious public debate over the reneging of the PASOK government of Andreas Papandreou on its campaign promise to oust the US military bases, a development that spurred the anti-American 17 November terrorist organization into renewing assassination attempts on US military and intelligence personnel and their purported Greek collaborators.

This was the environment into which Ueberroth and the LAOOC stumbled – with Samaranch in private manoeuvres offstage[37] – promoting their 'innovative' flame relay plan. Understanding nothing of this environment except that it was generically 'political', they could scarcely imagine the situation of the HOC leaders, crushed between their duty to the international Olympic movement to ignite and provide the flame to the world, overwhelming Greek public opinion against these American depredations, and their own individual attitudes towards collaborating with Los Angeles. Throughout November 1983, Filaretos sent a string of missives to Samaranch, notable for their nationalist and religious language. He appealed 'in the name of our entire country' against the LAOOC's 'contempt for the deep and sacred meaning that is symbolized by the Olympic flame and relay.' Noting that 'the Olympic Flame is for the Greeks … a second religion', Filaretos begged Samaranch to intervene to 'annul this planned sacrilege'.[38]

When these private pleadings brought no action from the IOC, HOC president Angelo Lembessis and secretary-general Filaretos formally complained by telegram to the IOC and the LAOOC on 19 December 1983, that the LAOOC was using the Olympic torch relay 'as a tool for collection of money for athletic resources'. The telegram, which quickly found its way into the Greek media, further stated that 'our protest reflects also the entire Greek public opinion which has the unshakeable belief that a "sacrilege" is attempted against an institution which Greece considers as sacred and is determined to protect by all possible means. In addition, we must emphasize that by such actions of the LAOOC, the country [of the United States] as well as the United States Olympic Committee are unjustly exposed, although they have no involvement or responsibility on the subject'. The HOC concluded by demanding that the LAOOC stop all selling of torch relay slots immediately. Ueberroth could only react with incredulity, counter-accusation, and 'resentment'.[39] He thought he was doing Olympic good, and could never understand how his way of doing so might violate another culture's sacreds. 'I couldn't figure out where we'd gone wrong'.[40]

It was in part a classic case of failed intercultural communication. The argument that all the funds raised would go to youth charities proved widely incommunicable in a Greece where national charities of the American sort were (and are) few and unimportant, and where youth development is the responsibility of the State and perhaps, to a much lesser extent, the Church. Coupled with a political environment of widespread anti-American suspicion, this meant that the LAOOC was simply never believed by many Greeks in its insistent claims that it was not raising money for itself but only for youth sport. Hadn't the committee simultaneously sold advertising rights to AT&T? Moreover, the LAOOC was completely blind to and did nothing to counter the neo-imperialist reading of what it was up to. Ueberroth was appropriating a piece of world and Hellenic cultural capital – it was inseparably both, so every Greek schoolchild was taught – and using it to raise economic capital for the USA alone. Even if the 'collection of money for athletic resources' to which the HOC objected was for kids and not US Olympians, these were exclusively American kids. The world's richest country, without a shred of compunction, was exploiting humanity's scarce symbolic and moral resources for its own material development.[41]

Throughout the early months of 1984, the outcry in Greece steadily escalated, with many groups and newspaper editorials insisting that the HOC and the Greek government refuse to light a flame for the Americans. In February, renewed negotiations, under IOC mediation, between the HOC and LAOOC at the Sarajevo Winter Olympics – for which an Olympic flame had been provided without incident – made little progress.[42] The LAOOC offered to suspend YLK sales in April 'in an effort to appease the Greeks', but then refused to sign a draft agreement they found too 'restrictive' in this regard.[43] The mayor of Archaia Olympia Spyros Fotinos[44] was now giving regular news conferences, attracting the international press, in which he insisted that 'The flame for us is a sacred thing. It is not for sale' and vowing that 'If the American organizers want the flame, they will have to come and light it themselves'.[45] On 18 February, the mayor of Los Angeles Tom Bradley visited Olympia, but refused to see Mayor Fotinos further enflaming the locals. 'Olympians Ready to Block the Streets' was a subsequent headline in the March 13 issue of *USA Today*. Fotinos's political affiliation – KKE, the Communist party of Greece, legalized only 10 years earlier with the fall of the Regime of the Colonels – was widely noted,[46] but the fact was that all three leading political parties in Greece were now competing with one another to show the appropriate level of outrage to the wider electorate.

After Sarajevo, the impasse continued, as the HOC continued to demand an immediate cessation of torchbearer slot sales, while Ueberroth resisted. His fundraising from the OFR had turned out to be much weaker than he had expected, but was beginning to pick up as the Olympic year progressed. Indeed, the LAOOC had even managed to convince itself that the fight with Greece was boosting sales![47] Thus Ueberroth would only agree to cut off torch relay fundraising 30 days after a signed final agreement, further outraging Greeks for whom there could be no 'grace period' for sacrilege. In late February with Samaranch and on 10 March with the HOC, Ueberroth added the conditions that the HOC must certify that the LA OFR was 'a non-commercial venture', guarantee that there would be 'no further interference' from Greek officials of any kind, and agree that the flame would be transferred directly by electronic means from Greece to New York 'to avoid demonstrations along the relay route in Greece'.[48] The first two demands were outrageous and impossible to meet.[49] As to the third, the HOC and other Greek Olympic leaders shared an aversion to having the OFR protested for the first time in its home nation, but many saw this new demand of the LAOOC as both ignorant and cowardly.[50] It was ignorant of that body of Greek opinion that regarded the electronic satellite relay of the flame from Athens to Montreal in 1976 as a violation of the human spirit of the ritual. It was cowardly, as the LAOOC was seeking to avoid any honest face-to-face encounter with the Greek people. In Greece, 'democracy' is fundamentally understood as face-to-face argument in public, as 'dialectic' in the older sense of the term.[51] Ueberroth had never come to Greece to argue his case himself, and his emissaries, on their infrequent visits, had taken only private meetings in Athens and refused to face the Greek press or otherwise to appear in public to answer for themselves.[52] Now they were proposing to receive the Olympic flame without a single American Olympic official having to set foot in Greece! It was a proposal going nowhere.

The struggle over the 1984 OFR was becoming increasingly internationalized, not only in the newspapers but also as a Cold War resource. The Greek flame relay controversy and the threat of a Soviet boycott were the two major international relations challenges faced by Ueberroth, who hinted in his book of some dark relationship between them. In fact, the only relationship was the one his torch relay plan created. On 18–19 March, the 'International Center for Peace and Culture' a self-described assembly of 'prominent athletes, peace activists, and intellectuals', held a conference in Olympia to express solidarity with Mayor Fotinos and progressives throughout Greece in their protest against the American commercialization of the OFR. This group and its Olympia conference were organized by the American Olympian, progressive activist, and frequent Soviet Union visitor Phil Shinnick, together with Yelena Petushkova, three-time Soviet Olympic medallist and at that time vice-president of the Soviet NOC and holder of several Soviet Communist Party honours. The Soviet *Tass* press service reported extensively on their activities: '"The International Conference of Athletes" meeting in Olympia appealed to the United Nations for support to prevent the commercial relay. 350 delegates signed the petition against this clear violation of Olympic rules'.[53] On 23 April, *Tass* reported from Greece that: 'the Olympic flame is to the Greeks, among other things, a national pride. The general feeling here is against anybody soiling things that are held sacred by the nation'. On 27 April, *Tass* continued in the same vein: 'Since the very first days after Los Angeles was awarded the right to host the games, the IOC has made one concession after another to the organizers who have misused their "private status" for the sole purpose of making maximum profits with minimum investment. The Torch Relay is no exception. IOC President J.A. Samaranch recently said that what was unacceptable in Europe was possible in the United States'.[54] My subsequent interviews in Olympia and Athens confirmed the Soviet source of funding for the Olympia conference and further suggested that money had flowed from East Germany to the KKE to help it try to maintain a leading presence in the demonstrations against the Americans. [55]

While the sale of torchbearer slots was finally ended by the LAOOC in early April, the HOC notified the IOC on the 26th of that month that it could not provide the traditional flame ignition ceremony in Olympia scheduled for 7 May.[56] The Greek government stepped in two days later to assure an Olympia flame lighting on that date. President Konstantinos Karamanlis took the public lead, issuing a statement 'regretting the errors committed by Greeks and the foreigners against this sacred institution'.[57] As *Reuters* correctly noted, the government action thus provided the necessary public cover for certain Greek Olympic personages to participate in the ceremony 'while the HOC decision not to take part theoretically stands'.[58] But this would hardly be a regular liturgy of Greek OFR rites.

Any thought of a relay from Olympia to Athens had long since been abandoned as completely impossible, given the refusal of many municipalities along the route to provide safe passage. Many voices vowed to prevent the Olympic flame from reaching the capital and to take revenge on anyone who consented to carry a torch for Los Angeles. Therefore, there would be no conventional handover ceremony in the Panathenaic Stadium either, even if LAOOC officials would ever dare to show up there. The ignition ceremony itself remained in doubt as protesters were streaming towards Olympia vowing that 'the Americans will never take the flame'. On 7 May, the day of the ceremony, the ancient sanctuary (*altis*) was, for the first time ever, closed to the Greek public. Hundreds of police and fully armed soldiers cordoned off the site, facing off against hundreds of demonstrators angrily denouncing the proceedings.[59] It was later reported that President Karamanlis had secretly arrived in Olympia and was prepared to personally step in between demonstrators and the army should violence break out.[60]

The small LAOOC delegation – not including Ueberroth, another insulting violation of protocol – had landed in a US Air Force jet in Athens and then helicoptered to Olympia, setting down in the ancient Olympic stadium. The high priestess Katerina Didaskalou, despite multiple and very credible and frightening death threats against her if she participated in the ritual, lit the flame in the prescribed manner from the rays of the sun on the altar of The Mother just outside the Hera Temple[61] (see Figure 1). The customary declamations in ancient Greek and classical choreography of Maria Hors were reduced to bare minimums. Instead, the first Los Angeles torch was lit and handed by a sombre Nikos

Figure 1. An authentic Olympic flame for the Summer Games must be lit by a priestess from the rays of the sun in a mirror on the Altar of the Mother just in front of the Hera Temple at Ancient Olympia. Source: IOA.

Nissiotis, flanked by an equally unsmiling Filaretos and Otto Szymiczeck, to the LAOOC's Dick Sargent.[62] The flame was then immediately transferred to the miner's lantern, and Sargent reboarded his helicopter and took off for Athens, skipping entirely the ritual visit of the flame to the Pierre de Coubertin monument. (This is a stele in a grove triangulated by the ancient stadium, the Kronos Hill, and the IOA in which Coubertin's heart had been interred in 1938 by Crown Prince Paul.) From Athens, the LAOOC officials took off immediately for New York, where, according to all subsequent LAOOC press releases, videos, and documents, 'the Olympic torch relay began'.

Nikos Nissiotis and the secret flame

When I arrived in Olympia to do field work a month later, the village was still seething with the controversy. I listened to the extended opinions and arguments of all of my friends there,[63] and of their friends, and I interviewed many of the principals: the present and two former mayors, the police chief, the IOC members in Greece, HOC officials and staff, local and regional political party leaders, past torchbearers on the Greek relays, key demonstration organizers, the head of the local business council, even the parish priest (who had declined to participate in the flame-lighting ceremony for Los Angeles). Opinions were multiplex and divided, but nearly everyone I talked with agreed on two things: the callous sacrilegiousness of the Americans and the relief that bloodshed at the world's peace ceremony had been avoided, narrowly as quite a few insisted. At the IOA, I was further able to sample a global cross-section of younger people in the Olympic movement as to their awareness – high throughout the Europeans, moderate-to-low among everyone else – and judgements of the Greek/American/IOC flame relay struggles. This ethnography is a key source of the interpretations I have offered in this article, and a key resource for my subsequent collaboration with ACOG.

I was in Olympia and set up with certain of these interviews, thanks to Nikos Nisisotis, IOA president and IOC member in Greece. After the flame lighting at Olympia, he had phoned me to say that I must come, so that there would be an independent scholarly record and analysis of the struggle by an anthropologist able to contextualize both sides. Moreover, in the context of their now announced boycott of the Los Angeles Olympics, the Soviet Bloc was sending an especially large delegation of famous Olympic champions and security handlers for the IOA session. I would lecture, of course, but Nissiotis told me that he also wanted a more mature and knowledgeable American presence on the campus than the feckless delegates typically sent by the United States Olympic Committee (USOC), to help him balance any propaganda campaign launched there by the Eastern Europeans.

Nikos Nissiotis was a world-class theologian and scholar of comparative religions. A one-time student of Karl Barth, Karl Jaspers, and C.G. Jung, he was professor of theology at Athens University, Associate General Secretary of the World Council of Churches, and the leading Greek Orthodox figure in the world-wide Ecumenical Movement. Nissiotis had taught at major universities all around the world, including in the USA, where he developed his particular passion for playing basketball.[64] He was by far the most scholarly IOC member at the time or subsequently, and one would have to go back to Coubertin's friend William Milligan Sloane, European historian and founder of the American Historical Association, to find a figure of comparable intellectual stature in the IOC. Had his life not been cut tragically short, Nissiotis, I am convinced, would have gone on to formulate a new Olympism for the global, intercultural world of today to replace the Eurocentric, modernizationist one the Olympic movement still largely relies on. Nissiotis was also an extraordinary teacher, an expert practitioner as well as a leading theorist of ecumenical discourse, the real object of the Olympic movement for which Olympic sport is intended to serve as only a means. After his death, the IOA never regained its status as a place for serious intercultural encounter and debate, and today it is largely a marginalized venue for the Olympic sport industry.

My book on Coubertin and the birth of the modern Olympic movement was barely out when I received, in 1982, a complimentary letter from Nissiotis and an invitation to lecture at the IOA for the first time. He understood completely the project of cultural anthropology and saw it as homologous with that of the ecumenical religious movement. We had subsequently spent many hours profitably debating the relationship between the general methodological positions of cultural relativism and universal humanism and their place in the practical affairs of the Olympic movement. Trained in many of the same literatures, we shared an intense interest in the place of ritual in transnational cultural affairs and political disputes. With the 1984 OFR battle, Nissiotis was living as a central actor through an extraordinary case example of these intercultural and transnational problems of ritual. Nikos wanted intellectual and moral company. I was honoured to answer the summons of a man I considered, after Victor Turner, to be my mentor.

Late one afternoon, Nikos and I quietly left the IOA for the deserted terrace of a taverna in the isolated village of Platanos. I had no inkling of what might require such a hush-hush setting, and I had never seen my friend so jumpy. 'There was a secret flame lighting. I want to tell you as an anthropologist and Olympic scholar about it, so that there is an independent record. Get out your notebook'. Nissiotis proceeded to recount how he had decided, as the senior IOC member in Greece, that no matter the offences of the LAOOC, it was Greece's duty as guardian for the IOC of the Olympic flame to provide an authentic flame for Los Angeles.

> I did not like what the LAOOC did, but I do not share the obsessive anti-Americanism of my [Greek Olympic] colleagues. So I took an action. There was another Olympic flame. We lit it in advance, in secret, in case the normal flame ignition [ceremony] could not be held. Then I had it carried back to Samaranch in Lausanne. You are an anthropologist of ritual. I am telling you this so that you will know the whole story, but also because you understand how important it is to always have a real Olympic flame. I arranged the ritual correctly. A young woman as priestess, the fire from heaven made in a mirror, on the altar slab outside the Hera Temple: I had everything done right. I was very afraid, but no one noticed us, thank heaven.[65]

I was stunned by what I was hearing. Nissiotis hardly needed to tell me that 'it was a very dangerous step to take, people's lives were placed at risk'. Samaranch had hand picked and sent the operatives from Lausanne, two 'Swiss students' as they were to come to be described. After the flame lighting in which one served as the priestess while the other took photographs, they drove the flame back to IOC headquarters. On 2 May, five days before the public flame ignition, Samaranch called Ueberroth to tell him Lausanne already had an authentic flame: 'Come and get it'.[66] On 4 May, this secret flame was presented by Samaranch in Lausanne to LAOOC press officer Greg Harney. On 5 May, it was driven to the Lyon-Satolis airport in France and flown out from there to New York on Air France cargo flight 1306.[67] As it turned out, the secret flame was not needed, as the LAOOC got its official flame from Olympia on 7 May. The second flame was extinguished and never used.[68] However, the matter did not end there.

In March of 1986, Peter Ueberroth published his Olympic memoirs from which I have been quoting. I secured an early copy and was shocked to find not just an account of the secret flame lighting but the actual photographs of it, taken by the second of the 'Swiss students' in order to document the provenance and proper ritual means of ignition. Though he professed to like and trust Nissiotis, Ueberroth did not shrink from fingering him as the first to suggest the solution of 'a private ceremony' at Olympia.[69] As it happened, I was leaving immediately for Lausanne and a conference on 'The Relevance of Pierre de Coubertin Today'. There I would see Nissiotis, who would be presenting a much-anticipated paper on Coubertin's *religio athletae*.[70] At the opening of the meeting at the Villa Mon Repos (where Coubertin had lived his final years as a charity case), I waited to approach Nissiotis until he was standing alone. We embraced, and I told him, 'Niko, Ueberroth has published the secret flame lighting and your role in it. Look, this is his memoir and here are the pictures'. Nissiotis took one look at the book page I was holding open and fainted, collapsing into an armchair that was fortuitously beneath him.

His first anguished words, as he came to, were 'How could he do this? Doesn't he understand he could get people killed?' My mentor and friend had a heart condition, and I was extremely worried as I watched his ashen face through the ceremonial opening speeches that followed. At the ensuing reception, Nikos grabbed my arm and rushed us up to confront Samaranch. 'Professor MacAloon has just shown me that Ueberroth has revealed the secret flame lighting and even published pictures in his book. How can this be?' Nissiotis was nearly in the president's face, sputtering with anger and anxiety, but Samaranch did not lose his characteristic sang-froid. Obviously, he already knew. 'Calm yourself, Nikos, there will not be a problem'. This unexpected riposte seemed to knock Nissiotis back a step, and as he began again to remonstrate with Samaranch, the president interrupted: 'Listen. You know that new seminar you two want for the Olympic Academy, the one just for scholars and graduate students? I think the IOC should support that'. I was just astonished. In a split-second in the heat of the moment, Samaranch had come up with a quid pro quo: let it go with Ueberroth, and I shall pay for your post-graduate seminar.[71] Stunned, Nikos mumbled something like 'you just don't understand', and we walked away.

As the evening came to a close, Nissiotis took me out a side door and into a waiting car. He had evidently made some phone calls in the interim. A woman whom I recognized was behind the wheel. We drove away from Mon Repos and pulled off to the side of a private road. It was made clear to me that our driver was the person who had acted as the priestess at the secret flame lighting in Olympia and who was now herself aware of being at considerable risk should her identity ever become known. 'Tell John what you told me about how those photographs got into Ueberroth's hands'. It was Monique Berlioux's doing, I was informed. In 1985, she had been forced out by Samaranch as IOC director and had taken IOC files with her. One contained the documentation photographs of the secret flame lighting, and Belioux had supplied copies of these to Ueberroth. She clearly expected that he would publish them to further thumb his nose at 'the Greeks' who had caused him so much trouble, while it was Samaranch whom Berlioux herself was seeking to embarrass and threaten. (The third photo showed him handing over the miner's lantern to the LAOOC official.) Herself caring nothing about Greek Olympic colleagues or the persons whose hands appeared in the photos, Berlioux had used Ueberroth to gain a measure of her own revenge.

When the official report of the Los Angeles Games subsequently appeared, it also mentioned the existence and possession by the LAOOC of 'a back-up flame for the torch relay'.[72] But these volumes – printed in limited number for the IOC and costing nearly a thousand dollars for anyone else – never came under journalistic or public scrutiny in Greece. The real miracle was that Ueberroth's *Made in America* did not seem to have either, and through the rest of 1986 and 1997, the months went nervously by without the Greek press, political parties, or terrorist cells seizing upon the book's revelations to provoke a new public outrage and recriminations. Whichever government and HOC leaders were aware of the secret ritual, if any, they later chose to keep silent about it too, doubtless in their own self-interests.[73] The fact that a personage like Nassos Kritsinelis had not heard of the secret flame lighting until it came up in our conversation for this volume indicates to me that the HOC leadership as a whole was never approached with and never discussed any 'Lausanne flame' ultimatum.[74] In any case, soon enough, Nissiotis was gone. The identities of the two 'Swiss students' remain carefully concealed to this day.[75]

ACOG: a different kind of American

No OCOG after the LAOOC ever even considered using the Olympic flame for fund-raising purposes. As for corporate sponsorship of the OFR, the practice became entrenched with Calgary, Albertville, and Barcelona and won complete support from the IOC whose own TOP programme of worldwide corporate sponsorship had been deployed in the years after LA 1984.[76] Though much Greek discourse continued to object, the Hellenic Olympic leadership grew resigned to OFR sponsorships in foreign host nations. However, it would not budge with respect to the Greek OFR ceremonies and segments. These would remain commercial-free. ACOG respected this policy and would never have allowed its OFR sponsor Coca-Cola to approach the HOC with a view towards any consideration in Greece.[77]

While the Athens/Atlanta contest for the rights to the 1996 Olympics left great bitterness and much alibiing in the Greek Olympic establishment, as has been discussed, paradoxically ACOG started out with a much greater knowledge of Hellenic Olympic leaders and traditions than the LAOOC ever attained. The latter did not have to work hard to get to know IOC, IF, and NOC officials personally, while the Atlanta bid committee did, in fact making an art of it in their own self-estimation. Rival bid teams come to have an intimate knowledge of one another, through mutual intelligence gathering but mostly from spending so much time together in hotel lobbies around the world, waiting for IOC members and other Olympic leaders to pass by in the hopes of chatting them up. The Greek IOC members and HOC officials and several of the 'Atlanta Nine' already had a good deal of mutual acquaintance, and ACOG was very careful never to appear to be gloating but always to be humble in the presence of the defeated bid leaders from Athens and the HOC. In private, ACOG leaders readily acknowledged that they had not so much won as Athens had lost, and several had sincere feelings of empathy for their Greek counterparts.

No one did more to set and maintain this tone in HOC/ACOG relations than Charlie Battle, the ACOG managing director of international relations. Many in Olympic circles, including the present writer, think Battle is probably the friendliest person they have ever met, someone utterly undaunted by social and cultural differences with his interlocutors because of his own good-natured humility and refusal to take himself too seriously.[78] But even the less naturally companionable and adventurous members of the ACOG inner circle firmly believed they had won the Olympics by becoming friends with even the most culturally different and personally difficult Olympic figures. This collective ethos meant that from the beginning ACOG was committed to the seemingly impossible task of making peace with and winning the eventual collaboration of the Hellenic Olympic establishment and through that to begin to alter Greek public opinion about 'Americans' in the Olympic movement. The OFR would necessarily be the centrepiece of their campaign.

The detailed analysis of where Ueberroth and company had gone wrong served as a kind of operating manual for ACOG. There would be grand gestures to honour Hellenic tradition and contemporary Hellenic Olympism, like designing the Atlanta Olympic torch in a bundle of reeds motif taken from the Greek vase paintings from which the ancient *lampadedromia* is chiefly known. Another was letting the HOC know early on that it would be choosing a Greek athlete to be one of the final flame bearers at the opening ceremonies in the Atlanta Olympic Stadium. Also, an entire segment of the cultural performance section of those ceremonies would be exclusively devoted to evoking and honouring ancient Greece athletics. Three hundred Greek schoolchildren and youth (including Pinelopi Amelidou, an author in this volume) were selected by the HOC and funded by ACOG to come to the USA to participate in the OFR celebrations. Special sculpture was commissioned from Greek artists for Centennial Olympic Park. The Centennial theme was carried through everything with an 'it all began in *modern* Greece' twist to it.

At Olympic meetings around the world, every effort was made to cultivate Greek IOC, NOC, and IF officials, always including special briefings on Atlanta's OFR plans and always emphasizing the importance of understanding and respecting Greek tradition. Often this meant having to listen to extended diatribes against the LAOOC and what it had done. ACOG officials were prepared for this and, though they did not speak out publically against Ueberroth, privately they had no trouble agreeing with most of what Greek voices had to say about 1984. As for the IOC, its moneymen Michael Payne and Dick Pound – the latter head of the IOC marketing commission as well as of the new Olympic Games Coordination Commission developed in part in response to the IOC's sense of powerlessness against Ueberroth in Los Angeles – were kept at arms length from the ACOG OFR, so as not to revive Greek suspicions.

ACOG worked closely with Greek–American organizations and individuals, not only from Atlanta, but from Chicago and New York as well. It listened patiently to every suggestion made by these groups and indulged their own, sometimes vigorous rivalries with one another. Greek–American communities and organizations were given precedence and marked roles in the US segment of the flame relay and in several other venues as well. But ACOG never made Los Angeles's mistake of allowing Greek–American voices to substitute for their own in communicating with the Hellenic authorities. All offers by Greek–American businessmen and religious leaders to 'mediate' for ACOG in Greece were politely declined.

But more important than anything else was ACOG's coming to clearly understand and accept that its top leaders had to be regularly seen in Greece and to behave there in ways that completely distinguished ACOG from the LAOOC. Again, the ACOG leadership's general ethos of sociability as organizational capital helped immeasurably in furthering this resolve, as did the fact that these leaders were for the most part middle class professionals – lawyers, realtors, public servants, bankers, civic association officials – used to dealing on a face-to-face basis with clients and antagonists alike. They were not corporate CEOs accustomed to, indeed proud of being insulated from all lesser personages and the general public. Still, it took a great deal of individual moxie for these Atlantans to stand undefended in Greece in front of the wave of animosity that was the recent history of Greek/US OFR relations. And we did insist that it had to be an open and unbunkered presence, befitting Greek popular understandings of democracy and sincerity and, again, in utter contrast to how the LAOOC had behaved. I had been circulating a message among my own networks, in Ancient Olympia and the surrounding region, among the HOC staff, within the academic community,[79] and with certain backstage presences in the Greek Olympic establishment whom I knew through Nissiotis and with whom I had grieved for him. Everywhere I could, I spread the word that these ACOG leaders were a much different kind of American than the people from Los Angeles and Colorado Springs. Now it was up to ACOG to prove it, and across a nearly two-year period, they did everything they could to do so.

Battle seized every opportunity to be in Greece, and his senior colleagues Andrew Young, Ginger Watkins, and the flame relay directors soon followed. Indeed, when they had business in Europe or the Middle East, they frequently diverted to Athens just to pay visits to the HOC, whether or not there were any pressing matters to discuss. While in Athens, ACOG officials, of course, made courtesy calls on US ambassador Thomas Niles, but they self-consciously did not spend any more time than was absolutely necessary at the US Embassy. The message was that we are ordinary citizens and sports leaders, not political agents of the US government, and we have no reason to hide behind its massive security. Knowing they would be photographed doing so, ACOG tried to take its meals in public restaurants with HOC and Greek Sports Ministry officials – the strategy on this point was professed innocence over Greek political party differences together with trying to balance contacts with PASOK and NEA figures.

Whatever meetings were scheduled at the IOA in Olympia, whether for young participants, journalists, physical education teachers, or post-graduate students (Samaranch's 'gift' to Nissiotis and me in 1986), ACOG wrangled invitations to them. Whether offered speaking parts or not, the important thing was to demonstrate sincere interest and investment in Olympic education and both to acknowledge and to add additional lustre to the HOC's and Greece's leadership in this area. On other occasions, ACOG officials simply arrived in Olympia as tourist-pilgrims come to be inspired by the ruins of the ancient Olympic games and the contents of the Olympia Museum. In either case, spending hours hanging out in the cafes, restaurants, and art galleries of Ancient Olympia – beginning with the Galérie Orphée, where Apostolos Kosmopoulos conducted his own alternative seminar on Greek Olympism and international affairs[80] – was of the greatest importance. The message delivered by ACOG was that we are here and we are happy to meet and talk with anyone and everyone about anything, including the unpleasantnesses of the past and why they will never be repeated. The citizens and political leaders of Olympia, who had been put through so much, were soon taking full advantage of these opportunities for informal conversation with American Olympic leaders, opportunities that were inconceivable in the days of the LAOOC. Indeed, ACOG was distinguishing itself from every other OCOG by these sustained practices. So thorough was their buy-in that I could send a message to Battle or any other ACOG leader in Olympia, 'take a taxi to the neighbouring village of "X" and at 7:00 pm take a coffee or an ouzo on the terrace of taverna "Y"' and they would comply without question, knowing they would there serendipitously be meeting a nomarch or mayor or regional party official or other local notable. These conversations were not always easy and inappropriate demands were sometimes made, but being rural Greece – indeed that part of it in which the flame would have to be lit for Atlanta and through which its OFR would first have to pass – the word quickly got around about these top American Olympic officials who properly understood the recent history and who behaved like honest, normal people. Some locals marvelled that they could approach a former US Ambassador to the United Nations, sitting by himself with no security men in a Peloponnesian village café and happy to talk about Olympic affairs.

With respect to formal arrangements with the HOC for the OFR ceremonies in Greece, ACOG was patient, accommodating, and respectful. The ACOG leadership had been thoroughly inoculated against the LAOOC canard, later retailed among other OCOGs, that 'the Greeks' were always trying to squeeze more money than necessary from the other side in the contractual negotiations for the OFR rituals.[81] Instead, ACOG assumed that the HOC had legitimate reasons for each of its requests and negotiated from that positioning, with no bean-counter back in Atlanta ever daring to challenge the manifest wishes of Billy Payne and AD Frazier as to relations with Greece. This attitude was of critical importance in 1996, for the HOC governors and Nassos Kritsinelis and his flame relay team, in collaboration with the sports, culture, and interior ministries of the federal government as well as with dozens of municipalities, had planned an extended relay through Greece and a particularly elaborate handover ceremony at the end of it in Athens. Greece might not have the 1996 Olympic Games, but the Centennial was its own. Celebrating the 100th anniversary of Athens, 1896, required out-of-the-ordinary arrangements, and Atlanta resolved to cheer them on.

Indeed, ACOG informed the HOC that in honour of the Greek Olympic Centennial and because it cared so sincerely for the OFR, it would be sending perhaps the largest delegation from an OCOG ever to appear at Olympia for the flame-lighting ceremony. Moreover, at least two ACOG officers, its flame relay directors Hilary Hanson and Rennie Truitt, and the present author would be travelling the entire route through Greece with the flame.[82] ACOG would be pleased to bear all the costs for these arrangements. In the past, the absence of any OCOG representation on the Greek segment of the flame relay had been a cause for irritation, particularly for Kritsinelis and his team on the ground.[83] In gratitude for this further testimony of respectful interest and enthusiastic participation, the HOC instructed Kritsinelis to ensure that each of the ACOG officials carried the Olympic flame somewhere on the Greek relay. It was an assignment he was happy to fulfil, having grown comfortable over the preceding months with Battle, Watkins, Hanson, and Truitt. The last two, Kritsinelis had come to regard as his junior protégés in the flame relay family, and they in turn warmly regarded him as the high priest of the Olympic flame[84] (Figure 2).

This campaign had by no means completely eliminated the problems. The Coca-Cola/CNN claim continued to be widely voiced, and there were scattered calls for Greeks to boycott the OFR rites for Atlanta. Kritsinelis's conversations with leaders of municipalities potentially on the route were more extended than usual.[85] But most of the Hellenic Olympic establishment had been won over and public opinion at least mollified,

Figure 2.   Athanassios Kritsinelis (far right), the dean of Greek flame relay practice, working with ACOG relay directors Rennie Truitt and Hilary Hanson at Olympia. Photo by the author.

and there was no longer any question about the normal ceremonies proceeding in Olympia. ACOG attention now turned to these.

Some weeks before our departure for Greece, I went to Billy Payne's office to talk about his speech at Olympia. I knew that the body of the speech was being written by George Hirthler, head of a small Atlanta marketing firm who had won his spurs with ACOG by designing its bid documents. Hirthler had become an enthusiastic philhellene and partisan of Olympism, and I was not worried about his part of the speech.[86] I knew Billy Payne would further personalize it with his trademark passion and exuberance. Delivering a vibrant and memorable ending was what concerned me.

- Billy, at Olympia, you have to say something in Greek at the end of your speech.
- I do?
- It's tradition. All recent OCOG chiefs have done this. If you don't, it will be noticed.
- What am I supposed to say?
- Here's my suggestion, Billy. You'll say: *Tin floga kai ta matia mas, tin floga kai ta matia mou.*
- What does that mean?
- Literally, it means 'The flame, our eyes; the flame, my eyes'. It's a traditional Greek expression, a curse really. You'd be saying 'If we hurt this flame, may we go blind. If I hurt this flame, may I go blind'.
- I can say that. I want to say that.

Billy Payne did not hesitate in the slightest. Whatever his Protestant faith might think about folkloric curses, his own truly religious devotion to the cause of these Games answered for him. I wrote out the Greek phonetically, and he began that day to practice, much to the wonder and amusement of some of his office staff.

The Clinton entourage in Greece

I arrived back in Athens as part of the first ACOG wave before the Olympia flame-lighting ceremony, scheduled for 30 March. We were billeted in the Grand Bretagne hotel on Syntagma Square, and I was not there long before I received a call from Gary Allison, who announced he was on his over. C. Gary Allison was a Hollywood screenwriter and producer, whom I had known since 1982, when he was working on his Columbia Television/NBC mini-series 'The First Olympics–Athens, 1896'. Gary had become so enamoured with turning up lost archives of pioneering American Olympic figures that he subsequently devoted himself to producing a *The Olympic Century*, a 25-volume popular series on the world history of the Olympic movement, working in episodic collaboration with the IOC and the USOC. But Gary had had a previous life as a White House aide, working in the Kennedy administration from 1961 to 1963 as a protocol specialist, and in the Johnson and Nixon administrations chairing a youth development programme. He was also a close friend of US Vice-president Al Gore, who was coordinating the White House's collaboration with the Atlanta Olympic Games. As a result, Gary had been selected to be the Olympic protocol expert to accompany Mrs Clinton's delegation to Greece. This turned out to be extremely fortuitous, as I was serving in something like the same capacity for ACOG, and we knew each other so well. (My international research team for the 1984 Olympics had rented Gary's house in Los Angeles.)

When Gary arrived at my hotel, he was accompanied by a man whom he introduced to me only by first name, 'Alexander' as I recall, but who I was immediately given to understand was a head of Mrs Clinton's Secret Service detail. We spent the next two hours going over in minute detail the site of Ancient Olympia and the liturgy of the Greek flame-lighting ceremony. After that, I took the opportunity to share my fears that the Secret Service and the rest of Mrs Clinton's entourage, by following their normal routines, might disturb and distort the ritual process in ways that would displease the Greek Olympic authorities and the local audiences and reflect badly on ACOG as well as the White House. (Most Greeks would not now make any distinction between the two.) On the security front, for example, it became apparent that the Secret Service was thinking of closing to the Greek public the narrow road stretching alongside and above the inner sanctuary at Olympia, at least while the priestess was lighting the flame. Mrs Clinton would be inside observing, and persons looking down from this road could have a clear line of attack, a 'head shot' in Alexander's term of art. I explained that while most of the audience would be inside the ancient stadium – invited guests on the stadium floor and the general public on the slopes that served the ancient crowd as bleachers – they would be unable to witness the actual flame-lighting from there and would only see the flame when the high priestess carried it in high choreography over the western berm and down into the stadium for the handover to the first torchbearer.[87] Veteran Greek ritual aficionados, including many residents of Olympia and Elis, knew this and preferred to gather on the road to view the most dramatic moment of the rite, the actual ignition of the flame in the mirror. They would be severely disappointed and angry, and might even create a disturbance audible from below should they find their customary venue denied them. Alexander agreed to consider these concerns, and in the end a compromise satisfactory to all parties was developed.

On quite another front, I explained how Nassos Kritsinelis worked hard to position the Greek broadcasters and all credentialed photographers to make it nearly impossible for them to show in the same shot the priestess flame-lighting choreography and the contemporary dignitaries inside the sanctuary. As he describes in his interview later in this volume, this practice was of critical importance to Kritsinelis, as well as to the choreographer Maria Hors, and the entire HOC, for it protects the dramatic illusion of an ancient world for the national television and international press audiences. It was imperative that the White House photographer and any White House press corps member allowed inside the sanctuary not violate this protocol by producing any shot incorporating both Mrs Clinton and the priestesses in action. ACOG had already been cautioned to the same end with respect to its officials and photographer in the inner sanctuary. Gary promised to take the matter up with the White House press officers, and no such photograph or video ever appeared.

This discussion led into another. Mrs Clinton was apparently keenly interested in the priestesses, and she and her daughter looked forward to meeting and talking with them after the ceremony. It occurred to me that, feminist that she is, Hillary Clinton always preferred to have some female Secret Service agents close around her. (I had even heard these bodyguards referred to as the 'killer women'.) A photograph of the High Priestess Maria Pambouki with her attendants together with Hillary Clinton and Chelsea Clinton with theirs could be very offensive to certain Greek audiences, if it was ever published. Gary was not sure if the White House press corps could be deterred from taking such shots. I reminded him that the Clintons were in a tough re-election campaign, and that by the time we left for Olympia, ACOG had received a two-inch stack of letters from Americans demanding that it not take part in 'this pagan ritual'.[88] Perhaps, it was not politically wise to have photos of Hillary Clinton communing with 'pagan priestesses' circulating back in the USA. Apparently, the point got through, because Mrs Clinton and Chelsea met only privately in the Olympic Museum with the priestesses, with only their personal White House photographer present.

In wrapping up our initial meeting, Gary insisted that Mrs Clinton's team understood our concerns and would do everything possible to minimize and discipline their footprint at Olympia.[89] Arrangements were made for Alexander and I to be able to quickly contact one another if necessary. (Though we did nod to one another several times in Olympia, we had no further conversations.) As he left, I remarked to Gary that I guessed I knew who the chief speechwriter was for Mrs Clinton's address at the flame lighting. He smiled broadly.

Meanwhile, Charlie Battle had been huddling with the HOC top officials, President Antonios Tzikas, a slightly baffling industrialist, and the very capable secretary-general Dionyssis Gangas, a lawyer, as well as with the Greek IOC members Filaretos and Lambis Nikolaou. Charlie reported back that Mrs Clinton's presence had created what Americans of his and my generation know as 'the Durante effect', after the comedian Jimmy Durante who was always complaining that 'everybody was trying to get into the act'. The HOC was overwhelmed with requests for official invitations to the ceremonies at Olympia, and it was scrambling to enlarge and sophisticate the traditional lunch it gave at the IOA after the flame had left on the relay. Above all, the uneasy condominium of the NEA HOC and the PASOK government was stretching to the breaking point, as Mrs Clinton's presence was to the latter sufficient reason to demand a larger government presence in what was nominally the HOC's ceremony. Greek presidents and prime ministers did not typically appear at the Olympia flame lighting – reports of President Karamanlis's concealed presence in 1984 were noted above – and would not be present this time, because the leader of the US government mission was the First Lady not the American President. After much last-minute argument over proper protocol, it had been decided that Mrs Simitis, the prime minister's wife, would accompany and sit next to Mrs Clinton as her official host in Olympia. Mr Tzikas had somewhat presumptuously been planning this role for himself, and he was miffed, and even more upset when it was discovered that the government Undersecretary for Sport was now insisting on being the first speaker in the opening phase of the ritual due to the State nature of the new protocol demanded by Mrs Clinton's 'leadership of the U.S. delegation'.[90]

The good news in all this Hellenic jockeying for position was that Mrs Clinton's visit was proving so interesting and attractive to a cross-section of Greek elites that the stakes were raised for any person or group thinking of protesting for any reason against delivery of the Olympic flame to 'the Americans'. The bad news was that ACOG was getting lost in the shuffle, and as we departed for Olympia, we realized that we were going to have to be zealous in guarding the organizing committee's own position at the flame ignition ceremony.

29–30 March 1996, in Olympia

Charlie Battle largely spent the day before the ceremony at the IOA, the HOC's headquarters in Olympia, ostensibly managing the final arrangements for ACOG accommodations and meeting space there, but actually keeping an ear wide open for any last minute programme changes that might disadvantage Atlanta. He was also in close touch with ACOG's government affairs person who based himself at the US Embassy, the Clinton team's headquarters. I spent the morning with Nassos Kritsinelis in the closed Olympic ruins watching and photographing the final dress rehearsal for the flame lighting (Figure 3), and chatting during breaks with Maria Hors, Maria Pambouki, and my friends on the technical staff. Security was intense, but not overbearing, and there was no indication that the police, the plainclothes Greek security forces, and US Secret Service agents moving about did not have their division of labour well sorted out. (That impression lasted throughout the next day.) Everything was focused and calm with the rehearsal until

Figure 3. The priestesses rehearse their choreography for the Atlanta flame-lighting ceremony. Photo by the author.

Lambis Nikolaou, the excitable and officious junior IOC member in Greece, arrived on the scene and began ranting and barking orders at Kritsinelis and his staff. Nikolaou had no use for me anyway, so as the arguments began to heat up, I left and walked to town to spend the rest of the day making the rounds of my network.[91]

Many of those I visited had talked with me during my research in 1984, and a number commented spontaneously as to the differences those 12 years had made. Said one, 'Who would have ever thought that so many people here would be happy to welcome Mrs Clinton and you Americans to come and get the flame'. Another, a thoughtful schoolteacher and poet who had been a leader of the non-communist anti-LAOOC forces back in 1984, insisted that the intervening fall of the Soviet Union 'had really changed everything. Now people here only fight about whether PASOK or NEA families are manipulating the system better than others'. A significant percentage of shops were making a point of displaying 'ATHENS 1996' tee shirts prominently in their windows, some original, some newly minted for the occasion. A couple of people I spoke with seemed still to believe that Mrs Clinton's motorcade down Praxiteles Street (it actually passed another way) would be followed by a parade of Coca-Cola trucks and an army of CNN journalists. And there were far fewer American flags on display than there had been Spanish flags in 1992. But I could detect no rumours of, much less any plans by anyone to protest at the site or during the relay the next day. A former mayor did caution that thousands of people were said to be en route, and 'with so many outsiders here, who knows what tomorrow will bring'.

In the course of my fact-finding peregrinations that afternoon, I ran into Gary Allison with other Clinton advance team members on the steps of the Galérie Orphée. 'I had it arranged', he told me, 'for Professor Yalouris to present the ancient games to Hillary and Chelsea at the Museum tomorrow, and for you to talk with them about the Olympic movement today at the IOA, but Ambassador Niles insisted that he would do all of their briefing. He's angling for a better posting next year'. I regretted the opportunity, but realized I had to stay free to do my part for ACOG. Indeed, the rest of the Atlanta delegation had arrived at the IOA, and when I returned there, Ginger Watkins and Linda Stephenson, another of the Atlanta Nine, took me aside and asked that I recommend a quiet but 'spiritually significant' place for the top ACOG leadership to meet together the next morning before the ceremony. The COO AD Frazier also found me to request an early morning tour of the ruins. It was going to be a crowded day.

ACOG was giving a party at a hotel restaurant in town, and after a few more conversations at the Academy, I decided to walk over there to see how things were going. What I found was an entirely different scene from what I was expecting. The entry was full of ACOG staffers whom I did not recognize, the pushiest of whom turned out to be from Dick Yarbrough's press relations group. They were all done up in credentials and acting as if they were the gatekeepers at a royal banquet, turning away anyone, myself included, who did not have a printed invitation. I was prepared to be amused, until they sent back out into the parking lot an important local politician who had been particularly helpful to us. Soon local dignitaries were piling up at the door, shocked at first and then growing more and more irritated at this most un-Hellenic inhospitality. (Printed invitations, indeed! Where did these people think they were?) It was threatening to become a major scene. I forced my way in and demanded of a guy acting particularly the boss that he immediately get Charlie or Ginger, or Billy over at the IOA on the phone. After a moment, Charlie came on and I explained what was happening, then passed the phone back to this fellow who took an earful. As he glowered at me, I retreated to the crowd outside, using my acquaintances in the group to assure everyone, with a gentle inside joke about the hotel proprietor, that they were just finishing the set-up inside and it would only be a moment. Soon, Charlie roared up in an HOC car and in his convivial way ushered everyone inside as if nothing untoward had happened. Billy Payne and the other ACOG officers, the HOC entourage, Mayor Deves of Olympia, and Konstantinos Rallis the nomarch of Elis arrived shortly thereafter, and the party proceeded as intended.

But my encounter with this 'other ACOG' was not finished for the evening. At one point during the party, I was chatting with an Olympics reporter from the *Yomiuri Shimbun*, an old friend, when another staffer from the ACOG press office rushed up and drew me physically aside to insist that no one was allowed to talk to journalists without Mr Yarbrough's explicit permission. I told this officious aide in no uncertain terms that he had just interrupted a personal conversation, and that if Mr Yarbrough had objections, he could come tell me himself.

These ACOG line staff who had just arrived in Greece for what was for most of them their first international Olympic experience had clearly been drilled in the 'rules and regulations' of their respective ACOG departments, but with no preparation for the actual context in which they now found themselves and were expected to operate effectively. It was typical bureaucratic stuff, but in retrospect it was also prophetic of the radical differences and degree of disconnection between the AOCOG officers and the line staff that were to so trouble the Atlanta Olympic Games themselves and to leave them with a poor overall reputation among many in international Olympic circles. While ACOG's small band of charismatic leaders were off accomplishing remarkable things, their lines of communication with functional managers in the bigger organization and their monitoring of the actual level of intradepartmental preparation and competence were not always what they should have been. As it was later put to me by one high IOC officer who acknowledges but does not share our prioritization of Olympic ritual, 'It's great what Billy and company accomplished with the torch relay, but maybe they should have been back in Atlanta making sure the computer system would work'. In the partial chaos of the opening days of the Games in Atlanta, when journalists could not get competition results and bus drivers were getting lost driving athletes to their venues, it was Hanson and Truitt and their team, exhausted and triumphant after 15,000 miles of flame relaying across the USA, who were rousted by Ginger Watkins and sent back out into the streets to try to direct Olympic Family traffic.

Of course, no one in Olympia was imagining any of this as the party broke up, and we returned to the IOA on the eve of the flame lighting. Battle and Watkins sat in on what they thought was the final meeting for the evening of the HOC flame relay committee, then retired to get some rest for the big day. I sat with Alexis Kostalas, going over Billy Payne's speech for the ceremony. Kostalas is a talented actor, ERT personality, and Ministry of Culture official who served as the HOC's translator on all important occasions.[92] Alexis had arrived at the IOA late, having been busy with the White House and Mrs Clinton's speech. Now we went line by line through Billy's, and when we got to the final sentences in Greek, he was clearly surprised by them. We determined to simply to repeat them in Greek in his consecutive interpretation. I nervously asked Alexis what he thought. 'I never expected such a thing; I think it could work'.

It was now very late, and I was about to retire myself, when bustling in came Martin Szymiczek (later Marton Simitsek, having subsequently Hellenized his name), the son of a long-time dean of the IOA,[93] who was now an HOC protocol official. Martin proceeded to convene another meeting to once again go over the ritual order for the next day. I figured I had better stay to listen and was glad I did when Martin announced, seemingly out of the blue, that only Mrs Clinton's speech would be translated into Greek the next day. I strongly objected that it would be completely against tradition and protocol not to have Billy Payne's speech consecutively translated as well. Martin responded that the OCOG chief's speech was never translated, and I told him this was absolutely incorrect, quoting some lines from Pascal Maragall's 1992 address. Szymiczek was angry at my intervention, but he backed off. All the next morning, right up until the ceremony, I checked back with Kostalas to make sure there had been no last minute change. A really terrible situation had been avoided.

The morning of 30 March dawned fair in Olympia, meaning that the flame could be lit anew in the mirror from the rays of the sun, and the back-up flame lit during an earlier rehearsal would not have to be used. It was the best of omens. I actually enjoyed my hour and a half in the ruins with AD Frazier, who was destined to become a good friend. The archaeological site had been swept again by security the night before and now was deserted. Even with our credentials, Kritsinelis had to intervene to get us through the cordon. AD Frazier was enthused to know everything and asked thoughtful questions, and it was a welcome relief from my anxiety about the upcoming day to be explaining the landmarks and practices of 2500 years ago.

Later that morning, about two hours before the ceremony, the ACOG officers assembled at the place I had selected for them, the terrace in front of the new IOA conference centre, overlooking the landscape. We stood under a contemporary sculpture of Winged Victory, evoking in an abstract way the masterpiece of Paionius, discovered by the ninteeth century German archaeologists on the exact spot the second century writer Pausanias said it would be found, and now conserved in the Olympic Museum five hundred yards away. With all the commotion over at the main IOA buildings, I had guessed correctly that this spot would be private enough for whatever ACOG had in mind. What they had in mind was prayer. They gathered tightly together, hands held, and one with preacher's roots improvised a blessing. After a prayerful silence, Billy said some words, then everyone dispersed to his or her duties. I caught sight of three HOC housekeeping staff staring out a window bemused at the strange doings of these Americans.

The crowds streaming into the stadium for the ceremony were huge. The entire north slope was eventually packed, and the crowd spilled over past the northeast gate and onto the eastern slope. Many others lined the road above or were arrayed along the relay route through the village. Nearly a thousand specially invited guests – including a substantial cross-section of Athenian government, military, business, and cultural elites, as well as acquaintances from Olympia whom I never thought I would see participating in an HOC event – took seats on the stadium floor. One local official later estimated the total crowd at 40,000. In HOC official memory, it was 30,000.[94] From going over videos and photographs later on, I would myself guess something more like 25,000. In any case, it was by far the largest crowd ever to come to Olympia for the flame lighting. Several of my local consultants were surprised, as it was March, so there were few tourists about, and Ancient Olympia is an effort to reach even in the busy season. The combination of Hillary Clinton, the drama of Athens/Atlanta 1996, and twelve years of OFR discursive struggle with America had proved powerfully attractive. Meanwhile, the national television audience was the also the largest ever for the flame-lighting ceremony. In the moments before the ceremony began, the stadium crowd was quietly buzzing. Not a shout was heard or any protest banner seen, though I saw some people wearing those 'Athens 1996' tee shirts. Everything was expectation, not rejection.

After the national anthems of Greece and the USA and the Olympic anthem, an opening invocation and brief welcoming speeches by Mayor Georgos Deves and the head of the HOC flame relay committee Ioannis Economou, and an address by the federal Secretary for Sport Andreas Fouras, Mrs Clinton walked to the podium, just off the ancient starting line in the southwest corner of the stadium floor. She addressed the crowd with a determined mien and in forceful diction that was a bit stilted. She clearly intended to be listened to.

The First Lady began by saying that she was honoured to be with her daughter 'representing the American people … in Greece, birthplace of the Olympics and of so many ideas and institutions that define our civilization today'. The tone of high *ellenismos* was thus set immediately in the speech and would be its explicit finale, while punctuating everything else that Mrs Clinton had to say along the way about the Olympic spirit. 'That spirit stretches back nearly 3000 years to the first foot race held here at Olympia and the presentation of a crown of olives to the victor. The same spirit grew only greater as the peasant Spiridon Louis crossed the finish line in the first Olympic marathon one hundred years ago in Athens, inspiring the princes of Greece to carry him to a place of honour in the royal box'. Applause broke out from the crowd: Hillary Clinton knew details about the ancient Olympics and was familiar with Spiridon Louis, Greece's first modern Olympic champion and the unrivalled hero of Athens, 1896. Standing about twenty paces away under the flagpoles, Gary Allison and I exchanged smiles. I had published the standard literary account of the Louis story; he had made a television film of it. I anticipated that Gary would feature Louis in Mrs Clinton's speech, and it had clearly made a hit.

'Every four years', she continued, 'the family of nations gathers to pursue excellence and to find peace and camaraderie through sport. That is the heart of the Olympic ideal. It is a testament to the power and vision of Greek civilization. In ancient Greece, warring city states called a sacred truce, so that all of Greece's finest athletes, warriors, poets, and artists could attend the games and honour the gods. In the modern Olympics, distinctions of class, nationality, religion, and race are forgotten in contests judged by individual speed, strength, and endurance'. Mrs Clinton could quote the IOC's version of Olympism as well, and if there was some irony in flattering Greek nationalism while suggesting the Olympics put people beyond national distinctions, ritual symbolism depends for its emotional effectiveness on such discursive ambiguity.

The First Lady then turned to the athletes, noting that they would come from a record 197 countries in Atlanta, be 'role models for children around the world', and 'build bridges of respect, tolerance, and friendship'. She concluded her address with the summary assertion that: 'The flame that leaves Olympia today on a four-month journey ... carries much more than light and peace. It carries the spirit of our family of nations, of the earliest runners, of Spiridon Louis, and of the young women and men who will convene in Atlanta this summer ... strengthening the ideals we share as part of our common humanity. God bless the Olympics, Greece, and all that you have given to civilization'. The applause from the crowd seemed sincere and prolonged. It had been a most effective performance for the Greek audience, not for any novelty in its content – this was ritual speech – but because an American of her stature, a figure whose identity mediated between the state and civil society, had said such things in this place and against the historical backdrop of the past twelve years.

As HOC president Tzikas rose to speak, I whispered congratulations to Gary and thought I detected a challenge in return: 'let's see Billy Payne top that'. I had plenty of time to grow more nervous about 'the speech', as Tzikas unexpectedly repeated his address himself in both Greek and English, being equally rambling in both languages. Finally, the ACOG chief took the podium.

> In honour of the Centennial of the Olympic Games, we have journeyed to the sacred grounds of Olympia today as a delegation of Atlantans entrusted with the prestigious honour of hosting the Centennial Olympic Games, to pay tribute to the greatness of Greece, and the dream you have given the world, a dream that had been embraced by all humanity.
>
> It is fitting that we all pay homage to Ancient Olympia, the birthplace of the Olympic Idea. The Olympic Idea is an idea of transforming power. It possesses the power to change lives, to exalt heroes, to rebuild cities, to shape history, and to unite the world. Those of us who are here from Atlanta today have experienced that power personally. Nine years ago, it inspired a dream that transformed my life and ultimately revealed the destiny of our city.
>
> In a few short weeks, you will entrust the flame to us to fly to America to begin the final leg of the journey that embodies the noblest aspirations of humanity. As we receive the torch from you, we will remember that it is your dream that we hold so gratefully in our hands. It is your gift that we shall share with the world. It is the flame of Olympia that burns within our souls. It is the idea of Olympia that lives within our hearts.

Here a large applause broke out among the crowd, and an even bigger one followed Payne's next line, delivered with a rising fervour.

> Out of our deep and abiding respect for the traditions that you have entrusted to us, we consider our mission as sacred as the ground we stand on today.

I thought to myself, this is a religious man delivering a religious speech, and even with the gap for most of them between Billy's emotion and Alexis's translation of his words, the crowd seems to be feeling it.

> It is our mission to ensure that when the cauldron is lit in Atlanta and the flame ignites the celebration of the century, there is an immediate and universal recognition that the Olympic ideal, the Greek ideal, is the source of humanity's greatest hopes for the future.

The big finish was now at hand, and I realized that my knees were shaking in fear that I had made some mistake.

> We shall guard the sacred flame on every step of its journey. We shall never take our eyes away from it. With you and your countrymen, we will proclaim: *Tin floga kai ta matia mas, tin floga kai ta matia mou!*

The first applause began with *ta matia mas*, and grew louder as Billy pointed directly at his own eyes, *ta matia mou*. He had inspired himself and nailed the delivery. The buzz continued through the translation, and when Alexis repeated the final line, a huge ovation broke out, accented by cheering people rising to their feet on the floor and slopes of the stadium.

Billy returned to his seat to warm congratulations by the Greek authorities and his comrades. Soon the VIPs were flowing towards the ancient athletes' tunnel into the sanctuary. Most of them were soon disappointed to find they lacked the special credential for entry and the usual status contests ensued. But security was unusually tight, and few dispensations were made. I did not try to enter. My ritual work was done, and I would watch Maria Pambouki light the flame late that night on video. Instead, I sat down in the stadium and waited with the crowd for the officials to return and for Maria Hors, the eighteen other priestesses, and two ephebes eventually to bring the flame over the west slope and down into the stadium to begin the final phase of the ritual. When the first Greek torchbearer exited the stadium to the east, accompanied by fifty multi-racial, multinational school children sent by UNESCO and heading for the Coubertin grove, and as hundreds of high school girls from all around Elis formed the Olympic rings on the south slope, Gary and Alexander pulled me into Mrs Clinton's entourage. They were exiting the site through the *krypte*, heading out to greet the priestesses at the archaeological museum. 'Hillary, here is Professor MacAloon'. 'Where have you been? she asked me, 'here, tell my daughter about all this'. Chelsea and I spoke briefly about the athletes' passageway between the sanctuary and the stadium, before her party was hurried away. I myself had to sprint out the main gate of the archaeological site to rendezvous with Kritsinelis, jump into his car, and commence the relay through Greece.

Around Greece with the flame

To honour the Centennial, Kritsinelis had arranged a much longer relay of the flame to Athens than customary, stitching together: famous antiquities (including the sites of the three other 'crown games'); important historical landmarks of the Hellenistic, Byzantine, and Revolutionary periods; and sites associated with the first modern games in 1896 and the birth of the OFR itself. Over the course of ten days, we travelled the following route: Olympia, Elis, Pyrgos, Kiparissia, Kalamata, Mystras, Sparta, Tegea, Tripolis, Naflio, Argos, Mycenae, Nemea, Isthmia, Corinth, Patras, Messolongi, Galaxidi, Dephi, Plataea, Thebes; by car north to Macedonia, then relaying Vergina/Aigai, Naousa, Edessa, Pella, Thessaloniki; by car again back south, relaying Marathon to Athens over the route of the first marathon race that Louis won. The flame stayed for a time in the Panathenaic Stadium, and then after the handover ceremony (which 50,000 attended and was entirely peaceful), travelling as well to Rhodes, Crete, and Thrace.

Crowds were everywhere large on the relay, and the celebrations were frequently extraordinary. Typically, the national anthems of Greece and the USA would be played, a rendition of the Olympic anthem would be presented by choir or recording, there would be an invocation, an HOC representative would make introductions, the mayor, nomarch, or archaeological service ephor would give an address, then Battle, Watkins, Hanson, or Truitt would give a slightly revised version of Payne's speech from Olympia, ending with the *tin floga* vows that the assembled were by now anticipating, having read about them in the newspapers. (I was privileged to give 'the speech' myself in Sparta.) Presents would next be exchanged between the municipalities and the ACOG representatives. The flame would arrive onstage and be passed from one local torchbearer to another, then depart for the next stage of the relay, or if it was a day-ending celebration, be placed in a cauldron while cultural performances of music and dance – elaborate festivals unto themselves in places like Patras, Delphi, Thebes, and Thessaloniki – unfolded late into the night. It would take at least another entire article to begin just to describe many of these scenes.[95] (For me, as an anthropologist, actually entering 'Philip's Tomb' in Vergina with the Olympic flame was a nearly unimaginable highlight.[96])

With regard to the main theme, ACOG was nearly everywhere greeted with friendliness and respect. Only at two celebration sites, that we were aware of, did any significant protest break out. At Argos, thousands of people were arrayed in the ancient theater for the ceremonial celebration that took place on its stage. There was some booing during the American anthem, and when Ginger Watkins was in the midst of 'the speech', a group of perhaps twenty persons made a vocal disturbance. Watkins persevered, as one must always do in ritual, and the applause as she finished completely drowned out the nay-sayers (see Figure 4). The ceremony concluded without any further incident. In Patras, as we neared the centre of town on our way up to the ancient acropolis for the celebration, a disturbance broke out somewhere in front of us, and the caravan was halted as the police rushed forward. After about five minutes, we resumed our progress, and I never learned any details about who was demonstrating there.

Of course, Greeks actively collaborating with the flame relay had their own political messages to deliver. Sometimes, it was in lyrical mode, as when a town councillor in Kalamata, the first provisional capital of liberated Greece, singled me out to present a parchment copy of 'The Proclamation of the Messenian Senate to the American Nation', signed by Commander Mavromichalis on 15 May 1821, appealing in the most moving and fraternal terms for American aid in the War of Independence. That appeal proved fruitless. The clear message in the gift was that the American government, in the 1960s and 1970s as well as back then, should have been more judicious in deciding which Greek military

Figure 4. Tuning out some hecklers, ACOG's Ginger Watkins delivers 'the speech' before thousands in the ancient theater of Argos. Photo by the author.

leaders to support. The message delivered could also be rather epic, from the point of view of the Greek state and public opinion. Ostensibly, we were with the flame in Macedonia, 'because it's the Centennial and it had never been there'. But obviously the intensifying struggle between Greece and 'The Former Yugoslavian Republic of Macedonia' over the name itself and Alexander the Great's ethnicity had everything to do with our route taking us around the province. We Americans were made party to the re-consecration of Macedonia as Greek through the Olympic flame (Figure 5). This was in fact how the archaeologists were persuaded to allow the flame as well as us inside Alexander's father's tomb. The little ACOG delegation could at best be said to represent American civil society. Turning to the American government, it was hardly accidental that when US Ambassador Thomas Niles was invited to carry the Olympic flame as a torchbearer, it was in Philip and Alexander's Macedonian capital of Pella.

ACOG, the flame relay, and the olympic movement

The special historical significance of the Atlanta OFR hardly ended with the flame's departure from Greece for the USA. As will be analysed in ensuing chapters, a new model of flame relay operations was to consolidate on the domestic OFR across America to Atlanta, a set of practices destined to claim the status of 'world's best' and to win the imprimatur of the IOC for global application. Greece herself was not done with 'America' yet either. ATHOC, the organizing committee for the Athens 2004 Olympics, decided to accept many of these practices for its own OFR, leading Greeks who had worked so closely with Atlanta in 1996 to complain in 2004 that the import of this 'American model' into Greece was destroying the very traditions that ACOG had so admired and respected.

But these new struggles would take place in the field of managerial and financial operations, not on the nationalist/religious plane of international relations and intercultural

Figure 5. ACOG's top leadership carried the Olympic flame in Greece. From left to right: Charlie Battle, Billy Payne, Ginger Watkins. Photo by the author.

sacrilege. In Greek/American flame relay relations, ACOG, in collaboration with the HOC and with an unexpected but ultimately welcome boost from the White House, had put an end to all that. When in 2002, Salt Lake City came calling in Greece for the Olympic flame, it might as well have been some city in Europe or Asia. 'Everything was completely normal'.[97] Obviously, Athens having its own games for 2004 eliminated one set of earlier tensions. But it was the hard intercultural diplomacy of Billy Payne and his OFR team, together with Hillary Clinton, who had finally erased Ueberroth and the LAOOC from Greek memory and made 'normalcy' possible.

As a social movement, Olympism is concerned with intercultural encounter, mutual understanding, and détente. The ACOG leadership's monumental achievement in the intercultural diplomacy of the Olympic Flame Relay, rectifying some of the most dangerous moments in Olympic ritual history, is a story of preoccupation with and commitment to the Olympic Movement. This story deserves to be better known. In the conventional discourse of the Olympic Sports Industry, Atlanta is today most frequently remembered for its managerial deficiencies in the areas of transportation, communication, press relations, and VIP hospitality. (Oddly, the fact that ACOG still holds by far the record for the most tickets sold to Olympic sports events is less frequently mentioned.) The contest over which story of Atlanta will eventually dominate is a microcosm of the struggle of the Olympic Movement today to survive the success of the Olympic Sports Industry.

Notes

1. MacAloon and Kang, '*Uri Nara*'.
2. The story has frequently been told, having acquired nearly legendary status in both Atlanta and international Olympic circles. See, for example Katz, 'Atlanta Brave'; Ruthheiser, *Imagineering Atlanta*; Yarbrough, *And They Call Them Games*. Aspects of Payne's story especially relevant to my narrative are: the fully religious nature (in the conventional, Durkheimian, and psychoanalytical senses) of Payne's Olympic inspiration and commitment; his deep and abiding status anxieties with respect to both the Atlanta power elite and all 'outside' Olympic experts; and his tendencies towards micromanagement of every aspect of 'his' Games. Payne exemplified the Weberian type of the charismatic visionary leader as against the rational-bureaucratic administrator. In Olympic history, one has to go all the way back to Coubertin and his youthful vision in the Rugby School Chapel (MacAloon, *This Great Symbol*, 51–96) to find a parallel in character and consequence to Payne's vision of an Atlanta Olympic Games as the next step for him after building a baptismal chapel for his Atlanta church. After the Atlanta Olympics, Payne made money as a rainmaker for a Southern bank, then emerged as chairman of Augusta National Golf Club and the Masters Tournament.

   Battle was another Atlanta lawyer. My first contact with him was when he barged into a reception of the Pierre de Coubertin Committee at the Seoul Olympics: 'Hi. I'm Charlie Battle, Atlanta bid committee. How y'all doing?' Dressed in standard American business casual, he was so outlandish, glad-handing startled Europeans and South Americans right and left, that I shrank into a corner in embarrassment and spoke only French while he remained in the room. Little could I have imagined then how much this unabashed and unapologetically friendly, Southern American style would contribute to eventually winning the Olympic Games for Atlanta, much less that I would come to befriend and admire this man and to work so closely with him on the Atlanta flame relay and other Olympic projects. In the aftermath of Atlanta 1996, Battle did civic development work for a time, then returned to Olympic affairs as a key consultant for the Beijing, New York, Sochi, Chicago, and Pyeongchang Olympic bids. Today, he is the most internationally accomplished and well known of this new breed of transnational Olympic actors. (See MacAloon, 'Legacy'.)

3. As, among US Olympic Games and bid chiefs, Peter Ueberroth (Los Angeles 1984) was before him, and Mitt Romney (Salt Lake City 2002), Dan Doctorow (New York 2012), and Patrick Ryan (Chicago 2016) were after him. Nor, during the 25-year period under study in this volume, was

the leadership of the US Olympic Committee (USOC) any more politically representative of the US population. The standing joke about the USOC was that it never had more than one Democrat and one speaker of a foreign language … who always turned out to be the same person! For the most part, these American Olympic leaders have been 'business' Republicans, sometimes socially moderate, a fact which makes some contextual sense given the tradition of principled distancing of the US government from sports governance and the consequent need to rely heavily on corporate funding and private philanthropy to support the American Olympic movement. (For the deep history of the political structuring of American Olympic affairs, see MacAloon, 'The 1904 Chicago-St. Louis Transition'.) Only in the past decade has the USOC begun to incorporate more linguistically competent, cosmopolitan, and politically representative persons, but only in its international relations office, not among its Board or officers.

[4] One consequence of being one of the few governments in the world without a cabinet or sub-cabinet level office of sport, or even a dedicated desk in an established department such as State or Education, is that there has been no continuity of knowledge and expertise about Olympic affairs anywhere in the US government. Every Olympic eventuality thus comes to be treated in an ad hoc manner by competing and uncoordinated branches of the federal government. (See Reich, *Making It Happen* for a detailed account of the difficulties that necessarily ensue for any American Olympic body seeking to coordinate with the US government). These facts are almost incomprehensible to other nations, which therefore persist in projecting their own utterly different conditions onto US actions. This effect has been clearly implicated in the Greek/American OFR imbroglios. Greeks could scarcely believe that some US government body was not implicated in the offensive 'American' initiatives with respect to the 1984 OFR. In 1996, most Greeks would simply assume that Mrs Clinton was the head of the American delegation, with Billy Payne relegated to the status of functionary. Yet, ironically, it was ACOG and not the White House who knew anything going in about the OFR ceremonies.

[5] In 1988 at a meeting in Seoul, I was one of a substantial multinational group of Olympic scholars and international relations experts who approached Greek IOC member Nikos Filaretos and then Education Minister (subsequently Prime Minister) George Papandreou to offer support and counsel. Despite this group's global contacts and long-time familiarity with Greece and Greek leaders through participation at the International Olympic Academy, it was curtly rebuffed. 'Greece has everything under control'. Others more influential than us ran into the same attitude again and again.

[6] The subsequent Greek bid for the 2004 Olympic Games succeeded in part because Mrs Gianna Angelopoulou and her team self-consciously and openly distanced themselves in every way from the rhetoric of the bid for 1996.

[7] When I had the temerity to confront this discourse by mentioning at a subsequent International Olympic Academy session Greek Coca-Cola's financial support for the Athens bid, Nikos Filaretos – IOA president, IOC member, and bid principal – interrupted from the chair to deny that any such contribution had ever existed. When I persisted, citing Mr Lavrentis and other Greek Coke officials, Filaretos backed down, while asserting that the Coke sponsorship had been very 'minor'. This episode clearly evidenced the complicity of top Greek Olympic officials in encouraging the Coca Cola/CNN/Samaranch conspiracy narrative as a cover for their own failures.

[8] Without the timely assistance of long-time HOC staffer Byron Amelides, I would not have been able to maximize this ethnographic opportunity. I remain perpetually grateful to him. This volume is dedicated to his memory and to that of Nikolaos Nissiotis.

[9] For further details on this 1992 fieldwork and the Barcelona/Athens relay itself, see 'My Programme Became Very Strict', my extended conversation with Nassos Kritsinelis in this volume.

[10] For Payne's views on the torch relay, see his *Olympic Turnaround*, 125–36. My many conversations with him over the years have confirmed the sincerity of his convictions that, as he writes in his book, 'at the heart of Olympic symbolism is the Olympic torch' and that the flame ceremonies have provided 'some of the most symbolic moments in Olympic history'. This is why it makes absolute sense for corporations to wish to attach themselves to it, in his view. Moreover, since Krupp, Zeiss, and Daimler Benz were official suppliers to the first relay in 1936, and even ancient Greek flame relays had 'sponsors' (so Payne anachronistically and tendentiously suggests), it is simply hypocritical for anyone today to object to commercialization of the OFR as 'a sacrilege against the Olympic ideal'. For further discussion of what Payne did or did not see

from his perch in Lausanne about actual sponsor and OFR relations, see 'Olympic Flame Relay Operations under a "World's Best Practices" Regime', my extended interview with Steven McCarthy later in this volume.

[11] In conducting the work reported in this volume, indeed throughout my entire career, I have made it a matter of principle never to accept any money beyond travel expenses from any Olympic body. Backstage ethnographic access and opportunities to advocate for Olympic movement causes and to mediate intercultural conflicts have been sufficient exchange value for my expertise. For a further discussion, see MacAloon, 'The Ethnographic Imperative in Comparative Olympic Research'.

[12] Reich, *Making It Happen*.

[13] *Los Angeles Olympic Games Official Report*, 805–17.

[14] Ueberroth, *Made in America*.

[15] Details on the role and performance of Hilary Hanson – today Hilary Hanson McKean of the Ketchum, Inc. public relations firm – as flame relay director will be found in the subsequent articles, 'Flame Relay Operations' and 'My Programme'.

[16] For a detailed after-action summary of what LA learned about staging such a complex and extensive 82-day relay, see *Los Angeles Olympic Games Official Report*, 805–17. For the internal struggles within the committee, see Reich, *Making It Happen*, 177, 180.

[17] Andrew Young is a former mayor of Atlanta, US ambassador to the United Nations, and co-chairman of ACOG. For his views today on the Olympic flame, human rights and political protest, see Tomlinson, 'Andrew Young'. AD Frazier was ACOG's chief operating officer, an investment banker who raised and supervised more private sector investment in an Olympic Games than any other person in history. As detailed in a later article, Frazier has told the present author many times that 'being in Greece for the Olympic flame rituals' was 'the only time he was certain' that his whole Olympic engagement was worth it.

[18] Payne, *Olympic Turnaround*, 126.

[19] Both of these relays demonstrated the OFR's capacity to generate larger historical significances. The Tokyo relay across Asia and Japan was memorably captured in the epic images of Kon Ichikawa's Olympic film, including the famous airborne shots of the Olympic flame passing through the ruins of Hiroshima and Nagasaki. These images were clearly intended to be juxtaposed with those of the flame entering the Berlin Stadium in Leni Riefentsahl's 'Olympia' and thus to bracket ritually the historical period of Second World War. As for Mexico's Columbian journey, with the flame residing on the summit of the Pyramid of the Sun at Teotihuacan the night before the Olympic opening ceremonies, it is striking how soon thereafter the new form of postcolonial consciousness would make any such celebration of Columbus politically inconceivable.

The 1984 OFR generated larger political meanings as well, as it was appropriated by substantial segments of its audience, with encouragement by Ueberroth and the LAOOC, as a patriotic and nationalist celebration of America in the context of the cold war. For many along the route, the Olympic flame became the American flame. I myself first heard the now common and notorious chanting of 'U ... S ... A ..., U ... S ... A ...' out on this relay. The USSR played its role in this by purposely choosing to announce its boycott of the Los Angeles Olympics on the day the American segment of the OFR began. In the aftermath of these Games, Ronald Reagan chose to make the Los Angeles flame relay across America a structuring motif of his presidential re-nomination speech at the Republican national convention. The flame relay, he suggested, had demonstrated the strength of his conservative Republican vision of an America that had put Vietnam behind itself in a newborn patriotism committed to winning the cold war, while iconically proving that collective achievement is the sum of collaborative individual efforts not of rivalrous group identities (the purported social theory of the Democrats). The main text is worth quoting as a master example of differential political appropriation of the social solidarity and *communitas* everywhere generated by the OFR.

'We came together in a national crusade to make America great again, and to make a new beginning. Well, now it's all coming together. With our beloved nation at peace, we're in the midst of a springtime of hope for America. Greatness lies ahead of us. Holding the Olympic games here in the United States began defining the promise of this season. All through the spring and summer, we marveled at the journey of the Olympic torch as it made its passage east to west. Over 9,000 miles, by some 4,000 runners, that flame crossed a portrait of our nation. From our Gotham City, New York, to the Cradle of Liberty, Boston, across the Appalachian springtime, to the City of the Big Shoulders, Chicago. Moving south towards Atlanta, over to St. Louis, past its Gateway Arch, across wheatfields into the stark beauty of the Southwest and then up into the still, snowcapped Rockies. And, after circling the greening Northwest, it came down to California, across the Golden Gate and finally into Los Angeles. And all along the way, that torch became a celebration of America. And we all became participants in the celebration. Each new story was typical of this land of ours. There was Ansel Stubbs, a youngster of 99, who passed the torch in Kansas to 4-year-old Katie Johnson. In Pineville, Kentucky, it came at 1 a.m., so hundreds of people lined the streets with candles. At Tupelo, Mississippi, at 7 a.m. on a Sunday morning, a robed church choir sang "God Bless America" as the torch went by. That torch went through the Cumberland Gap, past the Martin Luther King, Jr., Memorial, down the Santa Fe Trail, and alongside Billy the Kid's grave. In Richardson, Texas, it was carried by a 14-year-old boy in a special wheelchair. In West Virginia the runner came across a line of deaf children and let each one pass the torch for a few feet, and at the end these youngsters' hands talked excitedly in their sign language. Crowds spontaneously began singing "America the Beautiful" or "The Battle Hymn of the Republic." And then, in San Francisco a Vietnamese immigrant, his little son held on his shoulders, dodged photographers and policemen to cheer a 19-year-old black man pushing an 88-year-old white woman in a wheelchair as she carried the torch.

My friends, that's America.

We cheered in Los Angeles as the flame was carried in and the giant Olympic torch burst into a billowing fire in front of the teams, the youth of 140 nations assembled on the floor of the Coliseum. And in that moment, maybe you were struck as I was with the uniqueness of what was taking place before a hundred thousand people in the stadium, most of them citizens of our country, and over a billion worldwide watching on television. There were athletes representing 140 countries here to compete in the one country in all the world whose people carry the bloodlines of all those 140 countries and more. Only in the United States is there such a rich mixture of races, creeds, and nationalities – only in our melting pot.

And that brings to mind another torch, the one that greeted so many of our parents and grandparents. Just this past Fourth of July, the torch atop the Statue of Liberty was hoisted down for replacement. We can be forgiven for thinking that maybe it was just worn out from lighting the way to freedom for 17 million new Americans. So, now we'll put up a new one. The poet called Miss Liberty's torch the "lamp beside the golden door." Well, that was the entrance to America, and it still is. And now you really know why we're here tonight'. (Reagen, 'Convention speech'.)

[20] See my 'Introduction' to this volume and MacAloon, 'Theory of Spectacle'.

[21] All this was of a piece with his general strategy of greatly increased use of commercial corporations to finance an Olympic Games. The claim that the 1984 Los Angeles Olympic Games were 'entirely privately funded' is a piece of right wing business culture ideology. They certainly were funded more largely from corporate and philanthropic dollars than any prior Games. There is also no dispute that Peter Ueberroth's achievements in marketing the Olympics to corporations helped transform the entire Olympic system. See Barney, Wenn, and Martyn, *Selling the Five Rings* for a contextualized account.

[22] Ueberroth, *Made in America*, 190, emphasis added.

[23] Payne, *Olympic Turnaround*, 126.

[24] Ueberroth, *Made in America*, 190.

[25] Ibid., 191. I am not convinced that had Ueberroth attempted to clear the idea of an official commercial sponsor for the flame relay with Samaranch, that the latter would have recognized the problems this would necessarily cause with the Hellenic Olympic movement.

[26] In turn, AT&T corporate headquarters relied on its 'Telephone Pioneers of America' employee association for retiree volunteers and active employees across its several divisions who would staff the relay in their regions of the country. The AT&T 'cadre runners' actually carried the flame for over 60% of the route, mostly through unpopulated areas, and ran alongside the 'community torchbearers' who carried the flame the rest of the way. The role of these AT&T pioneers in shaping the 'world's best practice' model that consolidated in the 1990s is dealt with in the following article.

It must be pointed out that AT&T's advertising and self-marketing 'activation' of its sponsorship on its OFR was by any standard modest and tasteful. In comparison with the behaviour of Coca-Cola and Samsung on the subsequent relays to be analysed in later articles of this volume ... well, there is no comparison. The AT&T torch relay archives were donated to and are today held by the Special Collections Department of the University of California-Los Angeles Library.

[27] Reich, *Making It Happen*, 43; Payne, *Olympic Turnaround*, 126; Ueberroth, *Made in America*, 189–90. The subsequent success of the US domestic relay has led Ueberroth's hagiographers to offer this episode as high testimony to his visionary leadership. But that is because they jingoistically ignore or else trivialize the consequences of this 'vision' in Greece, the near bloodshed that ensued at Olympia, and the overall political impact on US/Greek foreign relations. In the years following, corporate OFR sponsors and suppliers have been chiefly concerned with the number of torchbearer slots their sponsorships buy, and these numbers are carefully negotiated and clearly specified in their contacts with the OCOGs. The OCOGs themselves assign torchbearer slots to their 'friends', including those who have materially benefited the organization. The controversial practice of offering his or her torch for sale to each torchbearer that came in with Atlanta will be discussed in ensuing articles in this volume. However, much one might want to see these practices as 'functionally equivalent', no one has anywhere ever again suggested openly selling the rights to carry the Olympic flame, even for the benefit of sports charities. On this point, history has judged very clearly that Ueberroth should have listened to his management team.

[28] Ueberroth, *Made in America*, 191. The original charities were the Boys Clubs of America, the Girls Clubs of America, and the YMCA, with the Special Olympics added later. Additional youth organizations eventually benefited as well. These charities eventually received a total of $11 million from the flame relay YLK sales, 'the largest single-event private youth sports fund raiser in the history of the United States'. *Los Angeles Olympic Games Official Report*, 807, 817.

[29] Ueberroth, *Made in America*, 192. Neither Samaranch nor Berlioux had ever been present in Greece for the flame-lighting, Greek relay or OCOG handover ceremonies, though both had visited the IOA.

[30] Ibid. A revealing slippage occurs further on in Ueberroth's memoir in which he appears to refer to the Session's reaction to the LAOOC's Delhi report as a 'signed deal'. Ibid., 196.

[31] This assertion is based on numerous and intensive personal conversations with both men in 1984, 1985, and 1986, and with Filaretos in later years.

[32] Ueberroth, *Made in America*, 196, 224.

[33] *Official Report*, 815; Ueberroth, *Made in America*, 192, 195; Nikos Filaretos, personal communication, June 1984.

[34] In a letter to Samaranch on 12 December 1983 (IOC Archives. Correspondence: JO-1984s-FLAMT), Ueberroth insisted that his raising money for youth was required to elevate the torch relay for 'the citizens of our entire country … substantially above the singular goal of a wholly ceremonial run'. Ritual to Ueberroth was 'mere ritual'.

[35] Peter Ueberroth was a businessman recruited through a headhunting firm to lead the LAOOC. While he had been a university athlete who once competed for San Francisco's Olympic Club, Ueberroth had no prior experience with international sport or with Olympic institutions and personalities, indeed, had never even attended an Olympic Games. As for Greek and wider European history, he had no formal education in such areas, and he tended to mistake his businessman's experience as head of an international travel company for substantive intercultural knowledge and sensitivity. One of the particularly curious features of the case is that Ueberroth's own wife (née Nikolaus) came from an immigrant Hellenic background. To my knowledge, no one has ever explored this factor in connection with Ueberroth's later relations with Greek Olympism and public opinion. *Made in America*, 41.

The problem of intercultural knowledge was not only Ueberroth's, but also that of his directors and larger management team, an artefact in no small part of the abnormality of their bid process in the first place. Because Los Angeles was the only real bidder for the 1984 Olympic Games, its bid team never had to get to know very many IOC members or much about IOC governance traditions or about regional differences and sensitivities in the broader Olympic movement.

[36] See Fermor, *Roumeli*; Herzfeld, *Ours Once More*.

[37] In a 9 May 1983, 'Dear Colleague and Friend', letter to Filaretos, Samaranch had pleaded for cooperation with the LAOOC because 'for the first time an organizing committee is entirely a private entity, having no government support as a consequence' (IOC Archives, JO-1984s-FLAMT).

[38] Filaretos to Samaranch, 18 and 29 November 1983, IOC Archives, JO-1984s-FLAMT, my translation from the French.

[39] Angelo Lembessis and Nikos Filaretos to Samaranch and Ueberroth, 19 December 1983, IOC Archives, JO-1984s-FLAMT. In his memoir, Ueberroth did not care to quote the sentence about

the contagion of guilt suffered by the US and the USOC (*Made in America*, 195–6). The degree of Ueberroth's narcissistic resentment at being thus impeded is immediately inscribed in his text, as he childishly and petulantly asserts that the umbrage of 'the Greeks' – that phrase again – over commercialization of the flame was not to be taken seriously, since in Olympia there is an 'Olympic Flame Hotel' and souvenir plastic torches for sale in tourist shops, while the national airline is Olympic Airways and 'uses the Olympic rings as its logo' (not true). Behind the scenes, the discourse could get even worse. LAOOC officials I subsequently interviewed did not shrink from insisting that 'the Greeks just wanted more money from us' in return for lighting the flame, and subsequent organizing committees came to hear this canard of HOC blackmail.

[40] Ibid., 195.

[41] In his 28 February proposal for a settlement, Ueberroth did briefly float the notion of sharing some of the torch relay proceeds with 'a sport organization benefiting Greek youth' that was 'to be selected by Mrs Papandreou during her US visit and accorded a deserving and dignified press conference coordinated by the Greek government and the LAOOC' (Ueberroth to Samaranch, IOC Archives, JO-1984S-FLAMT). Ueberroth clearly did not understand that any organization consenting to receive such funds would have no future in Greece. The whole matter of neo-imperialist capitalism in the OFR foreshadowed another huge controversy after the Olympic Games were concluded. Ueberroth, the LAOOC, and the USOC declared a profit of over $200 million, and then refused to even consider sharing any of it with the IOC, the NOCs that had participated, or the IFs. Instead, the money went exclusively to American non-profit institutions, a large endowment for the USOC and for what is today the LA'84 foundation for youth sport in Southern California. This outraged Olympic leaders worldwide and helped insure that Ueberroth would never be elected to the IOC, despite Samaranch's resolve to have him there.

[42] At Sarajevo, the IOC Executive Board generated a draft memo to the HOC affirming that the LAOOC's 'request for use of the Olympic Flame has the full support of the IOC' and demanding that the HOC cooperate with the LAOOC and certify in writing that it was doing so by a date certain. If not 'the IOC shall be required to take such steps as may be required to establish the Olympic Flame at the [IOC] headquarters in Lausanne or such other location as may seem appropriate in the circumstances' (IOC Archives, JO-1984s-FLAMT). The language could hardly have been harsher to the HOC. The IOC Executive now clearly felt that the dispute had called its own authority into serious question.

[43] Ibid., 204.

[44] Frequently transliterated in the foreign press as Foteinos, as many noted, the Greek word for 'light'.

[45] *Official Report*, 815. Ueberroth, *Made in America,* 204; Stanley, 'An Olympic Ideal Gets Burned'.

[46] See for example, 'Flame Campaign Close to Greek Communist Party', *Reuters*, April 26, 1984,

[47] Ueberroth, *Made in America*, 224.

[48] Ibid., 220–1; *Official Report*, 815.

[49] Ueberroth said nothing about AT&T's sponsorship contract at all, much less about cancelling it, and so the Greek authorities who had also always objected to advertising as clear 'commercialization' could hardly certify the LA relay as non-commercial. (Ueberroth does not mention this complaint in his memoir.) In their 19 December1983 telex to Ueberroth, echoing their formal 'sacrilege' complaint to the IOC, Lembessis and Filaretos wrote, 'Your argument that no commercialization exists whatsoever since no trademarks and no advertising on the outfits of the runners will take place is not valid' (IOC Archives, JO-1984s-FLAMT). Indeed, it was not. Ueberroth knew perfectly well that highly visible company logos would be on the togs of the AT&T cadre runners, who would end up covering 60% of the relay and who would run continuously alongside every YLK runner (with their commercial free shirts). Thus, the AT&T brand would appear in every video and nearly every photograph of the torchbearers. Ueberroth commenced this prevarication in early December (Samaranch to Ueberroth, 9 December 1983, IOC Archives, JO-1984s-FLAMT) and continued it throughout the negotiations in 1984. The lies ended only in June 1984, when the LAOOC sent a package of relay press clippings to Samaranch, showing the cadre runners Cathy Peterson, Dot Furley, and Kay Washburn carrying the flame in full AT&T kit and even including supplier advertisements using the OFR logo (IOC Archives, JO-1984s-FLAMT).

As to the second new condition, if he was at all serious in thinking that someone could by fiat command all Greek officials – 'federal, municipal, or Olympic' (*Made in America*, 221) – then

Ueberroth was once again betraying his conception of contemporary Greece as some Third World totalitarian country (the Greece of the Colonels?) and not a complex and vibrant democracy.

50 Interviews with Nissiotis, Filaretos, and three HOC staff members, June 1984.

51 A stereotypical complaint of foreign visitors is that 'Greeks are always arguing'. Few imagine that what they are actually observing is Greeks performing their own conception of popular democracy. In persistently seeking from 'the Greeks' a once-and-for-all deal with no subsequent discussion permitted, Ueberroth and the LAOOC were displaying their cross-cultural ignorance and, in Greek terms, their own authoritarian ethos.

52 Ueberroth did not usually even speak personally over the phone with Greek officials, leaving that to 'a successful Los Angeles businessman fluent in Greek' (*Made in America*, 221). Ueberroth doubtless imagined that the LAOOC was being progressive in this, but all of the key Greek interlocutors spoke excellent English, and two of them later told me they felt insulted by being asked to discuss sensitive matters with and through a volunteer intermediary without any authority or background in Olympic affairs. Moreover, there are generic tensions between Greeks and Greek–Americans in such intercultural filters as region of origin, dialect, party affiliation, and religiosity. Mr Caloyeras's business success was all Ueberroth and his colleagues were apparently interested in when they selected their go-between.

53 *Tass* dispatch 18 March 1984, IOC Archives, JO-1984s-FLAMT. This must refer to a circulated petition as there were nowhere near 350 people at the Olympic conference.

54 Press clippings file, IOC Archives, JO-1984s-FLAMT.

55 While not the chief plank in the international rhetorical groundwork being deployed to justify its eventual boycott of the Los Angeles Games, the importance of the LAOOC's flame relay to the Soviets was to made perfectly clear when they chose to have the announcement of the boycott precisely coincide with the relay's kick-off in New York.

56 'It is not possible to hand over the Olympic flame and to organize the Olympic torch relay according to the traditional way ... since, with few exception, it did not find the traditional cooperation of those public services [municipalities] the contribution of which were indispensable and since the sports organizations that had the duty to contribute to success declined to do so'. This was 'a serious blow to the Olympic Movement and to our country', and now it would be 'up to the IOC to give the flame' for the Los Angeles games'. (A. Tzantzanos to Samaranch, IOC Archives, JO-1984s-FLAMT.)

57 Press clippings, 3–6 May, IOC Archives, JO-1984s-FLAMT. As the IOC Archives show, Samaranch had been in direct touch with Kimon Koularis, the general secretary for sport in the PASOK government, at various points in the process. Though the archives not surprisingly are silent on this, it would be my hunch that Samaranch dealt directly with President Karamanlis (of the centre-right party) during the end game.

58 See note 52. In his memoir, Ueberroth boasted of an earlier 'deal' with Margaret Papandreou, the Prime Minister's wife in which she promised privately and on television 'an orderly transfer of the flame to the LAOOC' in return for accepting a troupe from the Greek National Theatre into the Los Angeles Olympic Arts Festival. (*Made in America*, 221). The actual importance of this episode, like so much else in this story, cannot be properly evaluated until we have a full scholarly account based on the relevant Greek government archives. There is no question, however, of the Greek government's leading role in providing, at the last minute, a flame to LA.

59 Some eyewitnesses claimed more than a thousand protestors, while others (such as Nassos Kritsinelis in 'My Programme', and ensuing in this volume) counted substantially fewer. In my interviews in Olympia, four weeks after the event, part of the discrepancy lay with those who counted villagers in solidarity with the demonstrators but were afraid to leave their homes and businesses unattended for fear of ensuing violence.

60 Nikos Nissiotis and local police officials are my sources here. Again, it would be helpful to have a full study of the event based on official Greek presidential archives. In his memoir, Ueberroth was completely silent about the dangerous and nearly tragic situation at Olympia. The LAOOC's *Official Report* noted only that 'heavy security was present at the ceremonial site' (816).

61 Katerina Didaskalou, like all contemporary Olympic high priestesses, was a classically trained Greek actress and model, and in her case later a television drama star. I did not get a chance to meet or to interview her in 1984. But we travelled together on the OFR for Seoul, for which she reprised her role as flame-lighting high priestess and was the honoured guest throughout Korea of the Seoul Olympic Organizing Committee and indeed of the entire Korean people (MacAloon and Kang, '*Uri Nara*'). We became close friends, and it embittered me to hear that no one from

Los Angeles had ever thanked her for risking her life to get them an authentic Olympic flame. 'I don't think they even knew my name. No matter,' she told me, 'I did it for the Olympic movement and for my country'. Samaranch, for his part, wrote to her on 23 May, 'You fulfilled your function with a great deal of dignity and solemnity, and the entire IOC is infinitely in your debt'. He also wrote individual letters of thanks to the HOC technical staff who had dared to assist: Kritsinelis, Georgos Moissides, Vasilios Karakisos, Perikles Paklatzidis, and Maria Horst [sic]. IOC Archives, JO-1984S-FLAMT.

[62] See Skiadas, *The Olympic Flame*, for the photographic evidence. Nissiotis was there as Samaranch's official representative, and Filaretos as IOC member rather than HOC secretary general. The HOC could thus, when it suited, maintain the fiction with the public that it had not taken part in the ceremony. Szymiczek was the dean of the IOA (and was later thanked by letter from Samaranch for his key role in making the ceremony happen). But, his salary was in fact paid by the HOC, thinning the committee's cover even more. (Samaranch to Nissiotis, 26 April 1984; Samaranch to Szymiczek, 21 May 1984; IOC Archives, JO-1984s-FLAMT.)

[63] I had been visiting Ancient Olympia since 1977, and had established networks and projects in the village. For a discussion of these and of Nissiotis, the IOA, and my relations with them, see *This Great Symbol*, 323–8.

[64] See Nissiotis and Grigoris, *Nikos A. Nissiotis*.

[65] Regretably, I did not ask Nissiotis to detail his communications with Samaranch in setting up this secret flame lighting. On their arrival in Athens, Nissiotis sheltered and carefully instructed the emissaries from Lausanne as to what they must do in Olympia, but he judged it too risky for him to be there with them.

[66] Ueberroth, *Made in America*, 242. Whether Samaranch really was 'chuckling' as he said this, as Ueberroth later claimed, it is perfectly clear from his text that Ueberroth himself was at the time and still years later chortling.

[67] 'Programme de remise de la flame olympique au LAOOC, 4–5 Mai', IOC Archives, JO-1984s-FLAMT.

[68] There was in fact a third flame. As Nassos Kritsinelis reveals in this volume (MacAloon, 'My Programme'), he had the back-up flame lit at the Olympia rehearsal secretly taken to Athens just in case demonstrators managed to overpower security and prevent the 7 May ceremony from taking place.

[69] Ibid., 196, 227, 241–2, 245. Samaranch clearly did not trust Ueberroth with the full details. The persons on the mission to Greece from Lausanne were not 'students on an Olympic project' and required no 'manual describing the ceremony for lighting the Olympic flame'. The photographs did not include their faces or torsos, only their hands performing the ritual acts with a small mirror, a candle, and a miner's lantern emblazoned with the Olympic rings, all with the unmistakable ruins of the Hera Temple in the background.

[70] Nissiotis, 'L'Actualité de Pierre de Coubertin du point de vue de la philosophie el le problème de la *religio athletae*'.

[71] Our proposal had been to add to the IOA schedule a four-week seminar for graduate students engaged in serious academic research on the Olympic movement. It took us until the summer of 1986 to begin to actually organize it, then in September, Nissiotis was killed in a car crash as he was returning from Olympia to Athens. A few years later, the seminar was actually inaugurated. As he was the IOA president at that time, Nikos Filaretos liked to claim credit as its originator.

[72] *Official Report*, 815.

[73] Once the LAOOC had the back-up flame, Ueberroth indicates that Filaretos was directly informed. In an outrageously vindictive and childishly triumphal passage in his book, Ueberroth recalls instructing his underlings to 'get Filaretos on the phone and make one last request for his help to arrange a flame-lighting ceremony at Olympia. If he refuses, tell him fine. Tell him we already have a flame, and we'd be pleased to tell the world how we snuck into Olympia and got it, if that's how he wants it. Also, mention that we've decided that Greece will march in alphabetical order at the opening ceremonies, instead of in its customary place – first in line'. Filaretos would never confirm with me that this conversation actually happened. But if it did, it is highly doubtful, as Ueberroth proceeds to claim, that this threat of using the secret flame rather than prior Greek government decision is the reason an Olympia flame ignition was agreed to. Indeed, if, as was reported to Ueberroth, 'Filaretos even guaranteed Greek government support', that could only be because the government had already decided there would be an Olympia ceremony. Ueberroth, *Made in America*, 242.

It is also uncertain whom Samaranch spoke with in Greece once he had an Olympic flame in Lausanne. Not surprisingly, the IOC archives are silent on this point. Michael Payne's account 20 years later reads like Chateau de Vidy office folklore, written in the same executive office master of the universe (schoolyard bully boy) tone as Ueberroth's. Payne writes that 'Samaranch presented the Greek Committee with a simple choice. The Greeks were told to either allow Ueberroth to come to Olympia and light the flame in the traditional manner, or the IOC would dispatch the flame from the IOC headquarters in Lausanne. The Greek Committee accepted Samaranch's proposal' (*Olympic Turnaround*, 127). Presumably, Payne means the HOC here, but I have my doubts that this is correct. Knowing Samaranch, it is far more likely that he was in communication with top Greek government officials over this, and not with Messrs. Lembessis and Filaretos for whom he had little political respect. Samaranch would have known perfectly well that by this point in the drama, the Greek government and not the HOC was calling the final shot.

[74] It is conceivable that as HOC secretary general, Filaretos received the secret flame ultimatum from Ueberroth, Samaranch, or both, and never communicated it to HOC president Lembessis or any others on the HOC board. If he had, I am quite certain that Kritsinelis (and other long-time HOC staffers I have talked with) would not still have been in the dark all these years later.

[75] After I published a summary account of these events in a new edition of *This Great Symbol* in 2008, I received an e-mail from the Olympic chronicler Wolf Lyberg, who had the temerity to request that, 'as so much time had passed', I tell him the two names so that he could enter them into Olympic history. Los Angeles businessmen and British brand managers at the IOC are not the only ones who sometimes just do not get it about Greece and the Olympic flame.

[76] See Barney, Wenn, and Martyn, *Selling the Five Rings* for a scholarly and Payne, *Olympic Turnaround* for a practitioner account.

[77] The LAOOC had been so bold as to have included in its 22 July 1983 contract with the HOC a provision (1.5) that the latter would 'render assistance in obtaining seats in the relay motorcade [in Greece] to a group of representatives from LAOOC's designated suppliers of equipment for the Olympic Flame Relay ... providing them with meals and other necessary service. No publicity whatsoever of said designated suppliers will be allowed in Greece'. IOC Archives, JO-1984S-FLAMT.

[78] Battle finished the Atlanta Olympic Games with the strongest international reputation of any of the ACOG officers. Because he is personal friends with so many Olympic leaders around the world, Battle subsequently became and is today a much sought-after consultant to Olympic bid committees, having worked with Beijing, New York, Sochi, Chicago, and Pyeongyang.

[79] One such ally was Nikolaos Yalouris, the famous senior archaeologist of the ancient Peloponnese, including Olympia, and long-time ephor of the IOA whom I had grown close to over the years. Steven Miller, the distinguished archaeologist and classical historian of sport from California-Berkeley, was another such ally. As the excavator of Nemea and the ancient Nemean Games, as well as the founder of the New Nemean Games, Stephen was (and is) highly respected and even loved in the central Peloponnese. He deployed his own networks on our behalf and brought a large and supportive delegation from Nemea to the Atlanta flame lighting at Olympia.

[80] MacAloon, *This Great Symbol*, 323–5.

[81] In fact, it was Ueberroth who could have been accused of cooking the books. After Samaranch requested to know the detailed LAOOC outlay to the HOC, Ueberroth gave a figure of $509,377.50, but $322,000 of this turned out to be for the chartered plane and other 'travel expenses for [the LAOOC delegation] to Greece'. Ueberroth to Samaranch 27 February 1984, IOC Archives, JO-1984S-FLAMT.

[82] As did two other Americans, Rusty Wilson an IOA graduate who was Kritsinelis's personal guest, and an American filmmaker making a documentary that unfortunately was never completed.

[83] For example, in 1992, COOB officials had flown back to Athens after the flame lighting, leaving no one to accompany the flame on its journey there through the Greek towns and villages. As a consequence, Kritsinelis had to ask the American anthropologist along on the relay to impersonate a COOB official in order that someone could politely receive the memorial gifts conventionally offered by the municipalities for a successful Barcelona Olympics. This ruse was embarrassing for both of us.

[84] See MacAloon, 'My Programme', in this volume.

[85] 'I stressed with them that this was our celebration of the 100th anniversary of 1896. If they didn't want the relay in their town, because it was a flame for Atlanta, then, fine, we would go through

another town. In the end, no one refused'. Personal communication, April 1996. The OFR celebrations in Greek villages and towns, of course gave local mayors and other dignitaries the opportunity to make speeches to large crowds who had had another festival day added to their calendars. Simply by doing his duty as HOC flame relay director, Kritsinelis became a key ambassador on ACOG's behalf through his unparalleled network of local contacts in southern and central Greece.

[86] Hirthler today makes much of his living as a transnational Olympic bid and Olympic Games marketing consultant.

[87] In this case, the Greek Olympian long jumper Kostas Koukodimos.

[88] Readers unfamiliar with the role of the radical Christian right in American politics might find such missives laughable, but the Federal Bureau of Investigation took very seriously some of the more threatening ones. After the Centennial Park bomber was identified, it appeared wise to have done so.

[89] In the event, the White House entourage presented a good deal of inconvenience for the spectators, but remarkably little for the ritual directors and personnel. Most citizens of Olympia were grateful for increased excitement, crowds, press coverage, and (so they believed) future tourist business the White House presence created.

[90] The first phase of the rite takes place on the floor of the ancient stadium and consists of the Olympic anthem, the national anthems of Greece and the Olympic host nation, an invocation by an Orthodox priest, followed by speeches by HOC, Greek government, municipal, and OCOG officials. After this first phase is concluded, the high dignitaries enter the sanctuary through the ancient athletes' tunnel (*krypte*) to witness from a respectful distance the high priestess's appeal in ancient Greek to Apollo as the god of light and the actual flame lighting with her own special torch held to the mirror. In the third phase, the dignitaries return to their seats in the stadium to await the high priestess, who accompanied by her attendants in highly stylized choreography, bears the flame in a vase into the stadium, lights again her own special torch, and after another declamation and the flight of a dove, reaches her torch across a symbolic boundary between the ancient and modern worlds to ignite the OCOG torch of the first flame bearer, a famous Greek athlete who sets off for the Coubertin grove and then on to the relay route to Athens.

Over the years, I have pressed NBC Television Olympics chief Dick Ebersol as to why he has never permitted American audiences to view the flame-lighting ceremony in its entirety. All that Americans, including Greek–Americans, have ever been allowed to see is a brief clip of the core dramatic moment when the flame comes alive in the mirror and the priestess lifts up her torch to the sky. Unlike all other national broadcasters in recent years, American network television behaves this way even when the flame is being lit for a US Games. Ebersol always answers that he saw the ritual once and found it 'boring'. When pressed, it is clear that he is talking about the first phase of anthems and speeches that, to be sure, would be a challenge to make into what the US commercial networks like to call 'good television'. But priestesses bringing down fire from heaven in storied ancient ruins can hardly be described as boring, so some other inhibition must be at play. And it is a general one, for even with no rights-holding barrier to doing so, neither Atlanta-based CNN nor any local broadcaster sent a camera team to Olympia or purchased footage of the whole ceremony from the Greek broadcaster ERT. All of them showed only the standard moment, a couple adding the briefest clip of Hillary Clinton at the podium. Though Ebersol for his part denies it, I am convinced that political fear of offending the American religious right and dealing with its demands for 'equal time' is the chief factor at play here, however consciously. I offer the influence of this threat on Mrs Clinton's behaviour at Olympia as evidence.

[91] Nikolaou had for some years avoided even speaking to me at the IOA or at OFR events in Greece. Perhaps I had somehow offended him. There was certainly the matter of my nationality, and in those days Nikolaou could be 'anti-hegemonist' when it availed him. But, I think the difficulty was first of all that I was so closely associated with the man he was trying to replace as IOC member, and second because I had such friendly relations with HOC and IOA employees, such as Kritsinelis and Didaskalou, and did what I could to make their work better known internationally. Nikolaou had Katerina replaced as high priestess after she outshined the other Greek Olympic leaders at the Seoul Olympic Games and, as discussed in 'My Programme' in this volume, Nikolaou subjected Kritsinelis to the same treatment in 2000 after all the international adulation Nassos received in 1996. Only in the past few years, while I was on the Chicago 2016 international relations team and when Nikolaou had become IOC vice president, a post Nissiotis had not attained, did relations warm up somewhat between us.

[92] Kostalas did his university work in philology and economics in the USA. A talented musician, he is perhaps best known outside of Greece as the long-time spokesman of the country during the Eurovision Song contest.

[93] According to the IOC Archives, Otto Szymiczek had played a key organizational role in the Olympia flame-lighting 'ceremony' for Los Angeles. Samaranch to Szymiczek, 20 May 1984. JO-1884S-FLAMT. So, there was a certain irony in his son's presence and performance here.

[94] Skiadas, *Thee Olympic Flame*, 151.

[95] Some details are provided in the ensuing article 'My Programme'. For readers of Norwegian, an anthropological study of local OFR celebrations and their cultural logics during the Lillehammer relay can be found in Klausen, et al., *Fakel-Stafetten*.

[96] Andronicos, *Vergina*, for the archaeology of this tomb.

[97] Personal communications, Steven McCarthy and Nassos Kritsinelis, 2002–03.

References

Andronicos, Manolis. *Vergina: The Royal Tombs*. Athens: Ekdotike Athenon, 1884.

Barney, Robert K., Stephen R. Wenn, and Scott G. Martyn. *Selling the Five Rings: The International Olympic Committee and the Rise of Olympic Commercialism.*, Rev ed. Salt Lake City: University of Utah Press, 2004.

Fermor, Patrick Leigh. *Roumeli: Travels in Northern Greece*. London: Penguin Books, 1966.

Herzfeld, Michael. *Ours Once More: Folklore, Ideology, and the Making of Modern Greece*. Austin, TX: University of Texas Press, 1982.

Katz, Donald. 'Atlanta Brave'. *Sports Illustrated*, January 8, 1996.

Klausen, Arne M., Ellen K. Aslaksen, Odd Are Berkaak, Ingrid Rudie, Eduardo Archetti, and Roel Puijk. *Fakel-Stafetten: Enn Olympisk Ouverture*. Oslo: Ad Notem Gyldendal, 1995.

Los Angeles, *Olympic Games Official Report* http://www.la84foundation.org/6oic/OfficialReports/1984/1984v1pt3.pdf Vol. 1.

MacAloon, John J. 'The 1904 Chicago-St. Louis Transition and the Social Structuration of the American Olympic Movement'. In *Sport, Politics, and History: Essays in Honor of Bruce Kidd*, edited by Russell Field. Toronto: University of Toronto Press, 2013.

MacAloon, John J. '"Legacy" as Managerial/Magical Discourse in Contemporary Olympic Affairs'. *The International Journal of the History of Sport* 25, no. 14 (2008): 2060–71.

MacAloon, John J. *This Great Symbol: Pierre de Coubertin and the Origins of the Modern Olympic Games.*, Rev ed. London: Routledge, 2008.

MacAloon, John J. 'The Theory of Spectacle: Reviewing Olympic Ethnography'. In *National Identity and Global Sports Events*, edited by Alan Tomlinson and Christopher Young, 15–40. Albany: State University of New York Press, 2006.

MacAloon, John J. 'The Ethnographic Imperative in Comparative Olympic Research'. *Sociology of Sport Journal* 9, no. 2 (1991): 104–30.

MacAloon, John J. 'Olympic Games and the Theory of Spectacle in Modern Societies'. In *Rite, Drama, Festival, Spectacle: Rehearsals Toward a Theory of Cultural Performance*, edited by J. MacAloon, 241–80. Philadelphia: Human Issues Press, 1984.

MacAloon, John J., and Kang Shin-pyo. '*Uri Nara*: Korean Nationalism, the Seoul Olympics, and Contemporary Anthropology'. *Toward One World Beyond All Boundaries: The Seoul Olympic Anniversary Conference*, 117–59, Vol 1. Seoul: Poong Nam Publishers, 1990.

Nissiotis, Nikolaos. 'L'Actualité de Pierre de Coubertin du point de vue de la philosophie el le problème de la *religio athletae*'. In *L'Actualité de Pierre de Coubertin*, edited by N. Müller, 125–71. Mainz: Schors Verlag, 1987.

Nissiotis, Marina N. and Grigoris, Mihail, eds. *Nikos A. Nissiotis: Religion, Philosophy, and Sport in Dialogue*. Athens: Grigoris, 1994.

Payne, Michael. *Olympic Turnaround*. London: Business Press, 2005.

Reagan, Ronald. 'Nomination Acceptance Speech to the 1984 Republican National Convention'. http://conservapedia.com/Ronald_Reagan's_1984_Republican_National_Convention_Speech March 2009.

Reich, Kenneth. *Making It Happen: Peter Ueberroth and the 1984 Olympics*. Santa Barbara, CA: Capra Press, 1986.

Ruthheiser, Charles. *Imagineering Atlanta*. London: Verso, 1996.

Skiadas, Eleftherios G. *The Olympic Flame, Torch of the Century*. Athens: Mikos Romios, 1997.

Stanley, Alessandra. 'An Olympic Ideal Gets Burned'. *Time Magazine*, May 4, 1984.
Tomlinson, Tommy. 'Andrew Young: Those Who Burn for Justice Should Respect Torch'. ESPN News, April 8, 2008. http://sports.espn.go.com/oly/columns/story?id+3334901.
Ueberroth, Peter. *Made in America*. New York: Morrow, 1985.
Yarbrough, C. Richard. *And They Call Them Games: An Inside View of the 1996 Olympics*. Macon, GA: Mercer University Press, 2000.

Olympic Flame Relay operations under a 'world's best practices' regime: a conversation with Steven McCarthy

John J. MacAloon

Social Science Division, The University of Chicago, Chicago, IL, USA

Steven McCarthy is founder, Chairman and CEO of Além International Management Inc., today's leading transnational provider of operational services for the Olympic Flame Relay (OFR). As operations manager for the 1996 Atlanta relay, managing director of the 2002 Salt Lake City relay, and operations manager of the international segment of the 2004 Athens relay, as well as the author of the IOC's official OFR technical manual, McCarthy has played the leading role in innovating key aspects and codifying the whole of today's 'world's best practices' model of OFR production. In this article, he discusses the origins of transnational OFR operations companies, the core ritual responsibilities of relay supervisors, security and safety issues, negotiation strategies with local authorities, and collaboration and conflicts among commercial sponsors, organizing committees, and operations personnel. A persistent theme in the conversation is just how universal or ethnocentric any world's best practices model turns out to be, and what the future role of the central IOC administration should be in protecting and replenishing the symbolic and moral capital of the OFR and through it the Olympic Movement. This conversation between the OFR's leading ethnographer and its leading transnational manager provides an unprecedented backstage view of one of the world's most important rituals, discussing dramatic issues and episodes equally unknown to Olympic publics and authorities.

John MacAloon: Steve, let's begin with some history. What was Além originally and how did you come to be involved with OFRs?[1]

Steven McCarthy: We love competition, being outdoors, and bicycle racing, and Boulder [Colorado] has been a main US centre for these things. We started working on bicycle races back in the late 1970s: the old Red Zinger bicycle race, then the Coors Classic, the Tour de Trump, the Tour Dupont, and a two-year stint with the Tour of China. We also did running races, marathons, triathlons. We were always involved in back of house organization for moving events, events that move.

I was doing this with a bunch of guys, most of them from law enforcement and defence services. They had been working in different venues, like presidential escort detail and the like, so I just started hiring them on a contract basis. That's how it grew until we finally said that we had better wrap some corporate entity around what were doing, because there is some [legal] exposure and some liability potential here.

JM: So you eventually incorporated as Além International Management, Inc.

SM: Not until February 1991. I was still doing some security work, executive protection consulting, and safety and security consulting, but the bulk of what we did was events management, and most of that for BMW. We did a lot of different things for BMW from trade shows to new product testing and launches, all kinds of stuff. I was still going to law school at the time, and others had day jobs. It didn't become full-time until much later, the end of the 1980s.

JM: You grew up in Golden, Colorado and went to the University of Colorado. What did you do between college, security work, law school and Além?

SM: After college, I joined the Pro Rodeo Circuit for a couple of years, but I wasn't a very good rodeo cowboy. I'd also worked in the oil business and was involved with an oil company in a regional land play in Arkansas. Then it was law school at Denver University. I left three days before graduation and moved to Brazil to work for the ConAgra firm. The CEO had a bad deal going in Brazil, and they needed someone to go down and sort it out. I'd already travelled a lot in Latin America and had been to school for a while in Medellin, Colombia. I stayed on working for ConAgra in Latin America.

JM: So when you returned from South America and started work on American events, it was mainly your security background you carried into the field?

SM: As much as anything, it was a simple interest in working on complex events. It was integrated oversight and coordination of law enforcement agencies, defence services, transportation agencies, and every other 'factor input' we could think of that would make an event successful.

JM: How did the Olympics enter in?

SM: We made contact with the people who were going to be in charge of the competitions in Atlanta for the [1996 Olympic] bicycle road race, the mountain biking, the marathon, the race walk, and a little bit on the equestrian side, the three-day event and the cross-country component. So, we were going to provide motorcycles and drivers, as well as shooters – videographers and still photographers – to cover those events live.

Part of what we were hired to do was the media side, but the biggest part was the operations side, working with police departments in Atlanta, the city and the counties, and the state police and transportation departments. So Além made a deal with the Atlanta competition managers, and that is where our Olympic work started. We went back to BMW and told them we needed 114 motorcycles to support our competition and media package, including establishing a photo delivery system from all the venues to the main press centre and international broadcast center. So we were in the transport business and the delivery business too. Besides the utility of motorcycles from BMW's sponsorship, we had the use of a lot of veteran guys from bicycle racing and marathons who continued to work for us on a contract basis.

JM: This was 1994, right, and you had already worked with BMW for some time, as you said?

SM: Yes, the end of 1994. We went back with BMW as our sponsor and client to the early 1980s, and we sort of brought them along to Atlanta. I have a lot to say about the distinction between the marketing side of the Olympic Games and the operations side, and why we think they have to come together and be truly integrated, because that to my mind is the future of the Games or of any major event, for that matter. We don't have that yet, and we certainly didn't have it in 1996. So, we brought BMW to ACOG [Atlanta Committee for the Olympic Games] on the motorcycle side. Another firm was already working on the automobile side, trying to get BMW in for a sponsorship category as foreign luxury sedan. When that finally happened, we consolidated motorcycles with cars and bicycles, and Além provided the management package for all the motorcycles.

JM: So you came to Olympic and flame relay work for 1996 with a commercial sponsor in tow. In retrospect, we can recognize this as exactly transitional between 1984 in

Los Angeles or Calgary, where the operational OFR team essentially *was* a sponsor [AT&T, PetroCanada], and post-1996 relays, when your company coordinates closely with sponsors, but is an independent subcontractor of the OCOG. How did you come to add the OFR to the sports events in your Atlanta portfolio?

SM: I was riding up an elevator in the old ACOG office building with [ACOG Torch Relay Director] Hilary Hanson, whom I didn't know at all, and she was saying to another woman, 'I wish we could find some people who could drive this torch across the country'. I turned around and literally raised my hand in the elevator and said, 'I don't mean to eavesdrop, but it sounds like you might need a hand, and we might be able to help'. It started from there.[2]

JM: That has to have been one of the more consequential elevator rides in Olympic history; it was destined to impact transnational Olympic ritual and governance processes.

SM: Our transportation manager Peter Bone and I subsequently met with Hilary and people from ACOG marketing. Then we went out on our first test event, just melding in with Jeff Cravens and the other operations and marketing people ACOG had already hired. One rain-soaked night in North Carolina, they asked us whether we wanted the job. It just grew from there. They went from wanting to hire seven drivers to drive the flame across the United States to having a crew of 145 people for the relay, most of whom Além hired.

JM: Hilary was hired by ACOG in May 1993, and Rennie Truitt came on as Senior Relay Advance Manager in February 1994, both with public relations backgrounds. They were reporting to Ginger Watkins, Corporate Relations General Manager, when I met them all in Spring 1994. I don't think the reporting line of the flame relay formally went to Corporate Relations until the end of that year, but, significantly, ACOG had the OFR organizationally classified with public relations and marketing from very early on.[3]

SM: That's right.

JM: With respect to the domestic flame relay in the US, I gave them a plan to have as much of the route as possible follow significant American historical journeys and symbolic centres, and not just a marketer's path connecting major population centres. Happily, that's what ACOG eventually did with so much of your American route: the Erie Canal, the Pony Express stations, the Voyageur river canoe journey, the Union Pacific rail lines, various Native American religious pilgrimage paths, the Selma Civil Rights march, and dozens of other significant American pathways. They didn't have anyone with any torch relay experience at all when I showed up. My experience with several relays and my tutelage in Greece under Nikos Nissiotis and Nassos Kritsinelis encouraged me to be a little forward with Ginger Watkins and her group at this early stage, despite ACOG's reputation for antipathy to outsiders. They really came through on this one.

SM: From the beginning, Hilary Hanson was great. Jeff Cravens was phenomenal. But I've always identified most, for some reason, with Ginger Watkins. For me, she was maybe the most extraordinary person in that whole 1996 Olympic setting, an inspiration to me personally and to my company. She reminded me of my mom, who died very young. Ginger had strong intellect and a passion for the torch relay project. She didn't suffer fools and was a strong manager, but she never said 'go do this' but rather 'what's your recommendation'. It was the first time in my life I had a boss who trusted me and said 'I'm not sure where we're going, but you'll figure it out'.

JM: How did you begin to figure out where you were going?

SM: We read books about Calgary and Los Angeles, some stuff about Peter Ueberroth. We watched torch relay film clips and read official reports and newspaper accounts. I did eventually talk with a California Highway Patrol guy who had ridden in the command car of the LA relay, the only veteran I talked with, but he was inspirational and a great source of information.

At ACOG, Rennie Truitt had obviously done a lot of research, and he educated us. But a lot was osmosis, things we picked up from the vision [ACOG President and CEO] Billy Payne and Ginger had, and [ACOG International Relations Managing Director] Charlie Battle was instrumental in giving us a global picture of the value of the OFR. Add to them [CFO] A.D. Frazier on the operations and finance side and you had a really formidable group of profoundly passionate and brilliant people. Like everyone, we had prior notions about the relay, but until we got into it, I don't think it ever occurred to us to wonder how that flame got from point A to point B. Now our job was to distil the software part of it, the philosophical and intangible parts of the relay down to the matter of how do we get from point A to point B in this amount of time with this number of people and this number of dollars.

JM: So LA 1984 was your most concrete point of reference. A huge Atlanta relay to outdo LA was planned from the beginning. I helped Rennie Truitt vet his confidential report on what had been done right on the Los Angeles flame relay and what absolutely had to be avoided this time around, notably the political disasters the LA 1984 relay created with the Hellenic Olympic Committee [HOC] and the Greek public. I'd gone out on the Greek relay for Barcelona 1992 to try to gauge whether Atlanta was going to be able to get an Olympic Flame from Greece at all. In those days, it didn't look promising. I ended up spending over two years working mostly internationally, mediating backstage among ACOG, the HOC, and the IOC. Charlie Battle was my chief ACOG collaborator in that period. I'd met him in Seoul back in 1988.

Since you didn't work on or come to Greece, I didn't really meet you, so far as I recall, until I spent time with you out on the domestic relay, first on a leg from Milwaukee to Chicago, where I was in charge of one of the celebrations, and then for a much longer stay on the East Coast. So I really had no idea how you assembled the bits and pieces of past relays with your own innovations into what became the core of today's favoured model.

SM: From what we knew then, LA 1984 was a great relay and their video was what we focused on, dissecting it frame by frame. Why is that guy there? What is that car doing there? Do you really need that? Where does the [broadcast] feed go that night? We also looked at the intangible, spiritual or philosophical moments of the Barcelona relay. Then we fast-forwarded to Lillehammer, because Vidar Eilertsen was going to join our team, and he'd been in charge of a lot of that relay, particularly the torchbearer component that ultimately drove the agenda.

Given the distance and the number of torchbearers Billy Payne wanted and the obligation to Coca-Cola for so many torchbearers, we quickly saw that the model ACOG had been using couldn't work. It was based on a straight eight to ten hour day, but they hadn't factored in food breaks, nature breaks, anything. So we got them to agree to assemble two whole crews, an A team and a B team to alternate, so we could go much longer each day. We were also going to split command control, but that didn't work, so I stayed with the relay pretty much all the way through, with Hilary or Steve Schriber filling in for me if I needed a nature break or just had to walk away for a few minutes. Hilary was a great leader and manager. Like Ginger, she was able to set her ego and self-interest completely aside and just get the job done.

JM: There's a tradition here. Maybe you became aware of it after you joined. The OFR attracts and probably also creates great leaders, like Han Guang-soo, the director of the Seoul relay, a military man but also a Korean traditional doctor, and to my observation a genius with his people. Or Jim Hunter, the Christian Olympian in Calgary, or the legendary Nassos Kritsinelis in Greece. Managers who care mostly about themselves couldn't survive the relay, could they?

SM: Absolutely not. It's all incredibly challenging day in and day out. But in the end we're all on the bus together, on the plane together, in the hotel and restaurant together. Everywhere you go, everyone is together 24 hours a day. I can't even begin to describe how strongly these people believed and how hard they worked.

You sit there in adverse environmental conditions – rain, heat, snow. You have the politics of sponsorship and marketing to deal with. You need the pure street smarts of how do I deal with this mayor or that police chief who is trying to prevent us from entering a city except on his terms. You get into these toe-to-toe contests of will in virtually every city. On top of that on the safety and security side for Atlanta, we had the Georgia State Patrol [GSP] join us at the last minute, and that was extremely challenging, not the officers who were a great resource of passion and pride of service, but their superiors. They just alienated a lot of people, when they started coming to our advance meetings with the Los Angeles, Washington, New York police forces, and the FBI.[4] But they did a great job protecting the flame, governing the lanterns, making sure the flame was lit properly, that it adhered to the sanctity, dignity, and purity that we felt the Greeks expected.

JM: While we're on the topic of moral leadership of the OFR team and the GSP, we lost two of these very officers to suicide within months after the end of the Atlanta OFR, James Robinson and Bubba Ball. I know you must have thoughts on this.

SM: Big ones. James and Bubba both … listen … you go from writing traffic tickets in Valdosta, Georgia, to sleeping in the White House watching over the Olympic Flame. That's a pretty big deal. And to have it all end and then to go back to Valdosta, I think it was just too much for some people. For Bubba and James to take their own lives was just devastating. You talk about a flame relay model and what you learn and learn not to do the next time. We promise everyone we hire that we know we will all be writing Christmas cards to each other for the rest of our lives. We couldn't guarantee anything else, but this we can promise. So that made it very difficult with James and Bubba, very difficult.

JM: I talked a lot with Hilary and Rennie early on about the moral stresses and elations out on the relay, and they quickly appreciated this dimension even though they'd never done anything remotely like this before. In my observation and to the many employees and volunteers on your relays whom I've debriefed, you are a master at appreciating that this experience changes people's lives and that to be a leader of a flame relay team, you have to monitor everyone's emotional condition at all times. This Atlanta relay generated the maxim that 'If you don't weep twice a day, you have to go home', meaning that you can't keep these powerful feelings bottled up inside you under these physical and moral conditions without risking psychological instability. When I met you out on your Salt Lake City relay, you corrected me, saying that 'now it's four times a day'.

SM: At least! You cry every day because there is somebody who is so inspiring, so motivating, and in some ways so sad, and in other ways so incredible in their power and strength and their humility about it. This mix of power and humility is an aphrodisiac to anyone who ever sees it. It is a total inspiration.

JM: Some can't ever really go home after this experience; they find it really hard to go home.

SM: At our Atlanta closing party, we just wandered around asking each other, 'What do we do now?' The post-relay letdown is just so overwhelming. You find yourself sitting in the middle of the floor somewhere just sobbing uncontrollably. These people have looked after you and you've looked after them, as we've all looked after the flame, and there is this compression that suddenly goes away. You are sad to see it go, but it is overpowering, absolutely overpowering, and the new obligations you have as a leader or manager of a company that is hired to do this stuff go well beyond pure operations and into the theoretical and spiritual, because to lose somebody like a Bubba or a James … I've had other people who are so close to the edge after this is over that you literally have to sit there and hold their hand, and have your hand held by them. It goes both ways.

JM: As evidenced by you and Além now moving from relay to relay, OFR production has become increasingly transnational. One advantage, clearly, is that there is less danger of being caught unaware of these potential impacts on staff mental and social health. You and the people you take with you each time have been through it and can educate newcomers, as presumably Di Henry and her copycat company Maxxam do on the relays they work.[5]

SM: People will drop everything they are doing to work one of these events, no matter where it is in the world. Athens was a showcase for that. Our people take sabbaticals or use accumulated vacation time, all because they believe that this is a great event and because they want that continuity you just mentioned. And not just for self-serving reasons, that this is a great event and they're going to get paid to ride a motorcycle around the world, or shoot videotape, or whatever. These are people who truly, absolutely, passionately believe in what the torch relay stands for. And that is the power you have over everybody. You could be a rotten manager, and people are still going to come together to make this work. No matter what has happened to them, whether they got fed or not or what hour of the day or night they've had to pull on their stuff still wet from a rainstorm and climb back on the motorcycle or run another 20 kilometres. They're going to come do it again.

I think that everybody we hired or represented recognized that this was much bigger than anything they had ever seen. Bigger in cost, bigger in time, geography, scope, and budget. The people were hired in 1996 and carried forward, through our consultancies in Nagano and Sydney, and those we added in 2002 for Salt Lake, they were already taking time off from their jobs and asking to be signed up before we'd even got the Athens contract. And many of them are with us again now in Rio for the Pan American Games torch relay.

JM: There was no such community of transnational flame relay labour when you started back in 1994, because each successive OCOG began afresh and learned pretty much as you did for Atlanta. The only real continuity in personnel was in Greece, where since 1976, Nassos Kritsinelis and his HOC team lit the flame at Olympia, relayed it to Athens, and handed it over to each consecutive OCOG. Once on the national territory of the host city, however, the flame relay was pretty much a national operation with entirely new personnel from the previous relay (one peripatetic anthropologist notwithstanding).

Back then, the IOC was almost nowhere to be seen in this process. Though things began to change after the controversies over the Los Angeles flame relay, IOC staff in Lausanne had little or no knowledge of or concern with what actually happened out on OFRs. Then in the later Samaranch years, the IOC began to adopt a so-called franchise model for the OCOGs. The idea was to help OCOGs by not leaving them alone to reinvent the wheel each time. With ACOG as the perceived negative model and SOCOG as the positive one in IOC culture, at least, Lausanne began to establish means of providing what they called 'Olympic Games Knowledge Services' to OCOGs: instruction manuals, software, and experts representing the 'world's best practices', to use the management school lingo that dominates the IOC staff today. The IOC is presently trying to assert itself as a central actor in the OFR, and things are becoming so codified that you have just completed, on commission from Olympic Games Executive Director Gilbert Felli, an IOC flame relay technical manual that all OCOGs will be expected from now on to work from.

Another part of this trajectory has been the provision of an experienced transnational management pool that moves from games to games. Manolo Romero pioneered this in Olympic broadcasting, and the model has subsequently developed in one functional area after another: accreditation, Olympic Village services, transportation, security, Opening and Closing Ceremonies, and so on. You embody the flame relay piece of this trend.

SM: Manolo Romero is the example I would have brought up. I know he was working long before Barcelona …

JM: He seriously began his operations in Calgary, as I recall.

SM: And he assembled an extraordinary team from around the world. But he really brought the model forward after Barcelona. He was the guy that I identified with as our mentor. Manolo was the guy who had been able to go to the IOC and the OCOGs and say, listen, I have a package here, you don't have to reinvent [host broadcast operations and the International Broadcast Centre] from scratch. We've already got it in place, just hire us and we'll go to town, and we'll do it quietly and with great humility, but with extraordinary power and experience. And we have a truly transnational team, not just Spaniards but people from all over the world. Same as Rick Ludwig on the finance side and others. Ludwig represents the best of the best, one of the quietest, most humble people I've seen, yet with plenty of reason to be otherwise. I think people like Romero, Ludwig, and Kritsinelis represent the true value of 'best practices' because all the best practices without the best people to execute them mean nothing.

JM: You're the first person I've heard in a long time speaking of Manolo doing things 'humbly', but it is absolutely true that he was the most important person driving the IOC's new model for transnational provision of Olympic Games management and technical expertise and services. It helped that so much of the IBC could now be black-boxed and in effect shipped on to the next Olympics. But in his movement from first dealing with OCOGs as an independent contractor, then as the owner of a transnational company strongly favoured by the IOC, and finally to being what is in effect an IOC joint venture partner with a more or less permanent franchise, he's been as important to the transformation of the Olympic Games on the management side as Horst Dassler, Juergen Lenz, and Peter Ueberroth were on the finance and marketing side.

SM: From a purely Além business model perspective, this franchise-ability was what we wanted in order to keep going, and not just for the revenue stream. We wanted to be known as the only people who could put together an incredible torch relay anywhere around the world. We decided to standardize all this, then formalize it into a package. Then we'll take it to the OCOGs and customize it to local operating conditions. There certainly are the spiritual or ethereal types of elements that are going to portray a different sort of message from Sydney, or Salt Lake, or Athens. You can tweak all that, but you do so on the foundation established by pure operations.

JM: So let's go back to the evolution of your model on the operations side.

SM: As I was saying, the main challenge is the jurisdictional one, dealing with the local authorities in all the places you move through. By Salt Lake City, we finally figured out that you never go into a jurisdiction and say this is who we are and this is what we're doing. Instead, you say that you have the gift and luxury of being appointed to look after the Olympic Flame, and you need their help. Can you give us some idea of what works here, about which streets to go down? What time of day would least intrude on your traffic flow, on your security planning? We want to make the smallest impact possible on your resources, while generating the largest promotional value we can. From a legacy standpoint, we want the people in your town, your city, your village, along your country roads to remember that they saw the Olympic Flame. Obviously most people cannot get to

Atlanta or Salt Lake or Athens or afford to buy tickets to see the Games. So this is their chance to be close to the Olympic Flame and the magic it represents around the world. But it's still hard because every local, state, and federal agency you come into contact with is protective of its turf, has its own professional routines and rivalries, and wants to get into the act. So you learn from the past and try to be ready to reinvent things every time you take it forward.

For Athens, we quickly discovered our biggest challenge in cities that relied more on law enforcement and defence services to dictate the passage of the 'icon', as they always called it, treating it like a presidential detail. They were like: 'You are from where again? Colorado? And you are going to come in and tell us how to do this? This is our place, son!'

JM: Well, that is hardly surprising. Greeks had never seen this national icon handled by foreigners on Greek territory, much less organized by foreigners, much less by representatives of an American company. All these local authorities were used to working with Nassos Kritsinelis, and he had already advanced the route with most of them before Além arrived and started reworking things for ATHOC, substituting elements from your model for those in the traditional HOC model. Even if you were an ATHOC subcontractor, your mere presence would be shocking to some Greek authorities and to many others an invitation to reopen negotiations on everything. And that's even before we talk about the visible sponsor presence, absolutely new to Greek relays. Your main job for ATHOC was the international segment of the relay.

SM: [On the international relay for Athens] Barcelona was maybe the most challenging for jurisdictional issues and negotiations on that segment, and Sydney and Melbourne were the first to say, look mate, we've done the Olympics better than anyone else, so you just leave the flame at the bottom of the aircraft stairs and take a nap, and we'll make a great relay and bring it back to you tonight. This is what you must deal with.

JM: But safety and security are also about *ritual* security and responsibility aren't they? At the end of the day, you have to be able to guarantee everyone that by god, it's the real flame they're seeing and carrying, the real Olympia Flame that is borne toward and arrives in the Olympic Opening Ceremony.[6]

SM: It is our first duty to guarantee that the flame stays lit from Olympia to Opening and through to Closing Ceremonies. We carried 13 separate safety lanterns on the Athens relay, and if I ever had needed to, I would literally have gone back to Olympia to get another one and start over. We wanted to be able to look anyone in the eye and say this is the flame we saw lit by the High Priestess with the parabolic mirror in Olympia outside the Temple of Hera or in the Coubertin Grove for the Winter Games. This is the flame that went to the Opening Ceremonies. In Salt Lake City, I could flat guarantee that happened. For Athens, I could swear a solemn oath that this was the flame that I watched over from Olympia to Heraklion, where we turned it over to the Greek operating team.

JM: And Atlanta, with Kritsinelis, Battle, and I guaranteeing that the flame that got off the plane in Los Angeles was the Olympia Flame?

SM: Atlanta, too. All three of them.

JM: I won't ask you to comment just now, but there are strong doubts within the OFR community as to whether another team at a recent Olympics can legitimately make such a claim. Surely, this is the single most important thing for maintaining the integrity of the OFR as a true ritual and not just a showy spectacle.

SM: It is the critical, essential thing.

JM: Let's talk about security in the more quotidian sense. As we discussed earlier, no one can fault you for the excesses of the GSP in 1996, but moving forward through your relays people point to the visible security presence as distinctive of what some European

Olympic people – including your experienced Greek colleagues Nassos Kritsinelis and Pinelopi Amelidou – now refer to as the 'American model' of flame relays. (Revealingly, no one refers to Romero's ensemble of broadcasting practices as 'the Spanish model'.) The large complement of motorcycles, that you've already referred to several times over, the two giant aircraft on the Athens relay to get these motors around, all the accompanying runners who are security people, the fact that so many of your people have American law enforcement or state security backgrounds, the language you speak to each other through your walkie-talkie and cell phone communication systems: all this has been labelled by some as having something essentially American about it. Whether or not that's the case, it is certainly a fact that this is distinctive of your practice. If you look at relay films, you know immediately that this one is Além and that one is not by the strength of the visible security envelope around the torchbearer. Your colleagues on ATHOC confronted the Greek people for the first time with all of these practices from your model – they had not existed in any HOC relay – while self-consciously reducing the number of motors and security men you might have wanted inside the envelope. I suppose this was one of those 'tweakings' of the world's best practices model to accommodate to local social and cultural conditions that you referred to earlier.

Do you question yourself about any of this? Is any of this really 'American' or even 'Anglo-Saxon' – the Australians, like the Greeks copied your general model but chose to be less visibly protectionist than you – or rather just an artefact of your own personal background and professional milieu? How do you determine how much security is enough? We'll get to this on the international segment of the ATHOC relay, where this question must have been exceptionally complex and vexed, but how about in general?

SM: First of all, on this American issue, we have never wanted to be viewed outside or inside the United States as this flag waving, patriotic, nationalistic kind of exercise. We want to be viewed as a company that quietly, in a back of the house sort of way, is going to look after, first and foremost, the safety and security of the flame and those who carry it. Second, we take our job to be looking after the message of the OCOG and the IOC and all the other Olympic Family stakeholders, and then the message of the sponsors. But we always want to be back of the house. We have never wanted to be labelled as the flag-waving guys with too much security presence and, specifically, too many motors and too many security runners.

We have always been aware and allegiant to the fact that this is a mission of Peace, number one; this is a mission that is a joyous occasion for that one person at a time who gets the flame passed to their torch or gets handed the flame. They are the only person in the world who is, right there, at that moment, entrusted with the passage of the flame. You can see it in the film clips of virtually every torchbearer. At almost the identical point, 30 metres out from where they accept the flame: they look around, they look up, and they finally look at the flame burning, and you capture the moment, almost the same moment every time, where you see them think to themselves 'Oh my god, I'm the only one carrying this Olympic Flame'. That is pretty powerful stuff. So we don't want to spoil this for that person by having the intrusion of security people. We want to make sure that if you are in a high-traffic area or a high-risk area, that we've identified through advance work and collaboration with local law enforcement agencies and the mayor's office, whoever knows their city best, the likelihood that someone may want to try to steal the torch, or put out the flame with a water bucket, or harm the torchbearer or his or her supporters.

Of course, the changes come, certainly in a post-9/11 world, and this was a big deal for Athens. Salt Lake City was the first post-9/11 relay, and we had been working on a very unobtrusive activation strategy, but we came to want more visibility as a deterrent.

Frankly, on the Salt Lake relay, virtually nothing happened. It was a raw, emotional time for everybody in America and this flame and those games generated support for this last sort of globally recognized non-religious icon that the Olympic Flame is, as well as support for post-9/11 America. When you look at the film clips of the flame on the ferry boat going around the Statue of Liberty or going past Ground Zero, actually anywhere in the country, it was a flag raving ... er ... waving ceremony like I've never seen before in all my life. I mean, it was very powerful. People coming out in the middle of a dark winter night, sometimes in sub-zero temperatures to cheer on somebody carrying the flame for 300 metres, whether they knew the torchbearer or not ... it's just ... I can't describe that ... I can't ... it's just a very powerful feeling.

JM: Part of the power comes from joining the most local meanings with host-country national meanings with the great international meanings of the flame and its relay tradition. Both harmonies and tensions among these layers of meaning build up that symbolic power you feel. In your Salt Lake example, you have a global peace symbol – perhaps now, *the* global peace symbol – being relayed in a war context, or at least what the US government was telling its citizens was a war context. And these are complicated tensions that enter into what you have to manage, whether it's your job to promote or try to damper the flag waving, for example. At the same time, the Olympic Flame is an open signifier, as we anthropologists say. To be sure, the flame comes with its history, tradition, and significations of Olympism, but these themselves are contested and in the end no one can tell people what the Olympic Flame is going to mean to them. I'm certain that just as many of the people you describe on the Salt Lake relay clearly distinguished between the American state and the American nation – the 'American people' in our vernacular – and were morally reinforcing the latter and not the Bush administration's view of the geopolitical situation. For them, therefore, this was a peace symbol in a peace context. All of this was replayed in the major conflict over political representations in the Salt Lake Opening Ceremonies, where your flame relay ended its journey.

The point is that to protect this symbolic power, you have to protect also the open-ended nature of this meaning making, and you are saying that this is your job as relay organizers just as much as physical security.

SM: Absolutely, within the limits of our mandate.

JM: Steven, let me press you a bit on the more general issue of security. You will correct me if you think I'm wrong, but having been around flame relays a little longer than you and having talked with many international security people and IOC monitors, and read the available IOC archives, there is no evidence that I am aware of that the Olympic Flame has ever been the object of any serious interest on the part of organized political terrorists. There is no after the fact evidence whatsoever of any terrorist plots against the OFR. Those of us who think about these things refer to it as 'the Munich effect', that all such persons have learned – as some Black September organizers themselves said subsequently – that you cannot win if you attack the Olympics, because you are attacking your friends as well as your enemies, you are attacking humanity.

Indeed, one could even generalize this effect to the Olympics as a whole since 1972. There are, of course, other security issues, like individual political criminals like the Atlanta bomber, and unstable people or pranksters who, as you say, might want to tackle the torchbearer, as one tackled the Brazilian marathon runner in Athens. And in Torino, for the very first time we did have quasi-organized disruptions of the OFR by Italians protesting against local development projects and world labour conditions they saw as promoted by the neo-liberal globalization represented by Coca-Cola, the main relay sponsor. But as to organized political terrorism, objectively, the risk is really about nil.

And yet there is almost a sort of blackmail of OCOGs going on these days by security agencies, businesses, entrepreneurs, and consultants: 'If you don't buy my equipment or hire my services, and something happens, just one mistake, you're going to be blamed, so you better give me a little business here.' I don't think I'm caricaturing how today's incredible investment in Olympic security in part comes about. You too say to OCOGs, if you hire us, because of our expertise and the way we conceive our mission, you won't have to worry about security. In fact, there is not very much to defend against, is there? Wouldn't it be exaggerating the threat to suggest there's anything but pranksters really to contend with?

SM: Yeah, well, touch wood, you are correct that there has never been, to my knowledge, any organized push to try to destroy anything about the flame, or about the games any more. Certainly there is always intelligence about people who might want to disrupt it just to get media exposure for themselves. But the torch relay has almost a sovereign immunity. Because this is such an enormous symbol, a universal symbol, it would be really out of balance if someone took a whack at the flame, the torch, or the torchbearer.

So we feel going into a relay that we don't have to ramp up a big security detail, or put together a big intelligence package, or buy a bunch of hardware. This is the greatest mission of peace. Our people don't carry weapons, our security runners and escort runners and our escort motorists don't carry weapons. Our job is to create a visual presence to prevent disruption so that we can keep going down the road. The job of local law enforcement is to create a surgically clean environment in the street that we are going down. Their job is to shut down the intersections and to keep this thing moving, exactly like a presidential or executive protection detail, so we can be out of their hair, and they can get back to everyday normal life as quickly and easily as possible, but with the memory of this grand passage of a universal icon.

You're absolutely right, from an OFR standpoint, there were people in the Athens case wanting to come in to ATHOC or the IOC and sell a big surveillance package, sell AWACs aircraft, sell everyone's latest intelligence gathering device, all kinds of things to guarantee the safety of the flame and torchbearers. But all that was properly pushed to the wayside. The torch relay affords an opportunity to individuals or groups to pronounce and promote a political or social statement simply because the relay commands a lot of global media coverage. In other words, people don't attack the flame or what it stands for; they consider using it as a low-cost vehicle to get their messages out.

Our job as the Além Company, hired to manage the relay, was never supposed to be the safety of the passage of that flame. That was always left to local law enforcement, largely because we didn't want the OCOG or the IOC to inherit that liability, risk, and exposure. We say to all the local and federal agencies involved, our job is to protect this flame, but if somebody intrudes on that and enters into the secure package, this envelope around the flame bearer, then you are free to do whatever you need to do within the confines of your jurisdiction. But if someone comes in to steal the flame or knock over the torchbearer, the strategy from an Além point of view is 'cover and evacuate'. This is the traditional presidential or executive protection defence, where you literally cover your protectee, then get him or her as quickly as possible out of the danger zone and into a secure platform, with minimum attention and risk.

So our job is to make sure that we just go through the streets safely. We've had great results with that: Atlanta worked out fine; Sydney had the torch put out and stolen a couple of times, but SOCOG took a really hands off, pacifist approach to this; for Salt Lake City, as I said, we truly felt like we had sovereign immunity, a gold pass.

JM: Even from the pranksters and frat boys?

SM: Absolutely. There were only a couple of water bucket incidents, but ordinary citizens took over, saying we'll take care of these guys, you just go on with the flame relay. And they did, and we did. There were a few people who came into the 'sterile zone' but, when you just quietly and quickly tell them it was a closed area, they left without problem. Athens became a bit different, because we went through so many different countries, cities, and cultures, and Torino certainly became different . . . .

JM: But flame and torchbearer security is still not an overwhelming issue, given the nature of the OFR itself and the success of your practices.

SM: It's always an issue if someone is in harm's way. While we don't invite confrontation or exposure, we certainly don't ever want to see anything bad happen to the flame, the torchbearer, or any other interests or parties that accompany us on the route.

JM: This still leaves the question of why you think SOCOG and ATHOC on segments one and three of the 2004 relay could get by just fine with fewer motors and security escort runners creating the envelope than Além used in the United States in 1996 and 2002 and on the second, international segment of the 2004 Athens relay. But maybe instead we should turn for now to another major piece of the 'world's best practices' model, the media relations piece.

SM: It has two fundamental elements, pure coverage and media public relations. How do you get a signal out around the city, the state, the country, even the world that excites people about the relay wherever it passes? How do you motivate people to be more interested in the Games and make them want to go visit the host city? For Atlanta, our model – driven by hiring Hilary Hanson with a terrific supporting cast and the Ketchum Public Relations company behind it – was to get this thing covered and on television and to send an advance team to really talk with local leaders about the pubic relations component and the emotional value it can create for a place that may not get that much national or global attention normally.

JM: Some people have the false impression that the relay inevitably gets lots of national press coverage. That's not typically true at all. Maybe a little squib in the newspaper or a brief shot on television that night, but generally if the flame isn't in your town, it doesn't draw much media attention. Of course, Greece is always different. Korea was different. Your 2004 international relay was different in the Southern Hemisphere cities you visited. But otherwise you have to work at it.

SM: That's right, and Billy Payne and Ginger Watkins addressed these issues very well for Atlanta in 1996.

JM: Billy Payne's 'community hero torchbearer' programme must have helped with this, right? There were precedents, in Calgary for example, and for Barcelona, where at least some of the torchbearers were selected for their community service records by the town councils and internationally by Coca-Cola, and 50% of the public torchbearers were mandated to be Olympic volunteers. However, in Atlanta, Payne and Watkins really pushed for and greatly expanded this programme of public torchbearer nominations, involving local offices of the United Way charity as their selection partner.[7]

SM: United Way was able to mobilize great people who were truly the cornerstone of the programme. The torchbearers they selected really were community heroes. Sponsor incentive programmes ran in parallel, of course, and Coke brought in deserving people from foreign countries to run the flame, as they had in Barcelona. But the media attention gravitated to these torchbearers who had made a difference in one or more lives in their communities, benefactors nominated by their beneficiaries. The media latched on to this early because it was a compelling story of the relay and it was real, not some fabricated deal, the very opposite of crass commercialism that critics focus on.

So you have the public relations side and the sort of advance work necessary to get the message out about the relay itself and Olympic history, and you come in with the activation. We brought everybody involved to the media platform vehicle to shoot every torchbearer, to shoot bureau footage and crowd shots of every city we passed through, to shoot a picture of the mayor at every celebration stop. ACOG had hired a company, the Texas Crew, who did a phenomenal job of capturing all these images into really inspiring compilation tapes of each day's relay. We've now worked together with them all over the world, and they truly represent the best of best practices, providing humble, accurate, and indeed magical coverage of amazing people, events, and places.

JM: While there were some precedents, of course, it seemed to me that you made much more effective use of these tapes than anyone else had until then. Back in Atlanta, the ACOG executives viewed these tapes each morning as a way to stay motivated in the final push to get ready for the Games. And you used them in your shuttle buses to psych up the torchbearers. (See Figure 1.)

SM: Absolutely, and we had them shown on local news and national news, and they brought a lot of people out into the streets, because we'd use these B-roll situations from the ceremony the night before at the media briefing before we started up in the morning. Seeing the tape, the media would figure they had better get on the press vehicle or out on the side of the road to cover it for local news or to spec shoot for the local newspaper. So the end result in every city was a torchbearer or celebration picture above the fold of every newspaper in town.

Figure 1.   One of the most appreciated innovations in the 'world's best practices model', is the torchbearer shuttle group in which torchbearers introduce themselves to one another, receive a briefing on OFR history, and debrief one another on returning from the ritual to their families. Source: John J. MacAloon, Jr.

We used motorcycles and retrofitted a BMW as a camera car, but to get these shots the Texas Crew and the still photographers needed a platform to shoot from, and it had to be in front of the torchbearer looking backward. So we retrofitted a motor home. It was sort of big and clunky and not very pleasing to look at, and the major criticism of it was that it blocked the view of the torchbearer from the side of the road. But it was a fabulous operations platform with its own power so people could keep their cameras and tape machines running non-stop. Transmitters could be mounted on it, and we went live to air on lots of occasions.

JM: Your media platform also allows you to ensure that each and every torchbearer goes home with quality still photos of his or her glorious moments, and by the time of Salt Lake it could even be an instantaneous video. Rather than Aunt Sadie on the side of the road screaming and crying and trying to get a snap with her Kodak, you go home with a professional record of the moment.[8] I'm sure that everyone who has these keepsakes treasures them as much as we treasure them in my family. Thanks largely to you, this is a very difficult personal issue with me.[9] The controversy abides. There is enormous public resentment of that media truck, and I've collected scores of testimonies about this. People come and wait all day, expecting to see this long shot of that little flame bobbing towards them up the country road or the boulevard and being able to anticipate where the exchange will take place, and then their view of the flame itself is completely blocked by this media vehicle until the very last seconds, when the flame passes directly in front of them, and then it's gone again behind other vehicles. This is not just the general critique of how big and loud and fancy the caravan has become, almost 20 vehicles sometimes, but a specific criticism of ritual disruption, the taking away of the ability and right of ordinary people to visually focus on the master symbol itself. There's real anger out there about this. It's a tough trade-off for you, isn't it?

SM: Yes it is, and I think that this is probably an American model too because....

JM: That certainly has been the accusation: that you Americans are so interested in media and souvenirs and elites that the whole ritual side of things is harmed. Many Greeks were shocked to have their view blocked by this media truck for the first time in 2004, and it was a particularly large and ugly truck by the way. I had parents who were so upset they were nearly in tears in Olympia itself, because they couldn't really see their child carrying the flame through their village. So fairly or not, this 'American model' is accused of serving media and material souvenirs ahead of the people and ritual experience.

SM: There is a trade-off, but we would still defend this media platform as a good thing to have to capture all those images that those people might not get and for the torchbearer to have a very clear, high definition photo or videotape (See Figure 2). We never want to block the picture your grandmother or your dad is going to take from the side of the road, and we feed pool footage to every local broadcaster so torchbearers and their families can be on local television. But you also have to look at this in the context of high- or low-density roads. On low-density roads or out in the middle of nowhere, we delivered on the lone torchbearer with no vehicle near. But when it's midnight coming down Peachtree Street through Buckhead in Atlanta, or through Mexico City, or Rome, or in half the other world cities where we had trouble with people entering the protective envelope, the media vehicle also serves as a blocking vehicle. Yes, it is a billboard and has some commercial value from a sponsor perspective, but it also helps us in the command car. When the crowd gets too big and gets your torchbearer in difficulty, we back that media truck literally into the torchbearer's face (See Figure 2). In large cities, particularly at the end of the day, people come pouring out of bars and occasionally even pitch bottles at you, so you close up the gaps in the caravan as tightly as you can.

Figure 2.   In the Além model, the Olympic Flame is always within a security envelope composed of the media truck in front, security men on motorcycles to the sides, and the command car behind. Steven McCarthy on his radio is at the far left. Photo by the author (John J. MacAloon).

Is the caravan too big? It all depends on what you need to get down the road. You've got your functional needs, your overnight services teams, and now we also get back to what I mentioned earlier, marketing versus operations and the need to integrate them. If the OCOG marketing department has promised Coca-Cola or Samsung or Chevrolet a lead vehicle and two support vehicles in the caravan – three each was the number in Salt Lake and Athens and seems to be the norm right now – what can we in operations do about caravan size? And our job is to keep things moving.

The worst moments for me in 1996 were summer nights when we came through a small town but had to collect the flame and put it behind the command car and just go, because [we] were behind schedule. And the people who had stood out there and gone to the store and bought disposable cameras, and we whipped by so fast ... these were absolutely the worst times for me on the relay. I felt we had let these people down.

JM: This must be the absolute bane of your existence, the thing that eats at you all of the time: that critics and journalists who completely stand outside this thing attribute everything imperfect to sponsor commercialism, media demands, or the convenience of elites. They have no idea of the operations team, of who you are and what you are responsible for in managing all these factors in order to get down the road.

SM: Not a clue, except when we are able to conduct our great tradition that we started in Atlanta and do wherever we can. In remote rural areas, it would be coming on twilight or we'd have just started out in the morning, and we'd find ourselves ahead of schedule. So we'd get off the highway and on to a little side road and start the real relay there, or we'd see 20 kids from a few families sitting by the side of the road and we'd just stop the whole thing, and create a photo opportunity for them. Great people who are sitting there, and we'd capture all that. These are the images in the photo archives that someone should carefully study some day. These are the magic scenes that will make you cry, and not just four times a day. Before long, we started building in cushions for these things, so we could stop and burn three minutes and accommodate these wonderful people. We want them to remember that day the relay came to their village and stopped at their 'mom and pop' barbeque on the side of the road or at their convenience store or trailer park, and they are the ones we most want to remember too.

We really perfected this on the Salt Lake relay, when we would stop at local Chevy dealers or Coke distributors or neighbourhood celebrations and just throw an instant party, walking that torch around from person to person, letting them capture that image with their grandparents, real local torchbearers who had just run in front of their home or office in a small town, with their relatives and friends sitting there, some in wheelchairs, some on crutches. I always regret that we can't manage to let everyone in the country see these things, because they are so valuable, so magic, so powerful. I think our whole crew feels this.

So we would wait, and we would wait, and people would ask for just one more photograph, and we'd look at our watches and say alright, we are already late, and then once we did get going, we'd have to pick up the caravan pace to above our legal speed limit. Sometimes, we'd just be an hour or more late getting to a town because we'd stopped to accommodate a lot of these people and it was so magical.

JM: Having had to fill in an hour and a half of programming waiting for you guys on the South Side of Chicago, I know. But when it comes to the OFR, I think people are enormously tolerant, don't you, compared with other events you have done?

SM: God, yes, though maybe not as tolerant as on the Tour de France.

JM: If the Olympic Flame is an hour late, so what? People know it's probably for socially benevolent reasons, or to use the anthropological expression of my teacher Victor Turner, that there's been a lot of *communitas* going down.

SM: We always do try to be on time, and for the Athens international segment, it was even more of a guarantee. We were forced into it by function, because we had a charter aircraft sitting on the tarmac with the engines running and we would literally run up the stairs with the flame to take off for the next city. It's always a trade-off, but everybody on our crew and on the OCOG feels good at the end of the day, because we are touching millions more people than we could ever touch with the just the Games themselves, and not only through broadcast and media attention, but literally face-to-face along the roads.

JM: Depending on whose figures you credit, there are perhaps 10 times more live viewers for the OFR than ever see Olympic sports events face-to-face; this is an extraordinary, extraordinary fact, one the IOC is finally waking up to.

SM: So, yes, people have that image and expectation of the lone torchbearer out on the road, a great image of purity, sanctity, and dignity. So what the hell are all of these motor homes doing here? You have to wrestle with that, and we do so every day. It does become a bit of a circus after a while, but I think it's getting better as they move deeper into the franchise model. We can't forget the view from Coca-Cola or Samsung or Chevrolet or SEAT in Barcelona or AMP Insurance in Sydney or whoever else is out there sponsoring and promoting the relay. They want to get their message across as well, and they don't just create advertising and promotions but also functional platforms that the relay management team can use from time to time.

JM: Let's move on then to marketing and sponsor relations and their integration, as you've said you'd like to see, with operations.

The rise of commercial sponsor interest, presence and influence over the OFR is a distinguishing and relentless, though not uninterrupted – witness Seoul 1988 and Lillehammer 1994 – characteristic of the transformation effected in the flame rites between 1984 and today. The LAOOC made far greater use of flame relay sponsorship in

1984 than any previous relay ever tried or imagined. There were financial considerations, obviously, but the sheer, or in my analytical language, the spectacular scale of the 1984 relay across the United States led Peter Ueberroth and company to essentially farm out to AT&T and the suppliers the actual operation of the relay. Yet, compared with what was to come, AT&T was in no sense a heavy-handed partner in 1984. There was little or nothing of today's elaborate, vexatious, and some would say polluting 'sponsorship activation' programming surrounding and disrupting the relay, perhaps because AT&T was not then so much a consumer products company.[10] Its situation was much more comparable to sponsors like PetroCanada for Calgary, the Norwegian Post for Lillehammer, or AMP Insurance for Sydney, and much less like Coke or Samsung today. AT&T's corporate effort in 1984 was more people-centred than product-centred. For example, AT&T pioneered the escort runners, but they were fitness boom AT&T employees, not security people, and so far as I have been able to discover, AT&T didn't even bother to contract for a definite number of torchbearer slots designated for its business purposes, certainly the key incentive for today's 'presenting partners'. So it was ironic, given what was to develop later, that the 1984 conflict with the HOC and Greek public opinion over 'commercialization' of the OFR was not really about sponsor logos and commercial marketing but rather about the LAOOC selling the right to carry the flame to individuals and institutions on a kilometre by kilometre basis.

After the non-commercial relay in Seoul, which had suppliers, but not major sponsors, SEAT automotive, Mito, and Coke were very visible in Barcelona and even played operational roles. Lillehammer was once again non-commercial, and then Coke took everything to a whole new level with its activation activities on your relay in 1996. What effect did this have on the development of your model?

SM: You have to meld operations and marketing to have all this begin to come out right. OCOGSs have to realize that they can't promise sponsors in a darkened room all sorts of activations out on the road, before knowing whether such things are even possible. Operations people have to be present as you are talking to the marketing people, to say, yes, you can fit a 13-foot truck under a 15-foot bridge, but not under an 11-foot bridge. This integration with operations has to be done in advance with whatever these people want to do as their activation strategy out on the road and whatever you are promising them in value for their promotional brand recognition. If they've already written you the cheque and think they know what they've got for their money, and then we can't deliver because their truck won't fit under a bridge, we've got a big problem.

JM: So integrated management here means using the operations knowledge an Além brings to keep OCOG marketing officials, who likely have never seen an OFR, from over-promising with – or, I would add, being suckered by – more experienced sponsor negotiators, like Coke's and Samsung's today. You really believe that a lot of the present difficulties and battles could be solved by your approach and with knowledgeable people like you in the room from the beginning.

SM: You go to the OCOG with simple logic and say, listen, it's great that you are getting these sponsors in, say Samsung and Coke for Athens, it's great that we'll have their support. We need their product, we need their money, we need their inspiration, we need their leadership, their management, their network. In return, we need to promote the messages that they are trying to put across, and often they are more effective messengers than we, the OCOG, are. So let's all sit in the same room before we launch this thing and figure out how to make it work so that everyone wins. So this is what our model comes down to in integrating operations with marketing, and this is also something we learned from Manolo Romero. But more importantly, we've learned it from the likes of

Peter Franklin and David Brooks from Coca-Cola. They've forgotten more than I'll ever know about brand and product activation.

JM: I guess it also goes without saying that without sponsor dollars, OCOGs would be less likely to be able to hire firms like yours to be in that room with them in the first place. You are pointing out that an independent operations contractor like Além can and should play a key role in mediating OCOG and sponsor relations, as well as sponsor relations with the public. That certainly has been the situation in the past, but not always a particularly pleasant one, as sponsors have also proven repeatedly to be an enormous burden on relay managers. Hilary Hanson has repeatedly told me that, as Atlanta OFR director, she spent over 60% of her time arguing, negotiating, disciplining, and otherwise coping with the Coca-Cola's activation teams out on her relay. You know this perfectly well, because you listened to her doing it hour by hour, day after day in the command car, as you sat beside her managing relay operations and the caravan on your walkie-talkies and phones, while she worked hers.

The tactical antics of these Coke teams could be almost unbelievable, as I saw for myself out on that relay: telling shopkeepers along the relay route that they had to take down their Pepsi signs, invading public spaces with unauthorized product vendors, trying to sneak Coke operatives among the speech-makers at celebrations, wilfully confusing local authorities as to who was actually running the relay. It was an omnipresent and never-ending struggle, so bad that by the time the relay reached Chicago, ACOG had secretly detailed a subgroup of the flame relay advance team to discreetly warn celebration organizers against what Coke would soon bring against them. The explicit ACOG message was: 'Whatever Coke tells you, you don't have to permit any of this, if you don't want to'. I know first-hand, because I was taken aside and briefed this way as the director of the OFR celebration at the University of Chicago, these ACOG 'special' advance people being unaware of my other OFR and ACOG relationships. Olympic critics who speak of a seamless takeover by corporate interests simply can't imagine the battles that go one between an OCOG and its own sponsors, with the relay managers squarely in the middle.

SM: We went from Atlanta where, after the Games, Coca-Cola was roasted as having been too commercial and too 'Red' in its sponsorship and activation to being with them in Athens where they were absolutely amazing and very cognizant of the fact that it wasn't just their relay and it wasn't just about them but about a much bigger picture. That was a magic time with Coca-Cola. [Senior Coke Relay Sponsorship Executives] Peter Franklin and David Brooks were great in Athens, but it was starting already with Stu Cross in Atlanta. I sat in the Closing Ceremony with Stu Cross, and we just sat there and cried when the flame went out. He had that same 'what do we do now?' experience we discussed earlier.

JM: I think you are making two points here, both of which are true in my experience also. First, that Coca-Cola executives going back to their pioneer Olympic 'brand manager' Gary Hite tend to be or to become, in the deepest sense, flame relay aficionados and true believers, no less than you or me. To put it a certain way, they know in their very souls what moral associations they are buying with their sponsorship. This may be an uncomfortable truth for structural domination theorists or general critics of corporate capitalism trying to help preserve things like the OFR from the further depredations of commercialization and spectacularization. But this is a truth that absolutely must be faced by anyone who is seeking to be an effective preservationist, in my opinion.[11]

The second point is that these transnational corporate elites and IOC interlocutors at their level, notably [IOC Marketing Director] Michael Payne in the OFR context through the 1984–2004 period, may have no idea whatsoever about what sponsor operatives – some in-country affiliates, some hired subcontractors – actually get up to out on the relay. The OCOG operations team, by contrast, sees, knows, and copes with these operatives first-hand and day after day. You have been the absolute front line of defence, whether you wanted the role or not.

SM: I think you have to balance dignity with the functional and fiscal. At the Olympic Games, you have a field of play in the stadiums that is clean of sponsor representations. In our minds, we have a clean field of play around the flame and the torchbearer, which is why there are no commercial marks on the torch or the torchbearer. Is it bad to have a commercial mark 20 metres ahead of the torchbearer? Is it bastardizing and demeaning? I understand why a lot of people think it is, but these same people often don't understand the costs of the relay or who pays. It just won't happen in this day and age that a national government, host city, or OCOG can just pay for the Olympic Games and the OFR. The relay is a big package, something higher that $20 million for Atlanta, closer to $23 million for Salt Lake divided about equally among Coke, Chevy, and SLOC, then perhaps $45 million for Athens. I'm far from defending everything the sponsors do just on the grounds that someone has to pay for the relay. But for us to be successful, the sponsors have to get value, you've got to give them something in return. I don't always know where the magic line is.

JM: But you and senior officials above you do have some lines that will or should bring sanctions, if sponsors try to cross them.

SM: If you don't have operations and marketing properly integrated in the beginning, there will have to be a top OCOG or IOC sheriff who rides in to settle disputes. The OCOG and IOC role now should be much more engaged with enforcement, but prior to enforcement, they should be in the dialogue in the meetings that determine what we're going to look like going down the road.

[ATHOC Marketing General Manager] George Bolos wasn't afraid to come out and dress down Coke or Samsung or a city or an NOC or a celebrity when we needed him to on the Athens international segment. He was willing to shut things down until there was a solution. His predecessor in that was Michael Payne who during the Salt Lake relay saw on television the Chevrolet logo across the windscreen of the command car, and all of sudden it wasn't a clean venue to him, because the Chevy logo was getting into every torchbearer photo and broadcast shot. Chevy had seen this with BMW in Atlanta and convinced SLOC that they had to have a windscreen presence. This is the most flagrant sort of target for commercialization. So Michael Payne calls me from Lausanne, as we're passing through a small Idaho town and tells me to shut the relay down immediately because of these windshield logos. Well, we could hardly stop in the middle of the street, and Payne wasn't the guy paying my salary and maybe wasn't aware of SLOC's deal with Chevy, but he's now announced himself the protector of the clean envelope around the flame, so at the next break we started peeling off the decals. Well, of course, the Chevrolet officials on the relay went ballistic, poking me in the chest and yelling who did Payne and I think we were?

JM: They were instantly afraid for their own careers.

SM: Yeah. Then [SLOC Senior Executive] Cindy Gillespie got into it on the phone with me at that point. I was told that I was going to put those decals back on immediately. This had all been set up in the early period when [SLOC CEO] Mitt [Romney] and [SLOC Marketing Executive] Mark Lewis had done the deal with Chevy, who later came back to SLOC with basically a sob story, 'millions of dollars of sponsorship and you've sold us nothing but a bill of goods, you're barely going [with the flame] to a fraction of our dealerships around the country'. The management of expectations just got shot at that point, and the bosses came back to us and said 'you guys aren't in control of this relay, we are. You don't talk to the sponsor representatives, you don't need to interact with them, you don't do anything with them. We sold them this package, so why don't you just go get into the command car and run the relay.' All right, fair enough, and this was a beginning of the end of that relationship. We had been trying to placate everyone and trying to explain at the same time. Listen, Coke, you can do that, but if you do, you'll piss off Chevrolet. And Chevy, you can do that too, but you're going to piss off the local city council or the mayor's office. So why don't we all sit down and talk about what we are going to do? But they silo marketing away from operations and never the twain shall meet. But what marketing sells to the relay, the relay inherits operationally. This is the source of so many of the problems, and until it gets fixed, we just have to get back in the car and start driving down the road again with the focus distracted from the main job, the safe transmission of the Olympic Flame.

JM: When I met you out on the Salt Lake relay, you told me that in some other ways things had gotten a little better with the major sponsors, that in return for letting them have what they were denied in 1996, the right to make short speeches during the main celebrations, that they had become more tractable in other matters. Is it going to always be two steps forward, one step back, with the operations team caught in the middle? How is this ever to be fixed on commercially sponsored relays?

SM: In 2002, [IOC Executive Board member and Marketing Commission Chairman] Gerhard Heiberg rode with us for a day in the Colorado Springs area, and we got to talk for a long time. It was the start of a great friendship that continues today. He saw what a big deal the relay had become. Where did all these people come from, he wondered? How does a relay run like this, because his hadn't. He, of course, had been the Lillehammer Olympic CEO, and their relay was very intimate, very romantic, very extraordinary. And you are right to say that having the Norwegian Post run the relay is an entirely different thing than having commercial sponsors subsidizing operating companies. He'd never seen the like, say, of all the Coke or Chevrolet activators out front passing out flags or promotional products. He was pretty amazed.[12]

These sponsor activation teams are young people who are instructed by their leaders to go out ahead of the relay and to sing and dance at the top of their lungs. They absolutely love and believe in what they are doing, and it is phenomenal to watch. Frankly, it's a bit of Americana more than anything else, but has real power and passion. So I don't discredit them, but for safety's sake there has to be some centralized control of the promotional and operational parts of the relay caravan. We have felt that some of this has to rest in the command car, because we are right there watching what goes on up front. But there has to be more self-enforcement on the sponsor side too, and that has to be dictated first of all by the OCOG with some sort of overlay from the IOC.

So we pushed Heiberg at the time to take better control of the IOC's own icons and property, its chief symbolic asset. If you don't want sponsors doing this or that, then tell them from the beginning and make sure you tell the OCOG before it makes its marketing deals, so you don't have a Michael Payne ordering a relay stopped for windscreen decals that didn't have to be there in the first place or should have been better integrated. So I urged Gerhard to franchise this, to bring the relay under the IOC knowledge transfer programmes. This is the way forward that I see.

JM: I think you are much too sanguine about the sponsor rah-rah troops that go out ahead of the flame on your relays. The OFR is and should remain a ritual, not become an American-style pep rally or a rock concert or a blaring television commercial. So much of their behaviour trivializes and tastelessly trashes, not just commercializes the atmosphere for the relay that comes behind them, in my opinion. The effect is the same, whether you want to talk about the cheap sponsor flags handed out, the hokey and juvenile pitchmen shouting from garish product floats, or luxury items whose material aura competes with the spiritual prestige of the flame. On the Atlanta relay, I spent a day with Além's Jill Arnone in the pace car, and it was pathetic to me how the waiting crowds were distracted into chatting about the merits of the BMW Z-3 rather than those of the Olympic Flame they'd turned out to see. And to suggest that crowds require this sort of hyping to be enthusiastic for the flame is to absolutely insult, in my opinion, the American or any other people who have turned out on their own to participate in the OFR.

Figure 3.   After the 2004 relay passed by, souvenir flags were proudly displayed in a Mycenae hotel, but only after the hotelier had carefully excised the Coca-Cola logo from the one on the right. Source: Sara Brewster.

And when this American commercial/cheerleader culture is taken overseas, the results can be ludicrous. I watched Greeks lining the roadways for the first Olympia to Athens segment of the 2004 relay absolutely mystified by and dismissive of the Coke operatives and fanfare in front of the caravan. They had never seen such a thing before. This is Greece! You need commercial hype for the Olympic Flame in Greece? Please! I won't forget coming back from the OFR celebration in Mycenae to find that our hotel keeper had made a little shrine to the 2004 OFR, including the promotional flag he had been handed and from which he had very carefully scissored away the Coke logo. (See Figure 3). So, I think you are taking too lightly the real contradiction between the ritual dignity you work so hard to protect and the commercial hoopla and rah-rah spectacle you are required to enable or at least to endure. I'm not sure I can see how stronger IOC engagement alone is going to assuage this contradiction.

SM: With these ground troops, it is a completely different matter on a consumer product-sponsored relay as against a relay sponsored by a conglomerate, a state-owned agency, or the government itself. For Atlanta, Coke was very active. They hired a company to put vehicles out in front of the caravan and to really activate the crowd. Their intent really was to activate the crowd, to bring people out on the streets and see this great, great thing Coke was supporting.

Since Coke was the only presenting partner in Atlanta, they didn't have anyone to temper them. Enter Chevy for Salt Lake and all of a sudden you have competing interests, not in the product sense, but for rights to media exposure. So the Chevrolet operatives kept trying to one-up Coke and vice-versa, until at the end of the day they weren't talking to one another, and we were drawn into the middle of it. Chevrolet wanted us to require that every police car in every jurisdiction we went through be a Chevy, when at that time 75% of all police cruisers throughout the US were Ford Crown Victorias or Plymouth Furies. So Chevy had these exorbitant, unrealistic demands, because they didn't know that there were established precedents and rules, so they never stopped trying to do this one more thing.

JM: That's the logic of the spectacle.

SM: More, more, more, more; bigger, bigger, bigger. But it really didn't reach its zenith until 2004 with Samsung, whose corporate headquarters in Seoul issued guidelines, a single operating standard to their people on the ground, their volunteers, and flag handers-out all around the world. This wasn't a sanctity, dignity, or class standard; it was about how they had to have so many vehicles, and people, and motor home sound boards to play music, and so forth. They got us into decibel-level arguments with the state and city police and into environmental and ground pollution issues. You need to be aware of the fact that people don't want to hear loud rock music coming through their streets, particularly if the relay is coming at nine in the morning or nine at night.

So that is when the commercialization became too much, and Samsung headquarters couldn't control what was happening on the ground, as evidenced in New York, or by the skydiver with a blue parachute with Samsung written on it who landed in the stadium in Munich, then landed in the Berlin stadium the next day. This was completely against the rules. We specifically said no air flights, sky-jumpers, inflatable balloons, nothing in the sky. We learned in Salt Lake how inflatables distract everybody from the message the OCOG was trying to send. So we continually enhance the model by saying look we talked about this generally nine or ten months ago, and even if we didn't say it specifically, you can't have 20 horsemen with 12-foot high Samsung flags riding out from behind the pyramids to escort the torchbearer through Giza.

JM: When I met you in St. Louis, you were still very upset about this one; it sounded like your greatest shock yet.

SM: One of them. It was precedent setting on both the OCOG and the commercial side. I was like, well, I've never seen that before. I guess maybe we should have planned for guys on horseback. But who could have thought that in the middle of Giza in Egypt that Samsung would be so brash. The OCOG has to be responsible for sponsor behaviour, subject to approval by the IOC. The IOC has to say listen, we really didn't want you to go to Egypt, let alone Cairo, let alone the pyramids with a big commercial activation campaign. You have superimposed blue Samsung flags against not just the pyramids but also the torch and the rings, which we own. So what are we going to do about it?

But the IOC has no enforcement mechanism on the streets during any relay, and frankly Samsung had no enforcement mechanism for its local distributors. You could slap their hands at Cairo, but the next day in Cape Town it was a totally different distributor and management, almost a separate Samsung franchise in Cape Town, and it would be another one in Rio. We can't punish Cape Town for what was done in Cairo, so we just hope that Cape Town will be civil and not over-commercialized. Instead, in Cape Town, we had Samsung balloons and flags, all against the rules of engagement. The co-presenting partners sort of discipline each other, enforce each other, but each looks to us and says, Steve, come on, [what the rival is doing] isn't called for.

JM: And you are in an ambiguous power position. You're the ops guy; you are running the relay. But as a subcontractor, some see you as an extension of the OCOG, ATHOC in this case, others as an extension of the sponsors, especially if you answer directly to the OCOG marketing department. In Nagano, it was not the OCOG but Coke – or rather their Japanese brand Georgia Coffee, the presenting and operational partner – that Além consulted for. As you've already described, you had these problems on the Salt Lake relay, even through you were both the director and operations manager for SLOC. On the international relay in 2004, the ATHOC chiefs popped in two or three times, but otherwise you had only Georgios Chalkides along just as an HOC observer and Spiros Lambrinidis, a somewhat obscure Greek diplomat basically there to make ceremonial speeches. You're an ATHOC employee and as an American citizen perhaps further weakened as a voice of authority for those trying to get around you to serve their own interests. Even though a handful of IOC members saw a bit of the international relay, including IOC President Rogge, this was a new and not necessarily typical expression of the normal challenges faced. By the way have you ever seen more than a handful of IOC members out on any of your relays? Five? Eight? Twelve?

SM: Maximum, though for the Athens international segment we had IOC members and large NOC contingents when we passed through their countries.

JM: Many other members watch a bit of the relay through the host city on the eve or day of the Olympic Opening Ceremony, and they all watch it enter the stadium for the cauldron lighting. Other than that, there isn't any reason to think they know what happens out on today's relays, except for what they might glimpse occasionally on television. Over the years, the IOC has largely ignored the flame-lighting ceremony at Olympia. The Greek IOC members are always there, of course, but Samaranch never came and, just to take one example, not a single US IOC member showed up for the Olympia lighting of the flame for Los Angeles, Atlanta, or Salt Lake. I persuaded the IOC 2000 Reform Commission and the IOC Session to pass a resolution that the IOC Executive Board should be present for this ceremony, one of the most important rituals of the Olympic Movement, but that resolution has subsequently been ignored. At least, Jacques Rogge did come for the 2004 flame lighting.

So it can't be the IOC membership or Executive Board that you are counting on, beyond the formidable figure of Gerhard Heiberg and even there, whatever he learned with you in 2002 doesn't appear to have changed anything in what you had to cope with in 2004. As far as the IOC administration goes, Michael Payne, in all his years of holding the dossier by default, never came out on the relay for any extended period for any careful observation. [IOC Olympic Games Executive Director] Gilbert Felli, who has taken over OFR oversight is an enormously talented, effective, and sincere administrator, but he doesn't have much first-hand, street experience of the relay either.[13]

SM: Frankly, there is no way IOC members or administrators have the time or inclination to monitor the daily operations of the relay. That is the province and responsibility of the OCOG and, notwithstanding the need for consistency in operational and spiritual integrity, the IOC shouldn't need to be on the ground every day. Gerhard instantly understood that the question was standardizing and formalizing, then customizing the relay so there is continuity and consistency from games to games on behalf of the IOC and under the IOC as the legacy protector of all the Olympic symbols and properties. We've got enormous respect for Gilbert, who is a very rare talent, and has just completed a draft of the IOC Flame Relay Technical Manual that the IOC commissioned from us. Once it is approved, we hope this will be the IOC's transfer of knowledge and standard practices manual for some time to come.

JM: Will this help insure that there won't be another Torino where . . . .

SM: The flame that lit the cauldron with fireworks wasn't remotely the flame that was lit in Olympia. This was very frustrating and disappointing to us, but we weren't engaged in the operations of that relay.

JM: Torino was huge scandal for the OFR community; the very thought that the flame runners carried might not be the Olympia flame is so shocking.

SM: Well, I guess it depends on your perspective. For you and me and the Nassos Kritsinelis' of the world, it's unthinkable that you would ever take shortcuts to keeping the flame lit.

JM: Then there was the opening ceremonies fiasco. Torino ceremonies co-chief Ric Birch phoned me two months before the opening completely upset because [the Torino Organizing Committee] TOROC had built their supposedly architecturally admirable cauldron tower completely outside the Olympic stadium, without any thought of how the final flame bearer was supposed to be able to light that cauldron. Ric had tried for months to get them to deal with this ritual problem, but they ignored it. In the end, they didn't even make a pretence of any real connection. In the stadium, the final bearer touched his torch to some silly contraption that spit our sparks like some cheap fireworks display, while outside the fire high up in the cauldron sprang to life. So this key ritual connection that all the torchbearers together are supposed to create between Ancient Olympia and the 'New Olympia' was just thrown aside. It was physically shocking to me; I was nauseated. Again, I suppose they will claim that the cauldron really was lit with a lantern-borne Olympia Flame, but even if one could have any confidence in that, it would still be the worst Olympic ritual profanation that I can remember. And, once again, where was the IOC in all of this?[14]

SM: I suppose they could say they had bigger things to worry about in Torino.

JM: Let's go back to Athens. Describe your first contacts with ATHOC.

SM: Our first substantive contacts were for Salt Lake City. We had already met [ATHOC COO] Marton Simitsek and some others when we went over in 2001 to negotiate with the HOC for the flame lighting and flame delivery to SLOC.

JM: In the book she co-ghost wrote for Mitt Romney, [SLOC Executive] Cindy Gillespie sort of implies that you were somehow double dipping in these meetings.

SM: It wasn't true, and I don't know where she got that. We documented every minute of every meeting for SLOC, and we had nothing but total success with the Salt Lake relay. Além didn't have any deal with ATHOC or the HOC and our only communication was to give them some operating protocol, because our interest at that point wasn't this or that OCOG but the legacy value of the entire OFR. Simitsek wanted to know how you do something like this, and can you do it off-shore, outside the host country? I said, certainly, we can do it anywhere you want in the world. So we'll just give you everything we've got that is open source now. It's yours for the taking. That was the extent of our conversations until during the Salt Lake Games themselves, when I met Simitsek and [ATHOC CEO] Mrs. Angelopoulou at the IOC hotel.

JM: Otherwise you were negotiating with Lambis Nikolaou and the HOC for Salt Lake. Simitsek and ATHOC were completely separate, and anyway Simitsek had hardly consolidated his executive position with ATHOC. He was often on shaky ground and nervous, as I saw when I talked with him briefly about the 2004 relay at the 2001 Moscow IOC Session.

SM: Simitsek, George Bolos, and Spiros Kapralos carried the flame just outside Salt Lake City, as representatives of ATHOC. Simitsek had already heard about us from Ginger Watkins, who eventually wrote a letter recommending us to ATHOC. She and Simitsek were friends going back to Atlanta. During the Games, they asked me to meet with Mrs. Angelopoulou at a hotel breakfast meeting, and I sat with them and talked during the Games. They asked me if I wanted to do the job for ATHOC, and I said more than anything else I can think of. They said good, come to Athens and we'll sit down and talk about it. Michael Payne helped facilitate these meetings. He told Simitsek and Bolos there were two companies to consider. So we went to Athens in March 2002, and I went out with Marton a couple of times and sat in his office talking very candidly about how we would be back of house and how he should forget that we are American, because we are not all Americans. We are bringing people from all around the world to activate this relay, Japanese, Chinese, Brazilians. So forget American, don't call us that. This is your relay, a Greek relay, and a global relay. We are the tiniest, tiniest part of this relay. I think this was important, because Di [Henry of MAXXAM, Inc.] had been lobbying ATHOC and trying to get the IOC to pressure ATHOC to hire her team, because they were Australian and . . . .

JM: Australians were the new top experts on anything and everything Olympic because of the overall success of Sydney.

SM: Right, but the reality of moving from one Games to the next as a contractor/consultant is that you are only as good as your *next* event, not your last event.

JM: And in its panic over the state of Greek preparations, the IOC had imposed on ATHOC quite a number of former SOCOG personnel, who were charging huge fees.

SM: I think Simitsek was also scared that Di would just put the Australian signature all over his relay. So they hired us, though it took a year to get the contract done. But the real reason I think we got the relay in the end was [ATHOC OFR Director] Nassos Kritsinelis. He supported us from start to finish. And the biggest tragedy, in my mind the only tragedy of the Greek relay, is that he eventually got pushed out. That was the worst thing I could ever have imagined, because they just treated him badly. We grew up with Nassos Kritsinelis, he was the guy that started it all for us, along with Ginger and Hilary. We were all concerned with the same things. Hilary absolutely adored Nassos. We realized that he didn't have tons of operational expertise, but who cares? This guy is the father of the freakin' flame relay. He is the heart and soul of everything we are doing with this thing. So Nassos' push for us was, I think, the final push that brought us on board.

JM: As I told Jacques Rogge and Michael Payne, if Athanassios Kritsinelis was the director, then ATHOC would handle a domestic relay just fine. But if the IOC was going to approve an international relay, then they absolutely needed your help. I told Nassos the same thing, and he agreed because he knew and trusted your commitment to the integrity of the Olympic Flame. He just expected to be the guy between Além and Simitsek.[15]

SM: Nassos has spent months and probably, ultimately his entire career preparing for that one relay. He knew every mayor of every city, every kilometre that the relay would take on its route throughout Greece. He was the first to admit that he wasn't so sure about Tokyo or Delhi, so that is where he was happy for us to come in, but he still wanted to be part of the planning process and to make sure that the sanctity and dignity would withstand the test of geography and politics around the world. All this made perfect sense. But then Bolos took over the OFR, and Nassos grew upset that they were going in a different direction. You could tell that Kritsinelis was going by the wayside, when Bolos came on board. Bolos was very aggressive and assertive, brash and bright in some ways about how the relay had to pay for itself and to stay independent of the government. This to him was protecting the Olympic ideals.

JM: But don't you think the difference between Bolos and Kritsinelis came down to the fact that Bolos came to perceive Nassos as anti-commercial? Bolos was a marketing guy whose job was to raise funds. That was his only Olympic success up to that point.

SM: Maybe it overstates things to say that Nassos was anti-commercial; maybe he just wasn't cognizant enough of the need to fund this relay. I think he felt that it was a mission from Zeus, and that somehow this would just float down the road and that people would just naturally be attracted to it. So he represented philosophically what we sort of did from a commercial standpoint. Bolos came in and put the real practical side to it and said listen talk to me about the sun and the moon and the stars lining up and the great value and spirituality and the magic and everything else, but somebody has got to pay for it, unless you Nassos or you Steve have a giant bank account and can take care of it. So this is the root of the division. Simitsek obviously was under great pressure at the time because the government was starting to say that you ATHOC people are out of time and we don't have any money for you so you had better figure something out. So Bolos became the lynch pin and he succeeded at it enormously.

JM: And he had Michael Payne behind him because of his general success in raising sponsorship monies for ATHOC.

SM: Yes. I called George the other day in New York, and I started crying on the phone. I wanted to thank George again, and I told him whatever disagreements we'd had over the two- or three-year period we worked together, that I would do business with him any time for the rest of my life. This wasn't just revisionist history, because now I understand better why George had to stand up to us and fight for things that we didn't philosophically believe in, all in the interest of paying for it and keeping the political wolves at bay. He had to do what he had to do. His methodology for doing it was sometimes a bit wacky, and he would surprise us sometimes, but in the end and now looking back at it, he was brilliant beyond his years.

JM: What about Penny Mikelopoulou who nominally assumed Kritsinelis' role on the Greek relay leg?

SM: She was a Bolos pick, having worked for him in marketing. She didn't have much to do with us on the international side, except to try to learn lessons on operations, risk analysis, or media relations that could be taken over to the domestic side. She was very strongly resented by some people because she had no operations or OFR background. Penny was a challenge and very much out of her league, and she recognized that. But at the end of the day, I think she came into her own a bit too. There was a series of people George brought in, and we felt passed around a little bit too over our years. We got through it. But with Nassos, when he was literally shoved aside, he was a broken man, and that was the saddest part of the whole relay.

JM: Why did this tragedy happen, in your opinion?

SM: I think he was so pure about the Greeks' final say on the relay and about the sanctity of the Olympic Flame that he couldn't be sufficiently aware of how serious things were on the political and financial side. He was so fixated on Greece's moment in the sun, and Athens' and Olympia's. He's a great historian and a great philosopher of the OFR, but he's not by his own admission a great ops guy who was going to be out there dealing with landing rights, visas, and airplane fuel. I think that's basically why he was told [to] focus on the domestic relay, and then he was totally out on the domestic side as well.

JM: Yes, his internal exile did happen in two stages. The question remains why – having created and advanced the route and knowing everyone that he knew along it – that he came to be pushed out of the third, domestic Greek leg.

SM: I think it just became a question of dysfunctional personalities. Nassos had assembled a crew of young, really enthusiastic and passionate people. He had a couple of women working for him who were bulletproof and loyal to the end, though others left for different ATHOC departments when management changed. Nassos felt that Bolos didn't see eye to eye with him, and Mikelopoulou didn't do well with him, and he must have thought he now had nowhere to go.

JM: And he didn't have the ability to fight politically and to save himself. Bolos and company didn't have sufficient respect for his history, experience, and international reputation to find some compromise or more elegant solution. So at a certain point, they just perceived him an old-fashioned barrier to be removed, however unceremoniously.

SM: I really can't speak to what George or anyone else believed, but you have to remember that there wasn't a lot of time left for 'ceremony'. We were scrambling every day to get this project on the road and protocol or feelings sometimes had to take a back seat to the practical side of the project. There are often tensions between the people who made the bid and those who come in much later on the games operation side. In Atlanta there was much more continuity between the bid and the organizing committee . . . .

JM: Though Billy Payne himself had to fight hard to survive for a time.

SM: Yes, and in Salt Lake there were very few people on SLOC who knew everything about the bid process; it was a completely different crew. Athens had these issues too, as Mrs. Angelopoulou was forced out after winning the bid, and then later brought back to lead the Games. Through every stage, Nassos was always this constant beacon as relates to the sanctity and purity of the OFR. Then all of a sudden, he was gone.

JM: I myself never anticipated how quickly and completely ATHOC and other Greek powers would shift over and accept so many aspects of the transnational relay style, including some that nearly contributed to bloodshed in Olympia only 20 years before. Even the HOC came around to accepting things like sponsor activation teams on the Olympia to Athens leg of the relay they controlled – it was a shock for me to see these things in the Peloponnese – though Georgios Chalkides insisted to me, and rightly I think, that the HOC had managed to dampen these things down compared with what happened on the third, Crete to Athens leg that ATHOC managed. So Nassos wasn't the only veteran who failed to see it coming. When Greece had nothing Olympic but the flame ceremonies, Greek nationalism was easily mobilized to defend their inviolability. Now Greece had the whole of the Olympic Games and that same nationalism could be neutralized or even turned to supporting anything that promised to be the 'biggest and best ever', the first worldwide relay. Their inward-looking national ritual had become their outward-looking global spectacle.

SM: At a meeting at Simitsek's house, Nassos was basically told, 'we're going in a different direction, go focus on the domestic [relay]'.

JM: Nassos asked me at the time where you were in all this. I said I didn't know, that I hadn't spoken with you, but that my bet was that, since you had utmost respect for him, you were not undermining him.

SM: No, never!

JM: To his credit, as much as he was hurt, Nassos never wants to believe that people like you can ever go back on what they experience on the relay.

SM: You don't ever go back.

JM: He did wonder about the sponsors, though, and I have to ask because of people seeing your relationship with sponsors in a way that sometimes makes it hard for them to recognize the difference. Did Coke or Samsung want Kritsinelis out?

SM: I don't think they ever thought about it. They definitely knew he existed in his spiritual and historical role, but you have to remember that sponsor negotiations weren't finished when Bolos came in, and the sponsors dealt with him and Payne. If the sponsors knew that Kritsinelis was still involved, they probably thought of him as in a senior adviser sort of role. It's true that Petros Charahalias, Coca-Cola's Olympic manager for Greece and specifically for the torch relay, didn't seem to get along with Nassos so well. Petros was probably one of those guys who saw Nassos not so much as an obstacle, but more as a non-factor. Yeah, Kritsinelis is the spiritual guy, the medicine man, the Zeus, and we realize we have to have that, but we also have to promote our relay and our activation of it. So no, I don't think there was any conspiracy or Machiavellian strategy, just something that morphed into what it was.

Which was Nassos getting fed up with being jerked around, which was what was happening. They didn't just hit him over the head with it and say, listen, we're going in a different direction, we're sorry that you won't be part of it. That is what they should have said early on. Instead they just kept injecting more of their people in there, until he finally sat in his office most days, I hope writing his memoirs or doing something beneficial to himself, because they didn't consult with him at all after that. He would come to meetings and start to say something, and Bolos would cut him short, 'Don't tell me that you've got it all and that it's in your working plan'. Because Nassos would always say, typical Nassos, that he had already documented whatever it was. This is one of the neatest things about him, that he had all of this stuff in his head, more than any of us did. But he is suddenly out in the cold wondering what happened. To Nassos' misfortune, Marton and George never just said, listen, old friend, we are going a different way. Best of luck to you and we hope you'll be a torchbearer and go to the Opening Ceremony. I don't think he was even invited him to the Opening Ceremony.

JM: He wasn't, or to the Olympia Flame lighting either. They humiliated him.

SM: I wouldn't say they intentionally humiliated him, I'd say they simply forgot him. I don't think they wanted to discredit him or humiliate him, any more than they set out to humiliate Chalkides or Zoides or any of those veteran HOC guys. Bolos just didn't have the time at that point with everything else that was going on leading into the start of the Games.

JM: There's probably another factor in why they didn't just fire him, but instead sent him into internal exile in his office. I can't speculate on Bolos, but Simitsek certainly understood how many friends Kritsinelis had in the Greek press and surely remembered how they had publicly rallied for Nassos when it seemed that he had been unfairly and unproductively set aside by Nikolaou on an earlier occasion. Judging from some phone calls Nassos got after the Games, during the period of government audits, this probably was a factor. What about Nassos blowing the whistle internally about the quality of the torches? He believes this was a key factor.

SM: I guess he was just telling it the way he saw it, which is that it wasn't for him a very good design or an adequate design to represent the post-relay legacy value in the Olympic museums. Coke had sort of volunteered at the eleventh hour to oversee the production and distribution of the torch as part of their sponsorship deal, because Bolos had said to them that the torch relay department was low on funds and didn't have the time or ability to shop for torch manufacturers. If the duty of selecting the company to design and manufacture it was passed on to Coke, everything theoretically could be expedited. So the FTC company from Australia ended up manufacturing the torch. Again, I don't think there was any backlash conspiracy against Nassos for questioning the quality of the torch. The quality ended up being visually OK, but we had some challenges operationally.

JM: You are putting it rather mildly.

SM: It wasn't perfect, and it didn't end up getting fixed until we got back to Athens. We went 30 days around the world with some problems [keeping torches lit], and as I told you, that led Bolos to come out on the relay to lower the boom on FTC. Even in the test events, you couldn't see the flame from this torch. The fuel canister had too much propane and not enough propylene to give it an orange burn. And that didn't get fixed either. Bear in mind that we were down to 'countdown sequence' on the relay and we were simply out of time.

JM: This company did part of the Sydney torch, so maybe here was more of that 'We're Aussies, we know how to do it, just give us the business'.

SM: It's important to note that making torch burner systems that fit into the creative concept is still an inexact science. FTC is one [of] the few companies in the world with this technology. And for Athens, this was the first time we were pre-shipping torches and fuel canisters around the world at various pressures and temperatures. Nassos certainly had the background to look at the fundamental elements of burn time, flame visibility, and related operational elements of the torch. We have nothing but the highest respect for him and nothing but the highest regret for how it was handled. You knew he was a broken man after this, everything that he had dreamt of and worked for all his life was suddenly gone, because of, ultimately, personality conflict between him and Bolos and Simitsek and the rest of them.

JM: Personality conflict or conflict over cultural and historical values, it literally almost killed Nassos. He got very sick after the Games.

SM: I didn't know about his illness, but I know he is one of the kindest, gentlest men I have ever met in my life.

JM: To go back, how did you react when ATHOC first spoke with you in Salt Lake about their proposed international relay segment.

SM: Oh, it was absolutely the dream of a lifetime and not just an Olympic lifetime. Having worked internationally for over 25 years, here was an opportunity to combine the academic and the practical, to work around the world but in the single project of the OFR. I couldn't have dreamt of anything more fulfilling. We'd heard about the proposal from Nassos and we'd also heard that in response to the Athens bid book, the IOC wanted to touch every continent, particularly those the flame had not yet seen.

JM: Actually, according to Michael Payne and some of my other conversations in Lausanne, the IOC was initially quite sceptical. Payne says he would have fought the plan if a major sponsor and an international operator hadn't been brought on board. The IOC liked the idea but was afraid of the execution.

SM: Well, we were worried about Salt Lake then, so we didn't act on anything. We just enjoyed the general buzz about the idea of an international relay and I talked about it with Heiberg. It became real for me at a mid-2002 meeting in Athens at the Lausanne Palace hotel when Payne, [IOC Director General] François Carrard, Heiberg, Simitsek, Bolos and I made lists of possible cities to go to and designed criteria for where to go and how to defend the costs, define the risks, and so on. By a sort of consensus, we'd pretty much come up with the same cities at the end of the day, former Summer Games host cities and a few others thrown in. Africa and South America, because they had not yet been able to host the Olympic Games. And it evolved from there, a couple more in Europe, a couple in the Balkans to show solidarity, including Sofia because it was fairly contiguous with Greece. For the future of the Olympics, the flame had to go to emerging markets. These were chosen somewhat randomly, with Egypt as a functional stop, because we were heading west from Delhi. But Cairo was much more than a refuelling stop, it was a great iconic city, with a great sports heritage. Mandela was, of course, a great part of Cape Town, but [IOC member and anti-apartheid hero] Sam Ramsamy and the [South African] NOC played a pivotal role in the flame going to South Africa instead of Kenya or Nigeria or another African country with a great sports heritage. South Africa made the most sense historically, culturally, and functionally, and going there was one of the most magical moments of the relay for the entire team.

JM: The moral heritage of the IOC's role in the anti-apartheid struggle is perhaps Olympism's strongest claim to successful moral activism, and Cape Town had bid for the Olympics and would host the football World Cup. IOC interests and political competitions among IOC members were feeding into this discussion as well.

SM: It's interesting that the cities with the least experience in global event management or global activation strategies became absolutely the best partners by far.

JM: Please elaborate. Given your past experience in Latin America, could you have predicted that?

SM: I think I could have predicted that Rio would be totally cooperative and totally passionate and excited about the passage of the flame. We never could have dreamed that it would come off as cleanly and powerfully as it did. Rio, Cape Town, Sofia, Delhi, Kiev: these cities were magical every step of the way. There were operational challenges because of the sheer mass of population crowding the streets at the same time, but these were the magic moment of the relay for me and I think for the whole crew. Rio and Cape Town outdid everyone's expectations.

JM: And what does that tell you?

SM: That those cities are ready to host the Olympic Games. The IOC should stop worrying about street crime and think more of the bigger picture. These are peaceful, quiet, well-organized, and serious people. What [IOC member and Brazilian NOC Chief Carlos] Nuzman put together in Rio I don't think anyone could have dreamt of. He had everyone who was going to be touched by the relay in the same room the first meeting we had: NOC and PASO [Pan American Sports Organization] people, defence services, intelligence, police, airport people, the mayor's office, the governor's office. Everybody was happy with everyone else. There was no bickering or ego insecurity. Clearly they intended to show the world a different face of Rio and of Brazil. And they did it.

JM: They had the Pan American Games coming up, with the 2014 World Cup and 2016 Olympic bids soon to follow. They needed a good showing, and the image of Pele with the tears running down his cheeks as he carried the Olympic Flame in Rio certainly didn't hurt the cause.

SM: Kiev was the same and Sofia and especially Cape Town.

JM: 'The Olympic Movement' were among the first words Nelson Mandela spoke when he was released from Robben Island, yet the IOC later judged that Cape Town wasn't developed enough to host the Olympics. The Olympic Flame is, shall we say, more sensitive to the values of Olympism than the Olympic Games are these days. It must have been extraordinary to see Nelson Mandela emerge from his Robben Island cellblock again, this time carrying the Olympic Flame.

SM: You just lose it. Coming into the celebration site that night in Cape Town, you could hear a buzz of music. You see people so passionate about something, so protective of it, so excited, and so terrifically organized. You see these little kids with the South African flag painted on their cheeks as the flame came through the townships. It reminded me of Memphis in 1996, when we were taking the Olympic Flame to the Lorraine Motel, where Martin Luther King was shot. Four or five blocks away, you could hear this buzz, and you couldn't quite recognize it until you rolled the command car windows down. Three blocks away, you recognized that it was definitely music. Two blocks away you could clearly make out voices singing. One block away, you were listening to the choir. Then we pulled into the circular drive of the Lorraine Motel, and there were people everywhere, all singing. I can't describe it; you can only feel it. The hair on the back of your neck just stands up, every hair on your body stands up. To the torchbearer's right is an adult choir, to his left is a children's choir, and straight ahead there's a black wreath on the door. We just stopped and sat in the parking lot. It was supposed to be a two-minute ceremonial stop. We sat there for 20 minutes and did nothing but cry. (See Figure 4).

JM: This is precisely how, through the OFR, the Olympic Movement replenishes its moral and social capital as a human rights and peace movement. It therefore follows that anyone or anything that interferes with, trivializes, or redirects this process is the enemy of the Olympic Movement. That can certainly include the Olympic sports industry when, for example, it lobbies against the very cities where the moral power of Olympism is most

Figure 4.   ACOG co-chairman Andrew Young carries the 1996 Olympic Flame with a company of children across the Edmund Pettus Bridge in Selma, Alabama, where on 'Bloody Sunday', 1965, he and 600 other Civil Rights marchers had been brutally beaten and gassed by police. Source: John J. MacAloon, Jr.

visible on the grounds that they are materially unprepared to host multi-sport festivals 'at a world standard'.

SM: It's disappointing and frustrating. I always recall that [IOC President] Jacques Rogge came aboard with a mandate to fight gigantism and to get down to the people and back to earth. I couldn't agree more, but now they have to execute that. People are concerned right now about Cape Town's hosting of the 2010 World Cup, just like they were concerned about Rio's ability to execute the Pan Am Games. Are they going to be able to do it? They'll have only one subway line open; will the stadiums be finished? You know what? Don't look at it from a Western perspective. The Westerners, because of money, have had the luxury and ability to produce both winter and summer games. But anyone can produce great games. It is not simply about how much money can be put into a new stadium, it's about the heart and soul of the people of the country, the culture, the region, and the continent. That is what the movement has to be about and why the torch relay is so valuable and why it has to be protected and promoted by the IOC. The people who say no, it's too expensive, we can't go to that many countries or cities, that we can't have that many torchbearers in one day, and we can't charge for the torch, they are totally missing the boat. It's the same as trying to understand the Chinese and the Chinese trying to understand us in the context of 2008. Wait a second. Don't put a Western mentality or perspective on this. Sit and listen first. I would hope that the administrative and management people in the IOC and the NOCs sit and listen to the people in the countryside, sit and look at the pictures of those children in Soweto and in other townships, or in the *favelas* in Rio. That's what we all need to promote. It has to ultimately go back to the ideals and visions of Olympia, not of any one developed city or region. It has to incorporate and encompass all of the views, all of the cultures, all of the future, and ultimately all of the kids around the world.

JM: I'm glad to hear you say that ethnocentric prejudice and neo-imperialism should not be allowed to mask themselves as 'world's best practice'. What else does the OFR need to be protected against?

SM: Against over-commercialization, as we've discussed, but also against politics, ego, insecurity, and ultimately gigantism. You need to stay away from one-upmanship. The torch relay adequately represents the spirit and the magic and the vision and the culture of the host city and the host country, and you can expand from there. But it can't be a neo-colonial exercise. There is also a point you can reach with the OFR that gives everyone a sense of 'been there, done that'. To do a global relay every four years, much less every two years is excessive. Gilbert Felli and the IOC made a great, proactive move when they said that, other than small forays into contiguous countries, they wouldn't allow an international relay for the Winter Games. To go around the world just to say that you went around the world is total folly.[16]

JM: The logic of the spectacle is hard to constrain, however. It's hard to put that genie back in the bottle. The IOC administration initially was sceptical of the global aspect of the Beijing 2008 relay plan, especially while the sponsor issue remained unresolved.[17] But beyond sponsor preferences, China had its own reasons not to accept a smaller relay than Athens, cultural and political reasons, including anti-colonial ones of the kind we were just discussing. Their whole Olympic mission was to finally overcome the colonial past by proving they could be as 'big' as anyone else in the world.

SM: Absolutely, and it will all be coming from the top down.

JM: There are other international relations dimensions to their OFR plans as well. In 1999–2000, I joined with [IOC member in China] He Zhenliang in promoting the Silk Road flame relay concept to BOBICO, the Beijing bid committee. This is an established

East-Asian motif, having been done for Tokyo 1964 (echoing a proposal of Carl Diem himself for Tokyo 1940) and producing those incomparable film images of Kon Ichikawa of the Olympic Flame passing through the ruins of Hiroshima and Nagasaki and merging with the setting sun at Mt. Fuji. Those were Ichikawa's answering images to Leni Riefenstahl's 1936 flame relay images and bracketed off the games-less World War II period. And there were Silk Road echoes in Seoul's relay, especially picking Cheju-do, mythic meeting place of East and West for the arrival of the Olympic Flame in Korea.[18]

We knew the Silk Road motif in Beijing's bid would resonate with many European IOC members. But I added something else backstage with BOBICO. When they asked me 'which Silk Road?', because of course there are many routes, I answered, 'The one with the votes!' I urged them to make a route including as many countries as possible with voting IOC members, focusing especially on the core Middle East, where the flame had yet to travel, the Indian sub-continent, and the former Soviet Republics. BOBICO sent out a special delegation to remind these members and NOCs that while their cities might never get the Olympics, they could have the Olympic Flame if Beijing won for 2008. Of course, we have no way of knowing how strongly IOC voters were influenced by this tactic, but Chinese leaders have told me they don't believe the effect was inconsiderable. So part of their resolve to do a longer world relay in 2008 than in 2004 had to do with some promises to be kept.

I have to say though, that even I was flabbergasted when they added Mount Everest to the flame route in BOBICO's final presentation in Moscow. Of course, there are contextual Tibetan political meanings here that could backfire on them, but also an underlying cultural history joined with the logic of the spectacle. We'll show you what China can do! And there's never been any doubt or hesitation since; they fully intend to get the Olympic Flame to the top of Everest in 2008. It's the same logic and deep structure involved in splitting the flame into three routes for the domestic relay. I helped BOCOG with a historical and cultural argument with the IOC for that; they understand there is resistance to splitting the flame in the West.

SM: The Chinese want to cover the whole of China and to share this with more people. It's a practical thing. To this day, Chalkides and others from the HOC claim they didn't know that Nagano was going to split the flame into three routes. To me that wasn't an Eastern versus Western historical thing, with the Greeks championing one side, though they were adamant about it even though they certainly knew the Olympic Flame was going to be split in Japan, as it had been for Tokyo in 1964.[19]

JM: As the Asian Games flame was for Seoul in 1986. Japan and Korea are small and rich countries. The flame wasn't split just for practical reasons. We had a long discussion of the cultural context for this at the Japanese National Olympic Academy in 2003.

SM: The Nagano people never mentioned to us any but the practical reasons.

JM: Well, your team is a little different than mine.

SM: This gets back to the IOC stepping in and saying listen, this is the operating plan, protecting either the unitary or the split-flame theory. The question ultimately, if the flame is split and you are the torchbearer, are you running with the real Olympic Flame?

JM: But there is no universal answer to the question in this case, assuming of course that all of the flames are taken from the Olympia Flame and return to it before the Opening Ceremony. It's completely a cultural question. In the deep, some would say 'Confucian' cultural logic of East Asia, the cosmos is tripartite – Heaven, Earth, and Humanity – and their relationship is complementary not contradictory. There is no problem with three in one or one in three. Each is co-constituted by the others, interpenetrates even at a distance with them, and is entirely complementary in relationships with them. So no one flame is ever any more real than the other two. In the modern West, a vastly different deep cultural logic dominates. True, we have Christian trinitarianism abstracted into a deep structure, but a monological realism dominates that on the religious level as it does on the cosmological level, particularly after the modern scientific and liberal political revolutions. So the question, as you state it, is largely a Western problematic – again speaking on the level of deep cultural structures – and if the answer for 'world's best' flame relay practice is only going to be the preferred Western one, then this is straightforward cultural imperialism, utterly antithetical to the intercultural understanding agenda of Olympism.

SM: That's why the IOC should step in at this point and say, listen, let's agree that in the interest of time and expenditure and so on, let's make this work for all of us, East or West, North or South, whatever. Forget culture for a minute, and let's figure out what the value of the flame is and how to promote it for the Olympic Family and Movement.

JM: I'm sorry, but what you just said is unacceptable to a cultural anthropologist. Just set culture aside?[20] Perhaps we can agree that world's best practice means universally that the flame that enters the Opening Ceremony and lights the cauldron absolutely must be the flame from Olympia, and that everything else along the way is culturally constituted, contextualized, mediated.

SM: Every OCOG has to put their signature on their games, and the IOC promotes that autonomy and creative license. It is not and should not be the operational team's mandate to dictate any element of that except insofar as it impacts the ability to deliver the flame on time, under budget, and with all the magic of the ages intact.

Notes

1 The interview took place in Boulder, Colorado, USA, August 15–17, 2006, supplemented by phone conversation through August, 2007. Jessica Robinson did the transcription, for which both parties to the conversation express their deepest gratitude. This article is edited and condensed from a much longer transcript and contains spliced quotations. Additional conversations with Além personnel Cheryl Cagle, Gillian Hamburger, and Simon Wadley were very clarifying.

2 Now Hilary Hanson McKean and a senior executive with the public relations firm Ketchum, Inc. See MacAloon, 'This Flame, Our Eyes: Greek/American/IOC Relations, 1984–2004', this volume.

3 Rennie Truitt, who had advanced political campaigns before working for ACOG, subsequently became Senior Vice-president and General Manager of the Edelman Public Relations firm's Atlanta offices. The significance of the ACOG organizational placement of the OFR and comparisons with other Olympic Games Organizing Committees (OCOGs) are discussed in MacAloon, '"My Programme Became Very Strict"', this volume.

4 Each state government of the United States has its own police force. With a quite dubious argument but strong political backing, the Georgia State Patrol successfully insisted that it should accompany the 1996 relay all across America. Their presence added a whole new level of jurisdictional disputes as the relay entered the territories of other local, state, and federal law enforcement agencies.

5 Di Henry was the director for the Sydney 2000 Olympic and Paralympic flame relays. Appointed early by the Sydney Olympic Organizing Committee (SOCOG), she was able to travel extensively on the Atlanta relay as an ACOG guest. Sydney adopted nearly wholesale the Atlanta flame relay practices. Di Henry eventually founded her own company Maxxam International Ltd, on the explicit model of Steve McCarthy's Além International, and the two firms are now friendly competitors for Olympic, Paralympic, and Regional Games flame relay business around the world. References in these essays to the 'world's best practices model' cover both Além and Maxxam since, while flame relay insiders recognize clear differences in culture and performance between the two firms, their operational models and practices are overwhelmingly congruent.

6 Individual torches can and do go out all the time. The point is that they are always relit from one of several 'mother flames' carefully guarded in multiple miners' lanterns from Olympia through the relay to the Opening Ceremonies.

7 Unlike 1984, no funds from the relay went directly to this or any other charity. Instead the 1996 OFR helped to refurbish the image of United Way that had lately been beset by management scandals. While beset with nothing remotely as controversial as the LAOOC's open sales of torchbearer rights to raise money for charities, ACOG's community hero programme was not entirely trouble-free. In many communities, the final torchbearer roster was not as economically and racially diverse as desired because of entirely inadvertent biases in the nomination and selection process.

   The comparative point with Seoul, Barcelona, Albertville, Lillehammer, Athens, and Beijing is that in the US, even local government would never, ever be accepted as being directly involved in torchbearer selection processes. In American culture, sport normatively belongs to civil society, not the state. Hence the involvement of charities and not government bodies in the 1984, 1996, and 2002 OFRs is perfectly congruent with other distinctive American Olympic practices, like the absence of a cabinet or sub-cabinet level sports ministry, the prohibition on direct tax money transfers to the United States Olympic Committee or American OCOGs, and so on.

8 This too became another sponsorship/official supplier opportunity on the American relays, with Kodak supplying torchbearers with their photographs through a website that, needless to say, offered additional promotional opportunities for the company.

9 My oldest son was a volunteer on the 1996 Atlanta relay and, like all such persons, he was rewarded for his hard work with the honour of carrying the Olympic Flame. I was preparing to watch him do so from inside a motor home in the OFR caravan, a platform normally assigned to carry ACOG officials and VIPs but kindly offered to me as my ethnographic base while out on the relay. The Além driver, Nancy Murphy, an accomplished arts marketing executive in her normal life, commented on how excited I must be as 'someone who knew all about what it feels like to carry the flame'. I laughed and said that while I had interviewed hundreds of torchbearers over the years, I had never carried the flame myself, so my son would have to tell me about it. She was astonished, but I explained that adults do not normally carry the flame in Greece, that officials on other relays just assumed, as she had, that I had carried the flame several times, and that it was quite beyond me to ever think of asking for this privilege. Nancy grabbed her walkie-talkie and called up to Steve McCarthy and Hilary Hanson in the command car, and, before I could quite process what was happening, a motorcycle pulled alongside and a torchbearer uniform was passed through the van window. A few moments later, I was bearing the Olympic Flame and then passing that flame from my torch to my son's, before he carried on through the streets of Raleigh, North Carolina. The photographs of these moments, together with those of my daughter carrying the flame and my younger son helping light a cauldron during the Salt Lake relay – Steve McCarthy's fraternal way of honouring my years of work on the OFR – are more precious to me than any other artefact of my career in Olympic studies, including the IOC's Olympic Order. These photos were all taken by the professional photographers on the media truck in question here, and I mention these personal details to show just how deeply vexed and ambivalent I am about this policy matter. Still, as painful as it would be, I would sacrifice these mementos to know that the public ritual participants on the side of the road would no longer have their views obstructed and their ritual experience truncated by this media truck.

10 'Activation' is the professional euphemism for 'self-promotion' activities among corporate marketers. Sponsors pay a large rights fee, in negotiated combination of cash and value-in-kind (VIK), for an exclusive in their product category. 'Presenting partner', a new category Coca-Cola demanded and eventually won for itself on the OFR, carries an even larger fee. Sponsors then spend additional monies, usually a significant multiple of the initial rights fee, to activate their sponsorship, that is to engage in promotion activities designed to publicize the sponsorship and leverage it for greater sales of the company's product or services. While basic matters like logo placement, proximity, and size are usually carefully set out in the sponsor contract, other activation practices are not, and it is in this domain that most of the conflicts between the OCOG flame relay managers and sponsor-hired activation teams have raged out on recent OFRs.

11 The congruence with Olympic broadcasters, at least in the United States, is very strong and just as challenging for activists. For example, anyone who thinks that Dick Ebersol, Peter Diamond, and the other principals at NBC Olympic Broadcasting are not themselves passionate partisans of the Olympic Movement and are deeply moved by the 'up, close and personal' athlete stories that have

for years centred their coverage has clearly never met these individuals. As with Coke and Samsung Olympic executives in the sponsorship field, it may be comforting in certain quarters to imagine media bosses as simple patronizers and manipulators of public taste for commercial gain, but this fantasy can never be politically progressive. It is no less a form of commodity fetishism, in the classical Marxian sense, than what it claims to criticize. Real political analysis and any potential for effective political action begins, in my experience, with the difficult recognition based on face-to-face, ethnographic interaction that such persons are both commercially interested and true believers.

[12] This Lillehammer relay has been carefully documented and analysed by a team of anthropologists from the University of Oslo, in the only book-length, fieldwork-based, scholarly study of a particular OFR. Sadly, this wonderful work has not yet been translated into English. See Arne Martin Klausen, et al., *Fakkel-Stafetten: en Olympisk Ouverture*. To further contextualize this relay in the overall Lillehammer project, see Klausen, *Lillehammer-OL og olympismen*; leaving just, project, see Klausen, *The Olympic Games as Performance and Event*.

[13] In a November 2006 conversation in Lausanne, Felli agreed that the number of sponsor torchbearers I reported to him for Athens 'was completely out of hand', and he promised to get after the problem. I take the formal and transparent announcement by BOCOG, in the summer of 2007, of precisely the number and percentages of sponsor torchbearers and escort runners for the Beijing OFR to be Mr. Felli keeping his word. Undoubtedly, he was assisted in this case by the very different underlying relationship between corporations and political, and public culture in China. However, in the same conversation, Felli was taken aback when I used the expression 'Olympic Flame Relay Community' in the context of discussing its shocks over ritual violations in Torino. Felli demanded to know to whom I might be referring. The professionals he knew, of course, but he seemed unfamiliar with and puzzled by the notion of a transnational 'laity' of flame ceremonies aficionados, torch relay pilgrims, former torchbearers, bloggers, memorabilia collectors, independent scholars, artists, school groups, and the like, who intensively follow all OFR developments. This lacuna is entirely consistent with the self-centred and, in my opinion, destructive way that the IOC defines 'Olympic Movement' in the *Olympic Charter* and related documents and attitudes today. If the Olympic Movement indeed were to consist solely of those whom the IOC authorizes, notably members of recognized sport organizations, sponsors, media, and athletes, then there would no longer be any Olympic Movement in the established sociological meaning of the term; an Olympic sports industry and Olympic sports system, yes, an Olympic Movement, no.

[14] Some months after this conversation with Steve McCarthy, a high IOC official said to me that while it was desirable that the flame that arrives in the Opening Ceremony and lights the cauldron be the actual flame from Olympia, the only really important thing to him was that 'the public believes it is the authentic flame'. Cynical pragmatism, perhaps. But what this statement certainly does represent is a further triumph of the logic of spectacle over that of ritual among the self-described guardians of the Olympic Movement. Ritual honesty, responsibility and sincerity – and therefore ritual efficacy – are less important than the spectacular appearance of these things. The simulacrum will suffice for Olympic leaders, and if the public partisans of the Olympic Movement are being truly fooled, well, how can it hurt them?

The IOC has frequently been compared with the Vatican, but episodes and attitudes such as these remind us that there is no Congregation of Sacred Rites in Lausanne. Nearly all other Olympic functions and properties have IOC commissions charged with their well-being, but not Olympic ceremonies. At a 1990 Olympic symposium arranged by the late Fernand Landry in Quebec City, IOC President Samaranch privately asked a group of scholars what governance initiatives they would like to see. When I answered that we wanted an IOC commission on ceremonies, he waved the suggestion away as 'insufficiently important'. So left to marketing and games operations, and subject to unchecked and ad hoc presidential intervention, it is little wonder that the OFR, the Opening and Closing, and the Victory Ceremonies today depend chiefly on other parties than the IOC administration for their ritual integrity. These other parties have frequently included OCOG officials and operatives, and this is one reason why the current IOC efforts to treat OCOGs as mere franchisees should not be accepted in any blanket fashion, in my opinion. In the area of ritual, OCOGs have been the main sources of both conservation and creativity in recent decades.

[15] See 'A Conversation with Athanassios Kritsinelis', this volume.

[16] In the aftermath of Beijing, the IOC banned global relays for subsequent Summer Olympics as well.

[17] Two months before these conversations with Steven McCarthy, I met with the BOCOG OFR director Zhang Ming and her staff in Beijing, and she was eager to discuss the enormous pressure they were feeling from the IOC to accept Coca-Cola as a relay sponsor, when they preferred to have 'only national companies'. I did not learn until an interview with Michael Payne in Lausanne in November 2006, that the IOC had already given Coke the right of first refusal of any OFR sponsorship for the duration of its new contract. This provision has never, to my knowledge, been publicly acknowledged. I do not know if Zhang Ming was aware of it when we spoke, but in any case it rendered moot our Beijing discussions and subsequent interventions.

The decision later worked out between the IOC, BOCOG, and these major TOP sponsor companies, made Samsung the 2008 international relay presenting partner, while reserving for Coke the domestic relay in China. A top IOC official presented this resolution to me as a wise compromise, giving each company what it most wanted, while cutting down on the risk of Torino-style anti-globalization demonstrations. Of course, as discussed elsewhere in this volume, the Beijing international relay was to face far greater and more important protests.

[18] Cheju Island is the home of both a powerful Korean origin myth and the famous *tolharubang* lava rock statues. The myth combines a chthonic emergence motif – the hunter brothers Yang, Koh, and Buk emerge from three holes in the ground – and an invading royalty motif – they marry three princesses who have come westward across the sea bringing with them agriculture and animal husbandry. As for the *tolharubang* or 'grandfather' statues, one branch of both scholarly and folk opinion links military aspects of their costuming as far back down the Silk Road as the empire of Alexander the Great, while their general sculptural form summons Polynesian parallels. In 1988, the Olympic Flame was taken for ceremonies at both the *Samong Hyol*, the Yang-Koh-Buk shrine, and to various *tolharubang* sites. Professor Kang Shin-pyo, who studied as well as contributed to the Seoul 1988 ritual designs, has shown how highly self-conscious the Seoul OFR planners were about performing this East meets West motif in a logic of hierarchical complementarity. See MacAloon and Kang, '*Uri Nara*'.

In this same article, Kang and I document and analyse several OFR practices that brought the ritual into conformity with Korean and East-Asian cultural codes but would find no place in today's 'world's best practices' model. For example, an individual torchbearer surrounded only by relay personnel, including security escort runners, would look completely wrong to Koreans. So in 1988, each flame bearer led a carefully composed and highly formalized group from six to ten accompanying runners. When shown films of this relay, Western audiences, in my experience, inevitably notice this practice and regularly wonder if it did not somehow take away from the actual torchbearer's experience.

[19] Another variant on unitary flame controversies concerns the use of national cultural flames and relays and their proper relations with the OFR. In Korea in 1988, SLOOC lit a Korea flame on Kanghwa Island at the traditional site of the descent to earth of Korea's mythical founder Tangun. This flame was then relayed to the Peace Gate in Seoul's Olympic Park. However, following a cultural logic Kang and I have called 'side-by-side, no mixing', the Korean organizers were extremely careful that this Korean national flame relay never intersected with or even approached the OFR, that the Korea Flame was extinguished by the time the OFR arrived in the capital, and that the Korea Flame received little or no international publicity. Greek flame relay officials whom I travelled with in Korea did express private disagreement when they learned of this Korea flame. Because of this experience, I warned a high Lillehammer Culture and Ceremonies Department official that a similar plan for a Norwegian Flame could run into trouble and create real controversy. Unfortunately, this warning was ignored, and LOOC went ahead with its plan to not only light a flame in the family hearth of the 'father of skiing' Sondre Nordheim at Morgedal in Telemark, but also to merge this flame with the Olympia Flame on the eve of the Games. As I predicted, this led to an enormous row with the Hellenic Olympic Committee and a sector of Greek public opinion. LOOC CEO Gerhard Heiberg and his team eventually backed down, and the Morgedal flame arrived in Oslo on a different day than and was not merged with the Olympia Flame. Instead the Morgedal flame was used for the Paralympic Games. See Klausen, 'The Torch Relay'; MacAloon, 'Anthropology at the Olympics'; Puijk, 'From Parish Pump to Global Village'; MacAloon and Kang, '*Uri Nara*'.

[20] For a general treatment of this opposition between universal humanism and interculturalism in Olympic affairs, see MacAloon, 'Humanism as Political Necessity?'.

References

Klausen, A. *Lillehammer-OL og olympismen*. Oslo: Ad Notam Gyldendal, 1996.

Klausen, A. 'The Torch Relay: Reinvention of Tradition and Conflict with the Greeks'. In *Olympic Games as Performance and Event: The Case of the XVII Winter Games in Norway*, edited by Arne Martin Klausen, 75–96. London: Berghahn Books, 1999.

Klausen, A.O., A. Berkaak, E.K. Aslasken, R. Puijk, I. Rudie, and E. Archetti. *Fakell-Stafetten: en Olympisk Ouverture*. Oslo: Ad Notam Gyldendal, 1995.

MacAloon, J.J. 'Humanism as Political Necessity? Reflections on the Pathos of Anthropological Science in Olympic Contexts'. *Quest* 48 (1996): 67–81.

MacAloon, J.J. 'Anthropology at the Olympic Games: An Overview'. In *Olympic Games as Performance and Event: The Case of the XVII Winter Games in Norway*, edited by A.M. Klausen, 9–26. London: Berghahn Books, 1999.

MacAloon, J.J., and Kang Shin-pyo. 'Uri Nara: Korean Nationalism, the Seoul Olympics, and Contemporary Anthropology'. In *Toward One World Beyond All Barriers: The Seoul Olympic Anniversary Conference*, edited by Koh Byong-ik, 117–59, Vol. 1. Seoul: Poon Nam Publishing, 1990.

Payne, M. *Olympic Turnaround*. London: London Business Press, 2005.

Puïjk, R. 'From Parish Pump to Global Village'. In *Global Spotlights on Lillehammer*, edited by Roel Puïjk, 27–58. Luton, UK: University of Luton Press, 1997.

'My programme became very strict': a conversation with Athanassios Kritsinelis

John J. MacAloon

Social Science Division, The University of Chicago, Chicago, IL, USA

Athanassios (Nassos) Kritsinelis is known and respected across the world as the dean of Olympic Flame Relay (OFR) practice. As OFR technical director and manager, first for the Hellenic Olympic Committee (HOC) and then for the 2004 Athens Olympic Organizing Committee (ATHOC), he has for over 30 years been the most notable on-the-ground guardian and innovator of Greek OFR traditions, as well as the chief Greek interlocutor with the succession of Olympic Games Organizing Committees (OCOGs) receiving the flame. Kritsinelis was the main ATHOC planner for the Athens 2004 relay. He was also a tragic casualty when the transnational, 'world's best practices' operational regime that had evolved out of prior, largely Anglo-Saxon OFRs was brought to bear in Athens.

John MacAloon: Nassos, I've been a close observer of your work ever since we travelled the length and breadth of Korea together on the 1988 Seoul relay, you as a distinguished collaborator and guest and me as an ethnographer. But I don't think I've ever asked you how you got started in all of this.[1]

Athanassios Kritsinelis: I went to work for the HOC in 1972, and was subsequently approached by Dimitrios Xirouchakis, then the chairman of the HOC Flame Relay subcommittee. As you know, I am by profession a mechanical engineer and electrical engineer, and they needed help with the 1976 flame for Montreal. First of all, they asked me to assist the quite elderly technical person on the flame-kindling ceremony at Olympia, especially with the lighting and the sound. I soon took over organizing this ceremony for the HOC. Secondly, the flame was for the first time to be transported electronically, from Athens to Montreal. I had to initiate discussions with Greek telecommunications in order to find a way. Conditions were completely different back then; we only had one satellite station in Thermopyles. So we had to install a special direct cable from the Panathenaic Stadium to Thermopyles, and special equipment had to be made to relay the laser signal to the satellite and back down again.

JM: How ironic that you who are known today as the man of simple, humane, traditional flame relay practice actually got your start with the high technology flame of 1976, when many observers felt that flame-by-laser wasn't a real Olympic flame at all. 'Mr Flame Relay' begins his career as 'Mr Satellite'?

AK: Well, it wasn't my decision to make, and there was heritage here too. In 1976, I worked with Professor Salteris Peristelakis, a physicist and my former teacher at the Athens University. He had been involved with arrangements for the parabolic mirror and the mode of lighting from the sun all the way back to Ioannis Ketseas and the original ceremony and relay in 1936. The mirror – you have seen it many times – was made with Zeiss and was once the property of the University. Prof. Peristelakis arranged to have it donated to the HOC.

JM: So your lineage as a ritual specialist extends back to the very origins of the OFR.

AK: And I read everything I could about the relay. I read all of the original documents of the HOC, I read everything published in official reports, and I talked with any Greek still alive who had been historically connected to the relay. You know that Ketseas is most remembered today as the Greek founder of the International Olympic Academy (IOA), but he was so much more. He arranged for the HOC to own the Olympic Stadium and he was the main originator of the torch relay practices in Greece that have been so admired, like the lighting from the sun and the selection of the classical dancer/actress Koula Pratsika as the high priestess, a controversial thing at the time. He worked in collaboration with the archaeologist Alexandros Philadelpheas. There was no television and not so much film in those days, so they were able to make a special ceremony, and this is the reason the ceremony became so nice and so acceptable all over the world. You will read all of the details when I finish my book.

Of course, the Germans of the Olympic historians society don't like to hear some of this. They haven't studied the Greek documents. They have only IOC and German documents and they want to give all the credit for everything to Carl Diem, who indeed had the main idea earlier and was the secretary general of the Berlin organizing committee. Diem arranged completely the international route, but in Greece mostly everything was left to Ketseas, Philadelpheas, and other Greek collaborators. They invented the main flame-lighting ritual practices still with us today. Also, the Greek citizens of Tegea played a strong role in encouraging the IOC to accept the relay plans in the first place. But you know my dispute with the Germans over this; I think you left the Olympic historians organization because of it.

JM: Well, my argument with them was less about the significance of the 1934 Tegea lunch than about kinds of historiography and presumptuous claims about who has the right to speak.[2] You, Karl Lennartz, and Walter Borgers certainly do agree completely on the historical grounds for fighting against the tendentious and iconoclastic polemic on the part of certain journalists that because the first relay was for Berlin, therefore the OFR 'was a Nazi invention'.

AK: This is one reason why the contributions of Greeks to the origins of these rituals must be emphasized.

JM: So from the late 1970s across to 2000, you came to take charge of the technical aspects, planning, and management of the flame lighting, the Greek relay segment, and the handover ceremony, for summer and winter Games. HOC bosses, including Greek IOC members negotiated and signed the contracts and made the speeches, but you did everything else. I wasn't able to meet you in 1984, when [IOC member in Greece and IOA President] Nikos Nissiotis asked me to come in a few weeks later to do an aftermath study of the terrible and very nearly tragic conflicts over the Los Angeles flame lighting and non-relay.[3] By the way, while I think of it, there have been widely discrepant estimates of the numbers of demonstrators and soldiers faced off against each other in Olympia that day in 1984. What are yours?

AK: They said about a thousand [demonstrators], but there were only two hundred persons marching from Olympia to the Pierre de Coubertin monument. The mayor of Olympia Spiros Fotinos led the march, and this is the reason I believe that he was never re-elected.

JM: That is way fewer demonstrators than many people say.

AK: Two hundred, maybe fewer.

JM: OK. And how many army troops and police?

AK: Too many. All of Olympia was full of army and police. Many, too many.

JM: We have talked about how you were at the time kept completely unaware of the secret flame-lighting arranged between Nissiotis and [IOC President Juan Antonio] Samaranch and the taking of this flame to Lausanne, weeks before these events occurred.[4]

AK: I still do not understand about this, but anyway, the day before the actual lighting ceremony for Los Angeles, I went out to Olympia and told everyone not to worry so much about the mayor of Olympia [the protest leader who insisted the Americans would not receive the flame], because I had the flame already in Athens. I took it there after the priestess lit it in the dress rehearsal.[5]

JM: So it too was a real flame, like Samaranch's flame, because it was lit under the required ritual conditions: by a woman, from the sun, upon the altar of the Mother outside the Temple of Hera.

AK: According to the *Olympic Charter*, the Olympic flame is the one that is lit in Ancient Olympia before the Olympic Games, is transferred by relay to the Olympic stadium, and stays lit until the Closing Ceremony, when it is extinguished. Therefore, no other flame can be an Olympic flame.

Given this very large struggle in 1984, it was something that made me very upset for [Athens 2004]. Because all of the very same people who were yelling at the Americans in 1984, now they accepted everything. The commercialization of 2004 was much, much worse than back then. I am very, very upset about this. In 1984, it wasn't so much a sponsor problem. Greek public opinion, some Greek authorities, and the mayors saw selling the rights to carry the flame in America for $3000 a kilometre as commercialization by the LAOOC [Los Angeles Olympic Organizing Committee], but it was a charity thing with much of the money going to youth sports charities and the rest to the expenses of the relay. So it was not so much for the sponsors. But [Greek officials] made 2004 more for the sponsors [than any previous] relay. This is still unbelievable and angering to me.

JM: We've jumped ahead to a main theme of this interview and the series of studies it is part of. But let's first talk a bit more about ritual continuity and change in the Greek OFR in the intervening period. After our many days of conversation out on the Seoul relay, I worked in close collaboration with you in 1992 and in 1996, so, of course, I have my own observations. But knowing your core commitment to ritual continuity in these performances, I wonder what you see as the important changes you and your colleagues introduced across the 1980s and 1990s.

AK: I did make changes in the scenario for the flame-lighting ceremony. Notably, I separated the priestesses and their ritual act of drawing down fire from the sun away from the contemporary audiences. I didn't want everybody to be in the sanctuary with the priestesses, standing all around them, mixing everything up, especially on television. So over the years, I reinforced the boundary between the ancient stadium and the *altis* [sanctuary], using for this purpose the *krypte* [ancient vaulted tunnel passage between the sanctuary and the stadium]. The crowd is present in the stadium for the first part of the ceremony, for the flags and anthems and the official speeches, while the priestesses are [unseen] inside the sanctuary. The crowd stays outside, and eventually the priestesses will emerge from inside, bringing the flame to the world.

Only a few persons should pass through the *krypte* to witness the actual flame lighting at the sacred spot next to the Hera Temple: six invited persons from the OCOG, the HOC members, maybe the Greek ministers and two or three other VIPs. It should be a small group. Of course, when your first lady Mrs Clinton came, we had some trouble about this.[6] But even in such a case, we successfully marshalled the guests and the television and photographers so that the cameras could never include in the same shot the contemporary people and the priestesses with their ritual actions in the ancient setting. This allows the choreography of Mrs [Maria] Hors and the actresses to create such a dramatic impression of invoking the ancient world.[7] (See Figure 1).

JM: And for many, perhaps most Greeks, this has been not just an Olympic ceremony, but a ritual of modern Greek national identity, with all its creative contentions over *ellenismos*, the cultural and political doctrine of strong connections between ancient and modern Greece.[8]

AK: You are absolutely right. Then after the dignitaries go back to the stadium floor, the priestesses come out in a procession bearing the flame. Here is the only space you see the priestesses together with the public, but here too there is an invisible line, across which the chief priestess lights the first torchbearer's torch with her own and speaks words to the first torchbearer and to the world.

JM: These changes certainly drew the ritual into greater conformity with everything anthropologists know about the structure of rites of passage, creation of liminal spaces and experiences, and generation of symbolic drama. But I know you don't work from any explicit ritual theory, but rather from a 'strict' attitude – one of your favourite English words – towards the small practices that make things look and be 'correct'.

AK: Yes, I became very strict with my programme. I made a change so that during the rehearsal, the antiquities were closed to the general public and even to most officials, just so the priestesses and the core team could make whatever we want in peace and creativity.

Figure 1. The Hellenic Olympic Committee marks the difference with Summer Olympic Games by lighting the flame for Winter Games in the Pierre de Coubertin grove rather than the ancient stadium. The stele containing Coubertin's heart is at the right. Source: IOA.

I developed a very good relationship with the police, and this process is still used today, so that the priestesses and the people responsible for the flame could get to their positions in the sanctuary without mixing with anyone else. For the Albertville Winter Games, I was delayed in my programme for the first time because I had to move 500 schoolboys and girls, ages 10–13, who were in the wrong place. For the television broadcasters, I built raised camera positions, so it became easier to confine them in their separate place. Official photographers are very strictly marshalled too, only 50 seconds in front of the temple.

JM: For the Sydney 2000 flame-lighting ceremonies you were sidelined, and your replacements had trouble lighting the flame from the mirror, because it was a cloudy day. They had to use the back-up flame lit during the dress rehearsal. There were other serious problems too, various delays and the decision to have the senior Australian IOC member's daughter be the first Australian to carry the flame just outside the *altis*, a nepotistic break with Greek tradition. Then there were problems again with the ceremony in 2004, when you were also not in charge.[9] I remember people calling out to you as we walked through the village of Ancient Olympia after both occasions: 'Nasso, where were you?'; 'Nassos, why did these things happen?' The Olympians have a hard time accepting that there can be a flame lighting without you, while their customary attitude towards top HOC and Greek IOC officials is notably different, as I know well from my many stays there. After the problems of 2000, some Greek newspapers came out saying that all of this was because Kritsinelis was not there. Even Athens Mayor Avramopoulos mentioned your name in interviews, maybe to politically embarrass Mr Nikolaou or [the Greek political party] PASOK.

AK: Well, I say nothing against my replacements, since I trained them all. But these difficulties were really unnecessary. As for Ancient Olympia, everyone knows me very well in the village, not only for the relay but for all my work as an HOC engineer and builder at the IOA. The journalists, after so many years, they know me. On both political sides, they know what I stand for. I did not have to give interviews to any of them. I always have believed it fair to be judged for my own actions and not to exploit for my own interest any bad moment somebody else had, especially when I am not involved. Some others judged that I should be excluded from these events, so let them be judged for the results of their actions.

JM: Turning to the relay from Olympia to Athens, I have always been struck by your commitment to continuity in the way you have managed it, for example: in the details of scheduling and preparing the route, the social composition of the torchbearers and their method of selection, the relative simplicity of the caravan, and the perpetual proximity of the flame-bearer or cauldron to the people.

AK: This is the way I am thinking and working. The flame cannot be separated from the people and still be the Olympic flame. If it is separated, it is the flame of someone's power, not of peace.

JM: Incidentally, this is why I so strongly object to the media truck that goes just ahead of the torchbearer in the so-called 'best practices' model of today. This truck blocks the people from seeing the flame approaching and only gives them a brief glimpse of it when the torchbearer passes directly in front of them.[10]

AK: I hate this too, and also all these motorcycles and security men in the American model who come between the people and the flame. Why do they want all this? This is the Olympic flame!

JM: Your relays have been secure, but very open. You also don't interpose security between you as organizers and the Greek people. It's easy for them to offer welcoming gestures – strewing palm branches before the flame, singing and dancing and praying for it – but also to tell you as officials what is on their minds. Your relays have seemed wide open to Greek democracy, that is, to traditions of people publicly speaking their mind. In 1992, there were many angry people who were not shy about telling you as a Greek Olympic official what they thought about Athens losing the centennial Olympic Games to Atlanta. They had plenty to say about the IOC, Coca-Cola, CNN, and so forth. The relay was an active and continuous conversation, not always pleasant.

AK: In 1992, the atmosphere was very heavy, you could say, but the people welcomed the flame and we didn't have any problems. We kept tradition and made the relay. We had to do that, and I think the flame was very good in the towns.[11] And, besides, you learned from the Greek people?the expression?that you later put into [Atlanta Olympic Organizing Committee President] Billy Payne's speech at Olympia for the flame lighting in 1996. The people liked it very much when Mr Payne and [ACOG Managing Directors] Ginger Watkins, and Charlie Battle used that speech in all the towns on the Greek relay. Remember, you gave it yourself for them in Sparta.[12]

JM: You showed me in 1992 how important the OCOG presence should be on the Greek relay segment, and ACOG eagerly accepted this when I told them. You remember that because [the Barcelona committee] COOB had thoughtlessly failed to send any official on the relay from Olympia to Athens, I as the only foreigner along had to pretend to be from COOB and to accept the small presents in the towns and to say brief thanks in Spanish. Happily, no one seemed to notice that I should be speaking in Catalan, if I really were from COOB. The absence of Catalan officials seemed even odder once they learned that Catalan Independence Movement demonstrators greeted the flame in Elis and elsewhere along our route.

AK: I can't remember the village we were in when I got a call from Mr Nikolaou, telling me that a certain Barcelona official was there and to give him a uniform and have him run. So I put him in for four or five hundred metres, and in the car afterward, you introduced me to him. He was the COOB Director of the flame relay in Spain, and I hadn't even met him until then!

JM: Antoni Rossich was a top man from the COOB marketing department, and this department arranged everything important for Barcelona, from design of the route to selection of the torchbearers, even though in the organization chart, the flame relay was formally under the Image and Communication Division not the Commercial Division. For Albertville earlier in 1992, the OFR was under the joint Marketing and Communications Department. So we can say that the flame relay had slipped again from the culture and ceremonies department where it was located in Seoul back into the purview of marketing and public relations in 1992. In 1994 and 1998, it returned to the Cultural Division in Lillehammer and Nagano.

In Los Angeles 1984, the OFR was a separate department, but with the relay basically subcontracted out to AT&T, Burson-Marsteller, and other firms, the real reporting relations were clear. The same was true with Calgary 1988, when the relay was basically subcontracted out to PetroCanada. For 1996, ACOG firmly placed the flame relay under the marketing communications general manager Ginger Watkins. The independent staging company Além International, rather than a government agency or a commercial company, handled logistics as an ACOG subcontractor. Things stayed pretty much that way with Sydney and Salt Lake and will do so in London, so I think we can speak here, of the consolidation, from an organizational point of view, of an 'Anglo-Saxon model', with several important Catalan features in it.

AK: For Athens 2004, we were originally with the Culture Division. When I went to ATHOC in January 2002 – I wasn't paid until June, but I started working in January – we reported straight through the Culture Division to [ATHOC Executive Director and COO] Marton Simitsek. But in 2003, we were suddenly transferred to the Marketing Division, reporting instead to the marketing general manager Georgios ['George'] Bolos. So you can say that we started in one model and ended up in the other.

JM: Of course, all flame relays today must accomplish the same functionalities, but this matter of classification and organizational assignment is highly revealing, I think. With the OFR back under culture and ceremonies in BOCOG [the Beijing organizing committee], we can speak of one model for countries, say in East Asian or Norway, where the relay is first of all classified as a cultural ritual and only secondarily as a marketing and public relations tool. And on the other side, we have the Anglo-Saxon/Spanish model, including Vancouver 2010 and London 2012, where the OFR is conceived first of all as a public relations and 'brand-building' opportunity and only later, sometimes after the fact, discovered and understood to be a ritual. As you say, ATHOC started with one model and ended up with the other. This was something I never could have anticipated, especially once your appointment as flame relay director was secured.

AK: Of course I did not myself imagine, when I joined, that we would ever accept in so many ways this American model.

JM: While Jacques Rogge was head of the IOC Coordination Commission for Athens, we saw each other several times in the context of the IOC 2000 Reform Commission and again in Moscow before he was elected IOC president. I knew ATHOC was quite unstable as yet. I spoke up for you and told Rogge that it would be a very foolish idea for the ATHOC bosses to bring anyone else in. I also spoke briefly in Moscow with Simitsek about your situation, but he seemed standoffish, probably, I thought, because of an argument we'd had in Olympia on the eve of the Atlanta flame lighting.[13]

At some point in Lausanne, Rogge told me 'Professor, I think the way you want to see it happen will happen'. Later I advised Denis Oswald, the next IOC Coordination Commission Chief, that in my opinion you would need extramural help for the operation of the international segment, but not for any of the relay in Greece. This was when Além International and others were trying to enter the picture. [The IOC Marketing Director] Michael Payne acknowledged to me at the time, and later said so in print, that he told ATHOC and Mr Bolos that the IOC would be happy if they accepted Coca-Cola and Samsung as relay sponsors and hired either Steve McCarthy and Além or else [Sydney Flame Relay Director] Di Henry and her Maxxam company to run the international relay. Payne's intervention was leaked to the Greek newspapers, presumably by someone at ATHOC displeased with this renewed IOC 'interference' in Greek flame relay affairs, and it even became a topic of parliamentary and public debate. You showed me those articles.[14]

AK: The point for me is that Simitsek from the beginning told me I had to make both the Greek relay and the international relay. There were all kinds of crazy suggestions coming from abroad, from people who wanted to get into the act but had no flame relay experience at all. For example, even [popular American Olympics chronicler] David Wallechinsky was pushing a plan of visiting 97 countries with the flame. Simitsek asked me, and I said this was not a good programme at all. First of all, I said, we have to go to places where the flame has never been, to Africa and to South America. Next, we have to go to all the previous Summer Games host cities. Finally, the programme had to be practical and doable. In 1992, the Spanish had wanted to do a global relay, but they came to realize that they couldn't afford it, and they soon saw all the difficulties.

JM: Atlanta also heard proposals for a global relay, especially from Greece, since it was the Centennial, and after that for at least a tour of former European host cities.

As I recall, Simitsek was a partisan of the first proposal and [Greek IOC member Lambis] Nikolaou was largely behind the second one, as part of his Olympic politicking of the European IOC members.

AK: Nikolaou did whatever he wanted to do, but he had only plans, no money or expertise.

Anyway, when the proposals from experienced people came in to Athens 2004, I told Mr Simitsek that Di Henry had made a good relay for Sydney, but there was another specialist she had copied nearly everything from. This was Steven McCarthy, and when his proposal arrived, I told Simitsek that this was really good. In the beginning I thought, of course, you should take Steven McCarthy to make the global, international relay, but I should be the man between Steve McCarthy and Simitsek. But Simitsek didn't want this; he wanted Bolos. Probably, given what you've just said, this was Michael Payne's idea too, and he used IOC approval of the global relay as a way to get what he wanted for marketing and for the sponsors.

JM: As far as the Greek domestic relay, 2004 would obviously be the biggest, but you had already done a pretty extensive Greek programme for the centennial in 1996. (See Figure 2).

AK: Normally the relay was from Olympia to Athens via Patras, though in 1976, we went through the southern Peloponnesus. For 1996, we did the south then went up through all the historical sites to Patras and then crossed over and went to Delphi, then on to the north, to Macedonia. After that, the flame passed through the historical town of Marathon and finally arrived at the Panathenaic Stadium, where the first modern Olympic Games had taken place 100 years before. There a big ceremony was organized to celebrate the Centennial. Using a special torch designed by the famous Greek jeweller Kostas Kaissaris

Figure 2.   Nassos Kritsinelis (centre) with the mayor of Nemea (left) and Prof. Stephen Miller (right), excavator of the ancient site and world authority on ancient Greek sport, during the 1996 OFR. The last two appear in their 'New Nemean Games' costumes. Photo by the author (John J. MacAloon).

and me – I designed the internal mechanism – the ceremony included a torch relay inside the stadium before the 50,000 spectators. The torchbearers were well-known representatives of all the cities that had previously organized Olympic Games, including, for example, Anita DeFrantz, the IOC member in the US, who represented Los Angeles. The actual transfer of the Olympic flame to ACOG took place 12 days later, so in the interim we had the chance to take the flame to Rhodes, Crete, and Thrace, so we covered a large percentage of Greece with this historic relay. In 2000, we followed much the same programme here in Greece, because it is something very nice.

For 2004, it was my opinion that after the flame-lighting ceremony at Olympia, we should make just a short relay to the Araxos military airport 60 kilometres from Olympia and from there go abroad. After going around the world, we would return to Greece and commence the relay all around the country, ending at the opening ceremony in Athens. The *Olympic Charter* says the flame is lit in Olympia and goes by relay to the Olympic stadium. But Nikolaou had a different opinion, because he wanted a leg to Athens and to make a ceremony in the Panathenaic Stadium, with him personally handing over the flame from the HOC to ATHOC.

JM: These ambiguities and this space for political manoeuvring were created because the *Charter* is silent about the handover ceremony in Athens, and few IOC members and directors have ever seen it or know the slightest thing about it. Moreover, in 2004, Greeks would be in the unprecedented situation of handing over the flame to themselves! In addition to being HOC president, Nikolaou was an IOC member and ATHOC board member, and in my experience, he is a person who never fails to exercise all of his prerogatives simultaneously.

AK: I followed tradition, but Nikolaou had a different opinion about the tradition, or rather he didn't have any interpretation about tradition, he just did what he preferred. I didn't want to go to Athens with the flame, because Athens was to be the final destination. This is the tradition. The flame doesn't go to the host city on the way to the host city! But I was the only person in the HOC who held this opinion. This was our first major difference. Looking back, I should have better read these, how do you say, clouds in the sky.

Bolos had come in during February or March of 2003, and naturally he wanted everything from me. I couldn't imagine that Bolos would turn out to be so different, so of course, as a dutiful and polite person, I gave him everything, all my programme, all my ideas, with good grace. When Nikolaou and the HOC decided they wanted a leg from Olympia to Athens, we had to accept it. What could we do? I accepted [HOC Flame Relay Committee Director Georgios] Chalkides because he is good and experienced, and Mr [Charalambos] Zoides, and they had all of the files I created for and left at the HOC about the relay. But despite my very deep feelings of solidarity with the HOC, where I worked for 30 years, I had arguments with their programme. They initially wanted to go from Olympia to Athens, via Tripolis, in just one day, with only two celebrations. Bolos had no knowledge, and he had to deal with Nikolaou, but I knew this was all wrong. Eventually, they used five days on this first segment of the relay.

As for the time of the lighting ceremony, we needed, let's say, 20 days for the international relay and 30 days in Greece, so we should make the lighting ceremony 50 days before the Olympic opening ceremony. But the HOC decided instead to light the flame three months before that, on March 25th. I strongly disagreed, and I asked Mr. Simitsek and other top ATHOC leaders why they had accepted this when it was not correct, not part of tradition, out of control. They said that they did not want to fight with Nikolaou; if Nikolaou wants it, we do not say anything. They told me to just make the lighting ceremony whenever the HOC wanted it. The flame would just have to stay on view in the Panathenaic Stadium in Athens until we needed to start the global relay.

But the point was that this flame would then become too familiar to the Athenian people, if it sat for weeks in the stadium! For all past Games, the drama for the people of the host city is when the flame finally approaches for the Olympic opening. Why would Athenians care about this, when the flame has already been around for months and they already had their pictures taken with it?

I tell you I am upset with these people, who were very angry with the Americans in 1984, and then they do these nasty things with our own Games.

JM: March 25th is the big national holiday.

AK: Yes, but it was hardly only that. It looked like the national elections were going to be in April, so they wanted to make the lighting ceremony on this date in March to help the ruling party [PASOK]. This would be a big ceremony in Olympia and the Prime Minister [Costas Simitis] and the Foreign Minister [designated PASOK leader George A. Papandreou] would be there, able to make propaganda for themselves. This is another thing I said to ATHOC, leave the politics out of the relay because this is – I used a very nasty word in Greek – a crime. For the first time, we will use politics in the relay, and this is not correct.

Then the elections happened earlier than they planned, on March 7, and it was another Prime Minister [Kostas Karamanlis of the New Democracy party] who was at Olympia for the ceremony.[15]

JM: And Mr Papandreou, there now as the opposition leader, created a public outcry by failing to wear a tie to the ceremony.

AK: Because the rest of the Hellenic Republic was there, you should dress accordingly, it was a violation of protocol. But I confess I was preoccupied with another protocol violation that day. I was not myself invited to the lighting ceremony by ATHOC. Here I had created the whole scenario for it and left the sketches, maps, and everything, all the details with the HOC, and then ATHOC, that is, Mr Bolos didn't invite me. Instead Nikolaou, the man who had severed me from the relay, he invited me to Olympia, clever person that he is, and I was forced to ask ATHOC for three or four days leave to attend.

I went and sat in the back, and everyone said Mr Kritsinelis, here, move up here, but I said no, I'll sit in the back. And there up front as a special guest was the Greek–Australian whom I had sent away from my office, telling my secretary to never let this gentleman approach again, yet he had gotten the business to make the torches anyway, and there he was sitting up front. I said in meetings that this torch will extinguish in the hands of [ATHOC President and CEO] Mrs Angelopoulou at the ceremony, and we will be embarrassed all over the world. And sure enough, that is precisely what happened. You were there. You saw it.

JM: It's probably a good thing that you were in the back, as you watched this scandal unfold. One more thing about the dates before we continue with the development of your ATHOC situation. Nikolaou tried to claim that the lighting date coincided with Olympic Day.

AK: This was only a partial truth. The 1896 Olympics opened on our national day, but we had subsequently changed calendars, so the real day was April 6, and here in Greece we have celebrated Olympic Day many, many times on April 6. But this was a date previewed for the elections, so they had to give this explanation. By the way, do you know what happened in 1948?

JM: Nassos, I was one year old then, so you better tell me.

AK: The HOC had given a proposal to the IOC to celebrate worldwide Olympic Day on April 6; I have the names of the authors of this proposal. But the IOC didn't accept and instead chose June 23.

JM: The date of the IOC's foundation at the Sorbonne Congress in 1894.

AK: Yes.

JM: So let's go back to the middle planning stage in 2003, when it was you, Bolos, Além, Coca-Cola.

AK: Yes, Bolos, me, Além, but not Coca-Cola. Coca-Cola and Samsung, they appear more towards the end.

JM: What were the discussions like? Tell me how things became more and more difficult. What were the major issues?

AK: In the beginning, the first year we had very friendly discussions. I made the programme, and whatever I said was acceptable and they liked it. I costed out all segments of the relay. We had to go all over Greece, including to the islands. I discussed all of the details of the helicopter flights to the islands with the Air Force: arrival and departure times, landing arrangements, and so on.

But after Bolos came in, things quickly changed. Além's man Simon [Wadley] disputed the timing that I had given. They took away six or seven islands, because Simon said we didn't have the time, but I knew my schedule was correct, because I had made the plan with the Air Force controllers and pilots. Anyway, they subtracted Milos, a very, very important place for Greek history, and instead they wanted to put in Mykanos, which I hadn't put in because Mykanos is famous for something else. They also didn't want Leros or Astypalaia. One of the first ancient Olympic victors was from Astypalaia!

JM: In other words, they were thinking more about population and tourist centres than about heritage sites. The 'world's best practices model', when it is in the hands of marketing and public relations people, seeks first of all to go where the most people are 'to spread the Olympic message most widely', as they like to say. Only secondarily, if at all, do they think about going to where the cultural and historical meanings are, in order to create new symbolic capital for the Olympic flame.

When it's feasible, you too like to take the flame to populations that have not had the flame, but mostly you have always composed your programme on the basis of the historical, cultural, and Olympic significances of the places you could take the flame to see.[16] Your admirers have always thought that this is your special gift and art. Just for myself, how could I ever forget the experience of symbolic power from being with the Olympic flame inside Philip II's tomb at Aigai, or in the ruins of Alexander's palace at Pella, or under the Lion Gate at Mycenae, or climbing to the temple at Delphi, or turning a corner to find the ancient theatre at Argos filled to overflowing, or at the Messolongi sacred sites of the Independence War. And these are just a few of the monumental, not even any of the lyrical ritual moments that you have created for the Olympic flame and that I have been privileged to share.

AK: I made you weep at Argos that time. I called to my team, as we rushed up to make the ceremony, 'Look, John is crying!'

JM: A 'Xerxes at the Hellespont' mini-moment, hardly my only one. But now suddenly in 2003, you were compelled to work with Greeks who knew nothing of this history of Greek flame relays and with foreign relay 'experts' who had no advance knowledge whatsoever about Greece, all with the explicit backing of the IOC Marketing Department and the commercial 'presenting partners'. So they are thinking mostly about marketing demographics, getting to the most people in the fastest and most convenient way....

AK: To sell the Coca-Cola.

JM: Simon Wadley is an Australian who worked on the Sydney relay and was subsequently hired by Steve McCarthy to work for Além on the Salt Lake relay. I've interviewed Simon. Whatever his technical planning skills, ritual, history, and culture are clearly not his things, unless there's some marketing angle.

AK: When Bolos wanted to make a disagreement with me, he used Simon. Simon would come and start the argument with me. They disagreed with the planned timing of the runners. In my relays, we plan and achieve five minutes per kilometre, because the runners are all students who are good athletes, aged about 17–25, boys and girls. For 2004, I planned six minutes per kilometre, because the relay would be more crowded, but we still expected young athlete flame bearers. But Bolos and McCarthy they wanted to let all persons have the opportunity to run, so they said we need seven and one-half minutes per kilometre. They wanted to be sure that older people who could pay for their torches and all the sponsors' torchbearers could run, regardless of physical condition. I didn't accept it, so this was another argument. Seven and a half minutes, that was too much. We should plan as if my grandmother or grandfather were running? So we had another argument.

Nevertheless, I am proud to say, and I will say this directly to anyone, that I never made any criticism or any suggestion for the international part of the relay, even though the attitude of Mr Simon Wadley gave me many opportunities to do so. I didn't do that because I really like Steven McCarthy, although he never contacted me after the Games, and I am really sad to say that.

JM: For the Anglo-Saxon model, these figures per kilometre are aggregates, involving more than one torchbearer. At least in urban areas, it is now rare under this model that any single torchbearer covers even half a kilometre, because they want to pack in as many torchbearers as possible, for several reasons, including those you mention. And all the exchanges and stops and starts of the caravan require more time.

AK: This is the reason for their delays all over the world.

JM: Let's distinguish two issues here, Nassos. The first is largely a cultural issue that you and I have often discussed. The contemporary Greek cultural context has always supported your having only teenage and young adult students (and, of course, Olympic athletes and some Olympic officials) carry the flame, as both befitting the educational goals of the Olympic Movement and echoing, with modern gender equity added in, a notion of the classical life stage of *ephebos* that is so closely associated with ancient sport and ritual education.[17] Persons in other age groups or physical conditions are instead honoured during your OFR celebrations in the villages, towns, and cities. To your team, HOC officials, and scores of thousands of Greek citizens I've observed along your relays, this practice had always 'looked correct'.

AK: This is accurate and I add that education is the reason for the Olympic movement and the Olympic flame relay. What can we teach an old person who runs? But the OFR teaches a young person. These young persons are your descendents and will have this memory all their lives, and they will represent this to other young persons in the future.

JM: Is this why you yourself have never carried the Olympic flame in Greece?

AK: I would never take away this opportunity from any young person.

JM: This way of seeing and doing things would be impossible in other cultural contexts, as you saw when you were invited by the OCOGs to travel with the OFR in their countries. In Korea, as you would have understood also in Japan, you saw how it was culturally undesirable and unacceptable not to have seniors carry the flame. Any torchbearer cadre strictly segregated by age-grade and physical condition would have been deemed inappropriate in Canada, the USA, Australia, or Norway, though it was indeed done for Albertville. In the US in 1996, you had to get used to the sight of grandparents, the disabled, and younger children as torchbearers.

At least you were able to carry the Olympic flame yourself the first time in this culturally different setting and on a long relay where there are always open slots out in the countryside. I remember how moved all the Atlanta leaders were about your carrying the flame for the first time on their relay. Not just the flame relay officials like Hilary Hanson, Rennie Truitt, and Steve McCarthy, but also the top ACOG executives. Billy Payne, Charlie Battle, A.D. Frazier, Ginger Watkins: they all call you their teacher. Billy flew home after the Olympia flame lighting, then turned around and flew back to Greece so that he could carry the flame in your relay. A.D. Frazier has told me over and over again that the only time he was ever sure that the whole Olympic thing was worth the effort was when he was with us on your flame relay in Greece.[18]

AK: He has really said that? That's very gratifying.

JM: So in 2003, what Bolos and McCarthy and their ATHOC and IOC overseers were saying to you, in effect, was that the way it has been done in those cultural contexts is now the new global norm, and you will accept it regardless of conventional Greek practice and understandings. And the HOC itself was made to, or chose to accept these new practices even on the Olympia to Athens leg that they and not ATHOC controlled. This leads to the second factor you bring up.

The selection of socially variegated torchbearers is also incentivized under the so-called world standard model by the desire to sell torches to the torchbearers and to accommodate whomever the sponsors choose to fill their contracted torchbearer slots. Young students – and often their families, if they were selected the traditional Greek way – are less likely to have 360 euros to buy their torches. And you're not going to tell Coke or Samsung or Alpha Bank, who have paid all this money to ATHOC, that some person they want to seduce or reward for business reasons is too old, too infirm, or too out of shape to carry the Olympic flame. That's become the main reason why they paid all the sponsorship money in the first place! So the argument for 'democratic' and 'progressive' expansion of torchbearer sociology is not only culturally contextualized, it can also serve as a convenient cover for commercial sponsors getting their torchbearer preferences taken care of.

AK: To have some persons from the sponsors run is fine, but not 60–70%.

JM: What? Are you telling me that 60% of the Athens 2004 torchbearers were sponsor torchbearers?

AK: Maybe more, international and national sponsors.

JM: Such a level of sponsor takeover is hard to believe. Maybe you are including in these sponsor torchbearer numbers whomever the Greek 'community hero' torchbearers – to use the Atlanta expression normalized into the Anglo-Saxon model – turned out to be? Maybe because Coke and Samsung funds paid for the selection process?

AK: Not at all. There were not really any such torchbearers in the Atlanta sense because, as you and I discussed early on, there is no mechanism in Greece to select such torchbearers like they had the charity [United Way] do in Atlanta. As I'm sure Panos [Amelidis] and Pinelopi [Amelidou] have told you, there was an open application on the Internet, where you could apply or nominate someone else and say nice things about them. But these lists went to the mayors to choose some torchbearers from their communities. ATHOC told them how many places they had.

JM: We always said that one way or another this would end up in the hands of the politicians. There is scarcely any other way in Greece.

AK: So for every 50 torchbearers, there were maybe 10 from the community, another 10 or so special persons [Olympians, ATHOC personnel or VIPs] and the rest were sponsor torchbearers, including their own selected VIPs.[19] For me, it should have been 90% from the communities, and 10% other persons.

JM: Marc Maes coordinated the Antwerp and Brussels stops on the international relay for the Belgian NOC, and he wrote the internal report to the IOC on the European NOCs' experience dealing with ATHOC and Além on this relay. He has told me these NOCs were shocked and angered at the small percentage of torchbearer slots they were given on their own territories, that they couldn't even get their top Olympians in because sponsor torchbearers took the most places.[20] But 60–70%? I could never have imagined this.[21] And, of course, the selection process for these people is not public at all. Did Bolos ever directly say, we'll have 65% sponsor torchbearers?

AK: He didn't say anything; no one said anything. Bolos is very clever, so nothing was ever written down.

JM: Did the Greek newspapers understand any of this?

AK: Some of them did, but because all the main journalists ran with the flame, they didn't write anything.

JM: Making journalists torchbearers is a tactic from Seoul, but there it was to serve national political interests not commercial sponsor interests.

AK: And especially, the point is that all the community torchbearers and those from ATHOC, if they wanted their torch, they had to pay 360 euros, but everyone who ran from Coca-Cola, they got their torch without paying.

JM: I suppose Coke would say 'we already paid for the torches as part of our sponsorship, we're not paying twice', but the point you are making is the unfairness to and hurt feelings among the citizen torchbearers and all the moral and emotional difficulties this practice creates for relay staff. To my knowledge, this unfortunate practice was invented by Barcelona, though there the torchbearers who were COOB volunteers or sponsor selections didn't have to pay, and the torches were supposedly sold at cost to the community torchbearers. Fifteen thousand pesetas, as I recall. It was on the Atlanta relay that the torches were sold for the first time at a price well beyond cost. There, relay staffers saddened or ashamed when a wonderful torchbearer couldn't afford his or her torch, they just paid for it themselves. I myself bought five torches for the torchbearers at our University of Chicago ceremony. Am I going to ask Chicago's greatest living Olympian to hand over $350 or she's not leaving with the torch she just carried into my ceremony? I don't think so. Steve McCarthy tells me that he personally bought about 50 torches in such circumstances for torchbearers on his Salt Lake City relay. And there are all kinds of other things torchbearers and line staff do in order to work through this moral quandary. Pinelopi Amelidou says the Greek staff members on the international relay sometimes took pity on torchbearers in poor countries who especially moved them and just told them to walk away with their torches.

AK: I have never paid a cent for any in my collection of all the torches, but the ATHOC torch, for this I had to pay. A journalist friend of mine was selected to run by ATHOC; he just told the caravan staff he was from Coca-Cola so he didn't have to pay for his torch. I know a lot of persons who said they will not pay, and they ran and they just went away with the torch.

JM: Pinelopi also reports that the official ATHOC notification to individuals that they had been selected to carry the flame included the means and strong encouragement to purchase the torch in advance. Perhaps this served to somewhat reduce the number of ghastly scenes after someone has just carried the Olympic flame under this regime. Here you are all aglow with this extraordinary ritual experience, and someone appears and asks you then and there to get out your credit card. Selling the torches is not just commodifying the ritual object, but also the experience itself.

Pinelopi also tells me that the national sponsor she works for had only 10 torchbearer slots in Greece in its initial contract. But each time ATHOC wanted something else from the company, they offered more slots. It's become like a private auction. This company ended up with more than 50 runners, dropped in here and there often at the last minute.

AK: And when they do this, they just add new slots and change the established relay schedule at will. Before, we had everything arranged, how many runners, the exact timing in each place, who would be running, and so on. This just makes a mess.

JM: Frankly, I always felt that it would be difficult if not impossible in 2004 for you to be in the command car and managing the relay, while being subject to call after call from headquarters, ordering you to change your programme on the fly to accommodate this or that torchbearer added at the last moment to serve some interest. And this model accommodates not just sponsor interests, but also the private interests of powerful people in the Olympic bodies and the government as well. It's true everywhere I have been that if you arrange for a powerful person or his daughter or his client to carry the Olympic flame – maybe even in his home village or in front of his business or club – well, you have, shall we say, made a friend for life. But given the especially intense clientelism of Greek political and social life, this aspect of the 'world's best practice' flame-relay model was sure to come to the fore here and even to be exaggerated in this local cultural context. It reminds us once again both of how 'local' the 'global' so often turns out to be, as well as how the global can be completely re-appropriated by the local.

You observed this kind of scheduling in action in Atlanta and Sydney. Maybe you still thought when they hired Além, that this model would be confined to the international relay, while the Greek model would still be followed in Greece. Other than briefly carrying the flame in Salt Lake, Bolos, Simitsek, and their superiors had no direct experience with flame relays outside of Greece, but I was sure they'd eventually figure out this radical power of being able to select and insert torchbearers. When they did, and when they also realized that you were going to stick with your 'strict' principles, pressure would mount to get you out of the relay command car. And this is exactly what happened. They 'retired' you to your office and gave the operational management of the flame relay to Penny Mikelopoulou, a licensing and sales manager in the ATHOC marketing department without the slightest experience in flame relays or public events. Someone who would take orders and effectively carry them out.

AK: You are right. I have never been anyone's chess piece in my life. Miss Penny was a protégé of Bolos. At one point, she said she would give me a car and let me travel along back in the caravan. How could I do that? Can you imagine? But I think the real turning point with them came about the torches themselves. After that I was, how do you say in English, 'a sitting duck'. The climate in 2003 was deteriorating day by day between Bolos and me. I got mad and told him one day that 'Mr Bolos, you suck the life out of other people, because you have no Olympic life of your own. You follow what the IOC tells you to do, and you sell out your employees as if your employers were the sponsors'.

JM: The IOC means Michael Payne?

AK: Yes.

JM: And the torches?

AK: You know I am an engineer and a specialist of the torches. I have worked with many experts, designers, and companies around the world.

JM: Yes, I was right there when you figured out the initial problem in Olympia with the Atlanta torches, and by the time we got to Pyrgos you had jerry-rigged a solution that kept the flame from going out and from melting the torch itself. In Kalamata, you gave the solution to the torch designer Sam Shelton of Georgia Tech University, and by the time the relay started in the States, the torches had been retrofitted to work well from there on. Yes, everyone in the OFR community knows your special competence in these matters.

AK: Well, Bolos asked me for the technical specifications, and when I gave them, he passed them on to be checked by Simon Wadley, and then they demanded two changes. They wanted a torch that would be efficient in 110 km/hour wind and at 2500 metres of altitude. I had given 50 km/hour and 2000 metres. You need a torch that is efficient in a storm, not a typhoon! If we ever would have such high winds and driving rain, we would take the flame forward by cauldron car. In Greece, we will not have any extreme rain, and abroad only so much rain and wind. And yes, Mexico City is 2400 metres high, but we should make a special torch for Mexico. To make a torch for 110 km winds and 2500 metres height to use everywhere on our relay, 11,000 torches, would hugely increase the cost. This was completely unnecessary. But Bolos and Wadley had me in a sandwich, and they insisted.

This Costas Manias from the Australian FCT company came to me. He had worked on the Sydney torch, and I have written that I appreciate this torch. But Manias was a specialist only for the canister and igniter, though now he wanted to make the entire Athens torch. Maybe you know that if you have a gas fuel and you turn on the jet, you feel the canister getting colder. If the gas goes up to the igniter this cold, you will have problems. So you need a special mechanism to warm and condense the gas to be ready for ignition. This special mechanism was in the Sydney torch, but not in the torch Manias was proposing to me. So I sent him away from my office, as I told you before.

JM: In his interview with me, Steve McCarthy said that one reason it was arranged for Coca-Cola to supply all the torches for ATHOC as part of their sponsorship was so that Bolos could get around the time required to follow the official rules for an open tender process. It was late in the game, and Bolos clearly had his own plans. As just an observer of the process, McCarthy says he does not know whether Coke ended up simply writing a check to FTC or instead gave the money to ATHOC to pay FTC.

AK: Who knows these things? Anyway, Bolos said the torches will be given by Coke, but to know the costs, we would have a purely internal, unpublicized competition, and the Australian Mr Manias and the Greek designer–manufacturer Mr Andres Varotsos were asked to present proposals. Mr Varotsos had a very clever engineer working for him who actually gave me a lesson about how to produce a torch. Varotsos gave us his proposed cost of 300 euros to produce the torch, but I never saw the FCT offer. Bolos said it was sent directly to Mr Petros Charahalias, Coca-Cola's sponsorship manager in Greece, and that it was cheaper than the Varotsos tender.

JM: How much did they end up paying for the torches?

AK: Nobody knows. I don't know who knows, or even where the torch was finally produced. It was not in Greece or in Australia. Maybe Taiwan. But it wasn't even close to half of 360 euros.

JM: Just to be clear, do you think Coke headquarters in Atlanta was playing a leading role in this?

AK: I don't think so at all. That's my opinion. I was ready to write a letter to [Coke CEO] Mr Ivester but I didn't, because it would have been against the Greeks.[22]

So there was this meeting with Mr Manias and Mr Varotsos, me, George Bolos, Steve McCarthy, Simon Wadley, and Mrs [Theodora] Mantzari, the ATHOC director of brand name identity. Bolos had the proposed torch in his hand, and I said, this is not the torch that Mr Varotsos has designed. It is completely different. Even Mrs Mantzari noticed this. It was wider; it lacked the ignition sheaths. It was poorer quality, not real wood. They put filler material inside. I saw what had happened, and I said so. They could not do the filler with the design of Mr Varotsos, and they wanted to use the same canister from the Sydney torch. It would cost a lot of money to make a new, thinner canister, and they had the Sydney moulds and they just wanted to reuse them.

I looked Mr Manias straight in the eye and asked was I lying? He said no. Bolos said we can change the specifications if we wish, but we have this so why not use it. I said, let's open this torch, and I did so and showed them the igniter and the canister. This torch, I said, will go out while it's in the hands of the president [Gianna Angelopoulou], and we are going to be nationally and internationally embarrassed.

JM: And that's exactly what eventually happened during the flame-lighting ceremony at Olympia. What was the reaction of Mr Varotsos to all this at this meeting?

AK: The torch he had made and showed to me was perfect. Now, he didn't say anything. Two days later, there was another meeting and Mr Manias was forthcoming for the first time. He said, OK, we will fix this; we will do better. But they didn't. After a month or so, they brought a prototype for testing, and we took it to a special laboratory in Athens. We checked this torch, and it seemed good to 96 km/hour of wind, but you couldn't see the flame in the sunshine. It was the wrong colour. Something had to be put into the fuel mix to add red colour to the flame. But they wouldn't change the mix, because the fuel was already produced. Nobody checked the torches they gave for the relay. In my opinion, the torch they gave for the test was better quality; it was different from the ones they supplied for the relay.

JM: That torch gave continuous trouble throughout the first and second relay segments. McCarthy and Amelidou have described this to me and also how Bolos was finally forced to go out on the international relay and lower the boom, cursing and yelling at FTC: 'What the [expletive] did you guys produce? Why doesn't it stay lit?'

AK: This was the way he usually talked.

JM: The torch was somehow improved for the third relay leg in Greece, but you were not out on the road to see it. Some members of your original team had resigned or gone to different ATHOC departments. Others were out on the relay under the direction of Ms. Mikelopoulou, together with all the newer staff she and Mr Bolos hired. You . . . .

AK: I was in my office with the door closed.

JM: Things had spiralled so far downward, but they didn't fire you or accept your resignation, they just took you off line. They put you into internal exile.

AK: I sent a letter of resignation to Mr Simitsek, but he said, 'No, no we couldn't go on without you. Just let the others do all the heavy work and you be above them'. I believe that they said this because they were thinking of the journalists. All the journalists know me, and what I do and what I stand for, and it wouldn't be good for them if the journalists found out that I had resigned. Right up until now, no one has given an explanation.

JM: Simitsek, for one, surely remembered how the newspapers got after Nikolaou, because of your forced departure from the 2000 relay.

AK: Perhaps. Some people said I should demand from them a lot of money to get out of their way after all of my work, but I respect myself too much for that. So I just went back to my office.

JM: To continue your work preparing for the Paralympic Flame Relay (PFR). Let's talk about that.

AK: I made the programme and I insisted on presenting it myself to the IPC [International Paralympic Committee]. After my presentation, the IPC vice-president called me and he said, 'Listen, I have three things to say. First, thank you. Second, thank you very much. Third, thank you very, very much. I never imagined that someone could make a programme like this for the Paralympic Games'. I had some problems with the archaeologists in the Agora and Acropolis over the flame relay opening ceremony, but I fixed them.

JM: How brilliant of you to start the relay from the Temple of Hephaistos.

AK: He is the disabled god. But the idea to start the PFR from there was not mine. It belonged to a girl who worked for the ATHOC Paralympic Division, and I accepted it. I thought we should start from Delphi, a well-known historical place, but starting at the Temple of Hephaistos was more emotional.

JM: And the Hephaisteion certainly lies on the route of the best-attested *lampadedromia* [torch race] of ancient times, the one from the Academy through the Kerameikos gate and up the Sacred Way to the altar of Athena on the Acropolis.[23] Vase paintings of this *lampadedromia* were a chief inspiration of the modern originators of the OFR, though this was a Panathenaic event of the Attic tribes and not in any way whatsoever associated with Olympia or the Olympic Games.

AK: I thought in this way to give a special authenticity to the Paralympic flame relay. I wanted the disabled people to have this special thing.

JM: You made the Paralympic relay on this occasion more historically grounded than the Olympic one, since the only sacred fires at Olympia were the ritual hearth fire in the *prytaneion*, and the sacrificial fires at the various altars, none ever associated with any torch race or relay in ancient times.

AK: Everyone said the ceremony was wonderful. I was not there to see it. My invitation arrived in the mail one month after the Paralympics were over. I sent it back to ATHOC unopened.

JM: What happened?

AK: I had prepared everything. All of the route was advanced, the torchbearer slots were filled, all the discussions had been completed with the government, with the ministers, the mayors, the police, everything was ready to go. Then the day before they bring me a letter saying that Mr Bolos and Ms. Mikelopoulou will supervise this relay, not me. (See Figure 3).

JM: The day before!

AK: The day before. This was just hateful. She came to my office to say that if I wanted, I could come out on the relay and ride in her car. I said, 'Lady, I have my own car. I don't want to come with you. You stole the other relay, so now just go make this one too. Please get out of my office, I don't want to see or hear you'.

JM: How could this happen again?

AK: I believe Bolos was afraid of this relay. There were going to be so many emotional torchbearer moments and new places visited on this Paralympic relay, and it was going to get strong attention. I'd arranged for the President of the Republic to greet the relay and the disabled torchbearers when they came to his house, and all the press would be there. I believe that Bolos worried that if this was so successful, everyone would ask why he had pushed Kritsinelis away from the Olympic relay. Maybe, it would take away from his claiming all the credit for the success of the other relay. So they waited until the last moment and then pushed me aside again.

JM: I think you are right about him wanting to preserve all credit to himself. The Athens Olympic Games had been an unexpected and nearly unqualified success. ATHOC

Figure 3. In 2004, Kritsinelis arranged to have the Paralympic flame lit at the Hephaestion, in the ancient Agora of Athens, because Hephaestos was 'the disabled god'. Paralympian Konstantinos Fykas carries the flame in front of the temple. Source: ATHOC.

executives expected they would get highly paid consultancies with subsequent Olympics, just as the IOC had forced Sydney officials on ATHOC in its early days. Bolos was lobbying BOCOG for work in Beijing almost immediately after Athens, and he went on to seek high-level work with London 2112. It served his self-interest to want foreigners to believe that he was now an OFR master as well as a successful Olympic marketer.[24]

AK: After ATHOC closed down and I had left Olympic work to return to engineering, there were some investigations. I got ostensibly friendly calls from a former ATHOC official suggesting why it would be a good idea for me not to talk with any auditors or lawyers, especially on the matter of the torches.

JM: Nassos, do you think the Greek OFR tradition can ever return?

AK: This is a difficult question, but my answer is right now 'no', because the new HOC president is a businessman in shipping and media companies, who is very involved in marketing. I met Mr [Minos] Kyriakou in Cyprus, and he said 'I've heard a lot about you, Mr Kritsinelis', but he didn't say a word about the relay. Of course, I didn't say anything. If he wants me, I'm ready. But I believe that in the future he will give this project of the Greek part of the OFR to a company. We will have to see what will happen for Beijing and London. I hope I am wrong.

JM: Probably not, at least for the moment, since very high-level people in Lausanne tell me that in negotiating the new IOC arrangement with the HOC on the flame relay, the IOC was willing to stipulate a non-commercial relay in Greece, but it was Mr Kyriakou and the HOC who rejected this. It seems that they wanted to be free to have sponsors and marketing again, if they so wished. They got a taste of this in 2004, and if they want more, I'm sure the sponsors and promotion companies will be right there to encourage them. This probably insures no future return of Nassos Kritsinelis to the OFR.

AK: If they have said something like this, then of course I have no future in the OFR. What new IOC agreement with the HOC?

JM: This has not yet been publicly announced, and the Greek people and now, it seems, even you are not aware of it. The HOC will no longer be making a contract with each successive OCOG for the flame lighting, Greek relay, and flame delivery ceremony. From now on, each OCOG will be making a contract directly with the IOC for these things; they will form part of the regular Olympic host-city contract. The HOC will still be expected to make the Greek ceremonies, but it will do so only as a kind of subcontractor to the IOC. Already, the IOC has told the HOC the timing Lausanne prefers for the Beijing relay in Greece.

AK: But how is it possible that we give up our historic rights like this?

JM: From the IOC side, as you well know, they have been trying to claim more ownership and control of the OFR ever since the troubles of 1984 awakened Samaranch and Payne both to existing Greek customary rights and to the marketing and promotion potential of the relay. Just remember the tricks they tried to keep a real Olympic flame permanently in Lausanne, even though this would violate the deepest principles of the ritual. And now under Jacques Rogge, the IOC has the huge pressure from Coca-Cola and Samsung as TOP sponsors ['The Olympic Programme' of IOC worldwide marketing] wanting to normalize their OFR prerogatives. Having won rights of first refusal for future flame relay 'presenting partnerships' in its new IOC contract, Coke would rather deal directly with the IOC in the first instance and not the OCOGs and certainly not the HOC. This all fits into the IOC's general impulse today to treat OCOGs more as franchisees than as autonomous partners, and to follow a 'world's best practices' managerial regime in Olympic affairs rather than the intercultural encounter ethos of Olympism. At the present time, this is chiefly centred in [Olympic Games Executive Director] Gilbert Felli's office, rather than in the IOC marketing department, and that is probably an improvement. Felli also commissioned Steve McCarthy and Além to write the IOC's official technical manual that will be imposed on OCOGs for all future torch relays. So everything has turned 180 degrees since 1984. The IOC is probably now the strongest not the weakest actor in the torch relay dramas, of course in contractual partnership with Coca-Cola, whom many in BOCOG didn't want for the Beijing relay but had imposed upon them anyway by the IOC.[25]

AK: OK, but that's the IOC, it still doesn't say how the HOC could give up our historical rights.

JM: Sources tell me that Lambis Nikolaou negotiated these rights away to the IOC during his last days as HOC president. When Mr Kyriakou assumed the HOC presidency, he was met with a *fait accomplit* about which he could do nothing, if he even understood its significance. Some wonder if it is entirely happenstance that Mr Nikolaou was re-elected as an IOC Executive Board member at the very same IOC session where these new arrangements were made. I don't know myself.

AK: This is all such dirty business. I have some ideas as to how we can get the emotions back to what they were. There are Greek specialists, like our biggest collector of Greek Olympic documents and memorabilia. I know you know him. Perhaps he will support renewing the Greek OFR of the past. If not, I will go on alone, like the 'solitary vine' that penetrates the wall, as we say in Greek.

Bolos used to tell me that we need money to make a relay. I always said, we need to make the relay more simple, then we won't need so much money. What is the point of making a gigantic relay? Just to say that we are important people? We were already important people.

JM: McCarthy and his Além staff and the Atlanta people refer to you as the 'Zeus' of the flame relay.

AK: On another relay, they called me 'the Eagle'. I like this too, both these nicknames. I guess they meant the Eagle of Zeus.

JM: I think Prometheus would be a better name for you. You gave this fire to so many of us, and then you have been made to suffer deeply for it.

AK: Thank you for your kind words.

Notes

[1] This interview took place in Athens in October, 2006, and was supplemented by phone through July, 2009. Pinelopi Amelidou collaborated in the interview and Jessica Robinson was chiefly responsible for the transcription, services for which both Nassos Kritsinelis and the interviewer are most grateful. This text has been edited from a much longer transcript and contains spliced quotations.

[2] There is no dispute among specialist scholars that plans for the relay well antedated the Nazi government and that the IOC gave final approval during its meetings in Greece in 1934 (see Borgers, *Olympic Torch Relays*, 13–26). Borgers does note that de Coubertin himself once thought that Philadelpheas, not Diem, was the chief author of the idea, and how concerned Germans were to correct him (*Olympic Torch Relays*, 18.) Barney and Bijerk, 'The Genesis of Sacred Fire', do a much better job of properly estimating the central contributions of Greek scholars and pedagogues to the ritual architecture of the flame relay. These facts condition still today the deep outrage among Greeks when foreign iconoclasts tendentiously assert that the OFR is 'a Nazi invention'. Arguments have instead surrounded which particular IOC/Greek meeting was most important in the approval process: the May 18 session in Athens, a May 22 lunch at Tegea where the relay was again discussed, or a May 23 banquet at Olympia.

In a speech to the IOA in 1996, Kritsinelis largely took at face value a memorial plaque erected in 1934 by the citizens of Tegea and their contemporaneous town hall register. The Tegeans understood then (and today) that it was in their town that the flame relay idea consolidated and the IOC took its decision (Kritsinelis, 'Lighting Ceremony of the Olympic Flame'). Kritsinelis did not deny the importance of the other meetings in this series, but felt that this local history, largely unknown outside Greece, should be honoured, as he also later did by arranging a special Tegea celebration during the 1996 Centennial OFR for Atlanta.

Karl Lennartz of the German Sports University in Cologne subsequently disputed the significance of the Tegea meeting in an article in the International Society of Olympic Historians (ISOH) newsletter ('The Genesis of Legends'). Fair enough, but unfortunately Lennartz did not stop himself from going on to suggest, rather rudely and without informing himself as to the identity of the author, that Mr Kritsinelis produced only 'nonsense' and, moreover, that non-academic 'historians' should not be published at all lest they generate 'legends'. As a fieldwork cultural anthropologist, I did indeed object to such presumption and disrespect for ritual experts and folk histories. Moreover, there was an element of the pot calling the kettle black here, as neither Lennartz nor most other ISOH members have advanced degrees in history. Instead they tend to be physical educationists or sportspersons whose historiography is limited to a radical originology. Rather than multiple historical narratives constituted by and relevant to understanding different cultural contexts and intercultural conflicts, for these writers there is but one point source of institutional origins to be discovered exclusively in documentary evidence. For practitioners of anthrohistory, this is naive empiricism of a kind that would make von Ranke blush (see MacAloon, 'Postscript').

No one disputes the usefulness of facts-and-figures history, but it can scarcely arrive at any challenging interpretive findings by itself and requires just as much inference as popular histories do to arrive at important significances. (It is hardly accidental that ISOH is presently the only research organization related to the human sciences that retains IOC patronage.) Under these epistemological conditions nationalist undertones inevitably creep in, and Greece and Germany are not just any nations in this context. The Kritsinelis–Lennartz dispute embodies a well-known deep structure of modern rivalry over the classical heritage memorably styled by E.M. Butler (in her 1958 book of this title '*The Tyranny of Greece Over Germany*'), here reactivated by Olympic invention of tradition. The continuing German archaeological mandate at Olympia, the joint foundation of the IOA by Diem and Ketseas, the large German presence at the IOA over the years: these are among conditions that have led to a widespread Greek perception of a tyranny of Germany over Greece. In summary, there remains still today a deep and bilateral tension between Germans and Greeks over a historically privileged right to interpret Olympic affairs, including especially the OFR.

[3] See MacAloon, 'This Flame, Our Eyes: Greek/American/IOC Relations, 1984–2002', this volume.

[4] See MacAloon, 'Postscript' and 'Introduction', this volume. Also, Ueberroth, *Made in America*, 241–5; Payne, *Olympic Turnaround*, 126–7.

[5] This was the brilliant and charismatic Greek actress Katerina Didaskalou, who endured serious threats of bodily and career harm for serving as the ritual priestess amidst the controversy with the Americans. Later, after she performed the same ritual services for Seoul, she was invited (indeed expected by Korean authorities) to tour South Korea with the flame. We travelled together and had many interviews and casual conversations, and in statements echoed by high priestesses before and after her, Katerina always said in public and in private that while she always knew perfectly well that she was a (classically trained) stage and television actress, when she performed as the priestess 'she became the priestess'. I was privileged to observe first-hand how the day-to-day adulation of Korean publics, both popular and elite, transformed Katerina Didaskalou's experience of herself in a way familiar to anthropologists from, for example, Lévi-Strauss' account ('The Sorcerer and his Magic') of how the Kwakiutl Quesalid became a shaman.

I also observed how irritated the top HOC officials and Greek IOC members could become when – to repeat the expression I have heard them use several times in such contexts over the years – mere HOC 'employees' garner greater transnational recognition and attention than their bosses do. I was assured by an IOC member in Greece, when I later enquired, that Didaskalou was not invited back as priestess after Seoul 'because we just like to change'. However, other insiders insisted that these male leaders felt she had become too well known and too 'big' for her role. The intense respect and friendship Nassos Kritsinelis himself had earned abroad, particularly in the Anglo-Saxon world, may likewise have contributed to the decision of Lambis Nikolaou to put Kritsinelis on the bench for 2000 Sydney OFR.

Of course, status rivalries between superiors and line staff are evident in any organization, but in this Greek context, ritual is involved. The relevant 'staff' are also ritual actors and become known to outsiders as such, not as someone else's 'employees'. Moreover, there is no official role for the IOC members in Greece in the conventional OFR rituals and the president of the HOC only makes a preliminary speech outside the sanctuary at the Olympia flame lighting and hands over the lantern to the president of the OCOG in the Panathenaic Stadium in Athens. Otherwise, these top officials are not ritually marked and are rarely to be seen out on the relay. In these facts and relations lie certain clues, I believe, as to why the Hellenic Olympic leadership was so surprisingly willing in Athens 2004, as Kritsinelis says, not just to capitulate to but even to augment the 'foreign', 'tasteless', and 'sacrilegious' OFR practices they had previously claimed moral authority for resisting.

[6] See MacAloon, 'Greek-American-IOC Relations', this volume.

[7] Ordinary spectators (and unaccredited cameramen) can choose to observe directly the actual flame-lighting moment by positioning themselves not in the stadium but on the road looking down on the *altis* from the flank of the Kronos Hill.

    The career of Maria Hors as a widely admired choreographer, ritual officiant, and senior priestess stretches back through the entire existence of the flame-lighting ceremony, her having appeared as a young girl in the initial performance in 1936.

[8] See Herzfeld, *Ours Once More*; Fermor, *Roumeli*; MacAloon, *This Great Symbol*.

[9] Institutional relations among the HOC, the political parties, and the government in Greece have been extremely complicated through recent decades. To simplify, the leadership of the HOC has changed with the governmental ruling party, except that if the government changes during an Olympic year, the existing HOC administration stays put until the Games are concluded. Entering the Olympic year of 2000, the HOC like the government was PASOK-dominated, and HOC president Lambis Nikolaou took the flame relay reins away from Kritsinelis in what was as much a gesture of arbitrary personal as of political power, somewhat typical of this mercurial Greek sports leader through his career. Though Nea Demokratia (NEA) won the government back from PASOK early in 2004, Nikolaou and his team remained in charge through the flame-lighting ceremony and initial relay segment from Olympia to Athens. By this time Kritsinelis was with ATHOC not the HOC and so would not have been formally in charge of these rituals in any case, the HOC guarding closely its own historical prerogative. ATHOC took control of the second and third segments of the relay, the international segment and the tour of Greece that ended in the Olympic opening ceremony, with the HOC having only a monitoring role. By the time of these events, as discussed in our interview, Kritsinelis had been effectively put under 'house arrest' by his ATHOC superiors.

[10] This 'media platform' made its appearance as a regular part of the caravan in 1984. It was present again in Calgary 1988, though it tended to stay well ahead of the torchbearer most of the time, thus blocking everyone's view less frequently. In the Seoul OFR, a truck full of media was allowed periodically to approach the torchbearer from the side, or occasionally to go in front, but then it was shooed away. It was by no means a permanent part of the caravan, always just in front of the torchbearer and, therefore, always blocking the crowd and the torchbearer's views of one another. This practice came into being with Barcelona and especially with Atlanta, where the media truck was a permanent presence, always just a few feet ahead of the runner. The justifications for this controversial practice are discussed in my interview with Steven McCarthy elsewhere in this edition. Perhaps not incidentally, Kodak, Inc. had become an official supplier of the media van and mounted its own promotions in Atlanta and later in Salt Lake City. The appearance of a lumbering media truck just ahead of the runner in the 2004 Athens relay caused some shock right from the beginning. For example, citizens of Olympia Dimitri and Franca Karabelas complained bitterly to me about the difficulty of seeing their son carry the flame, as one of the first 2004 torchbearers in Olympia. 'Why was this big truck there? We have never seen such a thing before'.

[11] Actually Kritsinelis tried an innovation on the Greek segment of the Barcelona relay that turned out to be more than problematic. He tried to copy a practice he saw and liked in Korea, where every handover across a marked civic–political boundary was formalized between the mayors of the cities or governors of the regions (see MacAloon and Kang, '*Uri Nara*'). But the prefects of Elis and Achaia did not collaborate the way Kritsinelis expected. In the very different political culture of Greece, they turned the episode in a representational power struggle with each other. Kritsinelis cancelled the innovation for the rest of the relay and was more careful about cross-cultural OFR borrowing thereafter. Ironically, unbeknownst to Kritsinelis, the Catalans later did the same thing at the boundaries of prefectures and autonomous communities in Spain, what they called the 'institutional relays' that in Madrid included the King and Queen.

[12] This folk saying really has the force of a curse. Literally 'the flame, your eyes', it means 'if you hurt this flame may you go blind'. I learned the expression after hearing many old people shout it at Kritsinelis and the other officials on the 1992 relay for Barcelona. When the time came to put some Greek into Billy Payne's Olympia speech, I suggested to him that he end with the statement 'The flame, our eyes; the flame, my eyes'. He understood immediately and at Olympia he delivered the line with a passionate sincerity that brought many among the 30,000 present that day to their feet amidst a general acclamation that put paid to long years of Greek and American Olympic conflict embodied in the OFR. See MacAloon, 'Greek/American/IOC Relations', in this volume.

[13] My experience with Kritsinelis had taught me that Olympic and government officials turned up late on the eve of the ceremony and often tried to change the arrangements already made. Sure enough, in such a late night session after all the rest of the Atlanta delegation had retired, Marton Simitsek arrived and announced that on the morrow only Mrs Clinton's speech would be translated from Greek to English. I objected and reminded him that this would entirely be against protocol. He argued that the speech of the OCOG chief was never translated. I told him this was completely wrong and mentioned some lines from Pascal Maragall's speech in 1992. Simitsek glowered and backed off, and Billy Payne's speech was translated appropriately into Greek the next day, my having worked closely on this with Alexis Kostalas, Greek television personality and the HOC's talented interpreter. Simitsek is the Hellenized version of Szymiczek, Marton's father being Otto Symiczek, the long time dean of the IOA whom I knew for many years.

[14] 'I recommended to Rogge that we allow the Greeks to proceed [with the global relay] but on two conditions. The first was that we find sponsors to fund the $50 million budget for the relay so that it did not put a strain on the operation of the Games. Coke and Samsung were quickly persuaded to back the project. The second precondition was that the Greeks outsource the operation of the global relay and getting the Olympic flame back to Greece on time to an experienced operator. It was not that the Greeks could not do it themselves, but every capable executive was required back in Athens to prepare for the Games. I gave the organizers the names of two executives who had successfully staged previous Olympic relays ... The ATHOC team ... fully accepted the IOC's dictate ... George Bolos, who had by now proved himself highly effective at delivering the Athens marketing programme, was tasked with taking over the management of the torch relay. He selected Steve McCarthy and his company Além' (Payne, *Olympic Turnaround*, 267—8).

This passage is disingenuous in certain respects. Coca-Cola and Samsung hardly needed to be 'persuaded'. Coke was fiercely lobbying on all fronts to get hold of this 'presenting partner' sponsorship. The fact that Di Henry was associated with the rejection of Coca-Cola as a sponsor for the Sydney relay, a development from which the company was still smarting, while Steve McCarthy had successfully cooperated with Coke during the Atlanta and Salt Lake relays contextualized the outsourcing deliberations on all sides. The notion that ATHOC simply accepted 'dictates' from the IOC is hardly true, as this Kritsinelis interview, the leak of Payne's correspondence to the press, and the parliamentary debate alone make plain. During his tenure, Michael Payne spent no time 'on the ground' with the flame relay. Moreover, his book was written after his departure from the IOC, and like many in his profession, he cannot always stop marketing himself. *Dictat* certainly does, however, represent the wishful fantasies of the IOC throughout the Samaranch years. As Payne acknowledges (*Olympic Turnaround*, 125–31), the IOC was slow to understand the power and significance of the OFR, and he correctly attributes, in my judgment, the IOC's growing attention to the relay and getting Greek relay forces under more control to the dramas of Los Angeles 1984.

By late 2006, Payne could be more sceptical of the IOC/Coca-Cola relationship around the flame relay, as consolidated in August 2005 contract extending Coke's Olympic sponsorship for an unprecedented 12 years. In a November 2006 interview with me in Lausanne, Payne revealed that this contract contains an explicit first right of refusal for all subsequent flame relay sponsorships. While for Payne, this only 'makes the *de facto, de jure*', it explicitly tied the hands – as Beijing was shortly to find out – of any OCOG wishing to follow Sydney and Lillehammer in refusing to give a consumer products company its flame relay sponsorship. In 2006, Payne himself was more concerned with other areas in which, in his opinion, 'the Rogge regime gave away the store to Coke' in this contract.

[15] The change of government was a key factor, many would say the chief factor, in the unexpected success of the Athens Olympics. The new government had every incentive to expose the actual state of the Olympic planning, construction, and finances left behind by the PASOK regime and to mobilize every resource so that NEA would not be tarnished by a failed Games just a few months after taking power.

[16] A succession of OCOGs has asked me where I think they should take the OFR in their countries. I always respond, 'What in your country would the Olympic flame want to see?' Relay officials have later told me that this suggestion has always turned out to be a useful guide, whatever eyebrows it initially raised. Listening to Nassos Kritsinelis' exegeses of his destination choices was one inspiration for this pedagogical slogan that has now become a part of flame relay community culture.

[17] See Miller, *Ancient Greek Athletics*. Unlike many classicists and classical archaeologists who shy away from any inventions of tradition evoking the ancient world in modern form, such as the OFR, Miller, the distinguished University of California excavator of Nemea, has been an ardent participant and producer of this sort of 'restored behaviour' (see Figure 2). He was, with Kritsinelis, the main designer of the powerful celebrations in the ancient stadium at Nemea for the 2004 OFR. When the flame caravan moved on that day, Sara Brewster and I stayed on in the excavation workshops for a deeply moving traditional party that the local villagers, priests, mayors, and Prof. Miller gave for one another. In other years, Miller's 'New Nemean Games' have given hundreds of Greek school children and ordinary people from around the world – not to mention the financial supporters of his excavations – the opportunity to race in sandals and tunic down the actual floor of an ancient Greek stadium.

[18] A.D. Frazier, Jr was an investment banker who became the chief operating and financial officer of the Atlanta Olympic Games, himself raising or managing over $1 billion in private financing. Since 1996, Frazier has subsequently stayed away from anything Olympic, except in 2002, when he carried the Olympic flame and made the end-of-day celebration speech in Chicago as a part of the Salt Lake City OFR.

[19] Non-Olympian celebrities are contracted by sponsors and in return for the privilege and publicity of carrying the flame appear at associated sponsor events and promotions. By focusing on these persons, media do their part to further highlight sponsor participation and 'value'. For example, on the licensed website of a for-profit supplier of relay photos, the international relay torchbearers highlighted include Naomi Campbell, Sir Richard Branson, Sean 'P. Diddy' Combs, Jon Kabira, Emi Takeuchi, Ellen DeGeneres, Sylvester Stallone, and Tom Cruise, some captioned as participating in a 'Samsung Olympic Torch Relay Celebration'. (www.wireimage.com/ GalleryListing, accessed May 14, 2007).

[20] Interview with Marc Maes, Beijing, July 2006. A respected sport manager and leader in the Olympic Academy movement, Dr. Maes was invited to contribute to this volume, but circumstances prevented him from doing so. In our interview, he further told me that in his report to the IOC, which has remained confidential, he complained on behalf of the European NOCs about eventual financial costs to them that they felt the ATHOC/Além advance team had promised would be borne by Coca-Cola and Samsung. In our August, 2006 interviews, Além president Steve McCarthy strongly denied that there was ever any confusion on financing or backtracking with the international relay NOCs after their advance meetings.

[21] A few days after this interview with Kritsinelis, I raised this matter with Gilbert Felli, Executive Director of the Olympic Games, at the IOC headquarters in Lausanne. Felli was also taken aback by these numbers and agreed that the situation had to be remedied. Perhaps in response, BOCOG's 25 June 2007 press release announcing torchbearer selection policies for the Beijing relay stressed 'transparency' and specified that among the 'selection entities', the 'presenting partners' (Coke, Samsung, Lenovo) would choose 6000 out of the 21,880 torchbearers and 750 out of the 5000 escort runners. (BOCOG website http://torchrelay.beijing2008.cn/en/torchbearers, accessed on July 2, 2007).

[22] M. Douglas Ivester, Coca-Cola Chairman and CEO. Mr Ivester had actually retired as CEO in 2000, but was still serving as a company adviser in the period Kritsinelis is discussing.

[23] Miller, *Ancient Greek Athletics*, 141–2.

[24] The increasingly transnational character of Olympic Games administrative work is a main theme of the essays in this volume. This trend can be artificially exaggerated by the 'world's best practices' managerial ideology and by specific interventions by IOC headquarters. After Samaranch issued his famous 'yellow card' to ATHOC over the worrisome delays in its preparations, pressure mounted on the Greeks to accept highly paid consultants from SOCOG who were being pressed upon them by the IOC managerial staff. Sydney was a successful Olympics and some experience is certainly better than none. However, the notion that good management practices are free of cultural context, that what worked in Australia will work in Greece, or what worked in Greece will work in The People's Republic of China can prove to be the height of naiveté and even folly. ATHOC certainly learned from watching SOCOG, but it also wasted a pile of money on arrogant and ethnocentric Australian consultants who added little or no value to the Athenian project.

Former OCOG officials who try to sell their services as consultants to subsequent OCOGs are rarely modest or precise, in my experience, about their past responsibilities and achievements. Instead they seem to count condescendingly on the supposed naiveté of the next group of foreigners down the line. I can testify first-hand how we in Chicago, during our recent Olympic bid, received on a nearly daily basis solicitations from would-be consultants the majority of whom seemed not to imagine that we already knew or were one phone call away from knowing just how exaggerated their claims of expertise could be.

[25] During interviews with high BOCOG officials in Beijing in July 2006, an experienced European colleague and I were repeatedly pressed as to whether there was not some way to avoid Coca-Cola as a flame relay sponsor in China. These Chinese officials were highly aware of the problems Coke operatives had caused out on past relays and were concerned by the fact that during the Torino OFR earlier that year, there had occurred the very first attacks in history on the relay caravan itself by political protesters. These included Italians who singled out Coke as the emblem of what they took to be rapacious neo-liberal globalization threatening their regional ecology with unwanted development projects.

I could only speculate as to what additional national political and cultural considerations were at work behind our Chinese colleagues' concerns, but I left convinced that such things were also very important to them. Our BOCOG interlocutors clearly indicated that they preferred only national sponsors for their OFR, but that they would need five or more to make this financially viable. The IOC, they told us, was insisting that this would be too many sponsors and would result in disruption and 'sponsor clutter'. So BOCOG felt pressured by the IOC to accept Coke and Samsung.

I only learned four months later about Coke's right of first refusal of flame relay sponsorship established in its most recent contract with the IOC, and I have no idea whether our BOCOG interlocutors knew about this at the time of our conversations. In any case, we sensed that our BOCOG OFR friends were pessimistic about the likelihood of evading Coke, and that they probably sensed the same pessimism from us.

Some months later, it was announced that Samsung would be the 'presenting partner' on the international segment of the Beijing 2008 OFR, while Coke would be the presenting partner on the domestic China relay. A high IOC official gave me to understand that this was a very positive outcome, because Samsung was far less likely to inspire protests along the international route than Coke, while Coke got what it really wanted, further prestigious exposure to the Chinese domestic market. BOCOG, he further asserted, would benefit from Coke's operational expertise in flame relays. Maxxam Ltd, Além's rival as an international OFR operations firm, collaborated on the international segment of the Beijing relay – which as we know and as is analysed elsewhere in the volume – was thrown into chaos by worldwide protests against China's crackdown on Tibet.

References

Barney, Robert, and Anthony Bijerk. 'The Genesis of Sacred Fire in Olympic Celebration'. *Journal of Olympic History* 13, no. 2 (2005): 6–27.

Borgers, Walter. *Olympic Torch Relays*. Kassel: Agon Sportverlag, 1996.

Butler, E.M. *The Tryanny of Greece Over Germany*. Boston, MA: Beacon, 1958.

Fermor, Patrick L. *Roumeli: Travels in Northern Greece*. London: John Murray, 1966.

Herzfeld, Michael. *Ours Once More: Folklore, Ideology, and the Making of Modern Greece*. Austin, TX: University of Texas Press, 1982.

Kritsinelis, Athanassios. 'Lighting Ceremony of the Olympic Flame: Technical Specifications of the Olympic Torch Relay'. *International Olympic Academy Reports* (1996): 159–69.

Lennartz, Karl. 'The Genesis of Legends'. *Journal of Olympic History* 5, no. 1 (1997): 8–11.

Lévi-Strauss, Claude. 'The Sorcerer and His Magic'. *In His Structural Anthropology*, 167–85. New York: Basic Books, 1963.

MacAloon, John J. *This Great Symbol: Pierre de Coubertin and the Origins of the Modern Olympic Games*. 2nd ed. London: Routledge, 2008.

MacAloon, John J. 'Postscript: History as Anthropology'. *International Journal of the History of Sport* 23, nos. 3–4 (2006): 666–86.

MacAloon, John J., and Kang Shin-pyo. 'Uri Nara: Korean Nationalism, the Seoul Olympics, and Contemporary Anthropology'. In *Toward One World Beyond All Boundaries: The Seoul Olympic Anniversary Conference*, edited by Koh Byong-ik, 117–59, Vol 1. Seoul: Poong Nam Publishers, 1990.

Miller, Stephen G. *Ancient Greek Athletics*. New Haven, CT: Yale University Press, 2004.

Payne, Michael. *Olympic Turnaround*. London: London Business Press, 2005.

Ueberroth, Peter. *Made in America*. New York: Morrow, 1985.

The 2004 International Relay: a Greek around the world with the Olympic Flame

Pinelopi B. Amelidou

Division of the Social Sciences, The University of Chicago, Chicago, IL, USA

This paper presents a first-hand experience of the 2004 Athens International Olympic Flame Relay (IOFR) from the perspective of one of the Greek team members who accompanied the flame. It provides a rich description of the mechanics of the relay itself, demonstrating that it involved complex international exchanges. It is about much more than the torchbearers. The author describes life on the road with the flame, highlighting the cultural, political, and personal challenges entailed in this endeavour. It explores the tensions: between sponsor interests and the spirit of Olympism; from professional 'world's best practices' implementation of the relay to volunteers' expectations of their roles and experiences; and in the division of labour between the International Olympic Committee (IOC), National Olympic Committees (NOCs), and Olympic Games Organizing Committees (OCOGs) as stakeholders.

Introduction

A few years have passed since 25 March 2004, when the Olympic Flame was lit in Ancient Olympia, in Greece, for the Athens Olympic Games. This flame would travel more globally than any other, before it eventually entered the Olympic Stadium of Athens on August 13 for the Olympic opening ceremonies.

I was in Olympia on the day of the lighting ceremony, and as I watched the flame on the torch of the first torchbearer, I received a text message from a friend that said: 'It started, there's no way back now. Good luck'. I still do not know if he meant the actual event of the Games – the lighting of the Olympic Flame is the inaugural event that leads to the Opening Ceremony – or he wanted to wish good luck to all of us that would be a part of the relay. I tried to imagine what it was going to be like to be a part of this epic relay. I think I had not then realized what would follow. Even though I had met with Além International Management executives Steven McCarthy and Gillian Hamburger in January for an interview about my volunteer work in the International Olympic Flame Relay (IOFR), it was only after April 2004, when I attended the test event of the IOFR in Colorado, USA, that I realized how unique this event would be.[1]

That was not the first time I was involved with an Olympic project. In 1990, I started working part-time at the International Olympic Academy (IOA) in Ancient Olympia. After 1995, having found a permanent job, I stopped employment with the IOA, but I returned there as a participant in 1997 and 1998, and between 1999 and 2005, I was invited as a discussion group coordinator during the main session for young participants. I also worked as a volunteer during the Sydney 2000 Olympic Games.

But although the IOA is a major cradle for understanding the Olympic Movement and the Olympic Games,[2] my initial exposure to the movement began much earlier. Both my brother and I grew up in an 'Olympic' environment as our late father, Byron Amelides, worked for the Hellenic Olympic Committee (HOC) from 1972 until his death in 2001. My attitude towards the torch relay up to that point was not only affected by my 'Olympic' past, but was also shaped by my own participation in the 1996 Olympic Flame Relay for the Atlanta Olympic Games in Greece and in Chicago as a torchbearer myself, when I travelled with an HOC delegation of young people to the United States as part of Atlanta's flame relay celebration of the Olympic Centennial.

The Olympic Flame Relay

The Olympic Flame Relay takes place every year the Olympic Games are held. The Olympic Flame is lit in Ancient Olympia, Greece, at the archaeological site,[3] some time before the Games. It is carried by torchbearers, or kept in a lantern when transported by other means, and finally enters the Olympic Stadium, on the night of the Opening Ceremony, to mark the beginning of the Games in each host city.

Ever since the 1936 Berlin Olympic Games, a torch relay has been organized under the auspices of the Hellenic Olympic Committee (HOC).[4] However, in the International Olympic Committee's (IOC) *Olympic Charter*, this relationship is obscured, as it is stated that 'the Olympic Flame is the flame which is kindled in Olympia under the authority of the IOC' and the document recognizes the HOC only as the contracting party with the Olympic Games Organizing Committees (OCOGs). In practice though, the HOC is responsible for the lighting ceremony and the execution of the relay up to Athens. The Olympic Flame, after arriving in Athens, is handed over to the OCOG for that year. After that point, the OCOG is responsible for the transfer of the flame to the country which will host the Games, the execution of the torch relay up within the country, the transportation of the flame within the Olympic Stadium, the lighting of the cauldron there for the duration of the Games, and finally for its extinction during the closing ceremonies.

During the Athens 2004 Olympic Games an interesting 'split' of torch relays took place, a split that highlights the different perspectives within the Olympic Movement. The HOC followed tradition and organized the Olympic flame-lighting ceremony in Ancient Olympia, on 25 March 2004. Although they faced a lot of criticism from the Greek public for choosing this date for the lighting ceremony – March 25 is a national holiday, in commemoration of the Greek revolution against the Ottoman Empire in 1821 – the HOC went ahead with their decision, since they also wanted to commemorate the date of the first modern Olympic Games which were held in Athens, in 1896. The HOC president and IOC member in Greece, Mr. Lambis Nikolaou, announced the decision of the HOC during the presentation of the Athens 2004 Olympic Flame Relay at the Athens Organizing Committee (ATHOC) offices, on 26 November 2003:

> The Torch Relay Committee has decided after detailed discussions to suggest the 25th of March 2004 as the day of the lighting of the Torch in order to link the 2004 Games with those of 1896, when that date was chosen for the Lighting Ceremony. The decision of the Torch Relay Committee on the 25th of March was an absolute need[5] because the opportunity to organize the Olympic Games in 1996 had been lost. So, we wished to link up with 1896. Thus, for the Games of 2004, the only way to link up with 1896 was to have the coincidence of dates of the lighting of the torch with 1896.[6] This was adopted unanimously. So the procedure that we suggest is that, after seven days of running, it will be brought by helicopter from the Temple of Aphaea in Aigina to Zappeio, Athens.

The seven days of running, as was announced in Mr. Nikolaou's speech, were organized by the HOC as is usually the case. The flame was then passed on to the ATHOC president, Mrs. Gianna Angelopoulou-Daskalaki and was then kept in a cauldron in front of the Panathenaic Stadium until 2 June 2004.[7]

On June 2, the flame was brought to the airport by the ATHOC president. There, she handed the flame, in a lantern, to the IOFR manager on the 'Zeus' airplane that would take the Olympic Flame around the world (see Figure 1). The international journey lasted 37 days until July 9, when the flame landed on Greek soil again, on the island of Crete. There, the ATHOC president was again present. She stepped down the airplane stairway with the flame in a lantern and gave it to the first torchbearer for this third and final segment of the relay. After that point, a different team from ATHOC itself was responsible for the execution of the torch relay, which lasted 35 days until August 13, when it entered the Olympic Stadium. In summary, the HOC team organized the first segment of the relay that visited Peloponnesus and the islands of Saronikos bay, near Athens. Then, a company called Além International Management organized the IOFR, and finally the ATHOC team executed the torch relay throughout the rest of Greece, culminating on the night of the Opening Ceremony.

The two latter teams were organized under one manager in ATHOC, with two divisions, the international part operated by Além and the Greek part operated by ATHOC's personnel. Both divisions were under ATHOC's General Manager of Marketing. Neither of these two divisions was responsible for the first segment, which was an exclusive organization of the HOC. The only common factors were the official sponsors of the relay, Coca-Cola and Samsung, present, although with some minor differences, throughout all three segments of the relay.

Figure 1.   The 'Zeus' aircraft that ferried the 2004 Olympic Flame around the world. Photo by the author (Pinelopi B. Amelidou).

My role

The IOFR started its global journey on 2 June 2004 from Athens, and the first stop was Sydney, on June 4. After visiting 33 cities in 27 countries it ended on 9 July 2004 in Crete, Greece. I was a member of the team that took the flame around the world, and my job description was 'VIP coordinator'. This meant that in cooperation with another member of the team, we would take care of the VIP guests of the IOFR. When I joined the team on June 2, I realized that I would mainly escort the HOC representatives, Mr. George Chalkides and Mr. Andreas Arvanites (Mr. Arvanites left the relay in Paris, and he was replaced by Mr. Charalambos Zoides), acting as their translator. Of course, there were ATHOC representatives too, Mr. Spyros Lambranides and Mrs. Dimitra Evans. However, early on Mr. Lambranides distanced himself from the 'Greek' representatives, and from Seoul onwards he usually travelled in another vehicle, and not with the official VIPs.

I will describe here an interesting event that took place that morning in Seoul. Mr. Lambranides, out of the blue, attacked me, yelling at me in English, for 'not doing my job properly, and not taking good care of Mr. Chalkides and Mr. Arvanitis'. When I asked him to keep his voice down and talk properly (I also spoke in English), I pointed out that I was a member of the Além team and that my boss Steven McCarthy would not tolerate this attitude. Furthermore, neither would I. He insisted that *he* was my boss. I said 'No, Além is paying me, and if you have a problem with me, go talk to Steve'. I also pointed out that neither 'Mr. Chalkides nor Mr. Arvanitis had ever expressed any complaints about my performance'. I then left him to deal with another colleague who was telling him 'to stop now treating people like this'. I went to the bus where the HOC people (along with Mrs. Evans) were and asked them if they had ever expressed any complaints about my work. They denied such a thing. I have to add here, before giving my explanation of this situation, that McCarthy and Hamburger gave me their full support that evening and reassured me that Mr. Lambranides was not my boss. I was almost sure even from the moment he started the row that he had other motives. In fact, he wanted to be set apart from the HOC representatives, and he was trying to use me as a pretext to keep them away from him. Lambranides wanted to play what he took to be the superior role of ATHOC representative, when Mr. George Bolos was not with us.[8] Lambranides wanted to listen to no 'grumbling' if things were not done the 'HOC way' or to have any association at all with the HOC people, whom he regarded as not 'polished diplomats' such as he was. By the middle of the trip, even his relationship with Mrs. Evans had soured. I share this anecdote to show that common nationality and pride in this global exposure for Greece were not enough to overcome institutional tensions and personal status contests among the Greek delegation on the IOFR.

The team

The team had about 100 members ferried by two jumbo jets: the official airplane called 'Zeus' that was painted with the logo of the IOFR (see Figure 1) and the second one, that was called 'Hera' and did not have any special markings.[9] The crew was divided between these two airplanes with approximately 65% of the personnel on Zeus and 35% on Hera. Hera was generally flying two hours ahead of Zeus. The idea behind this was that if for any reason one of the two airplanes could not take off from the previous city or land in the next city, the IOFR could still take place with a back-up team. All events went according to plan and the Hera back-up plan did not have to be activated. The official ceremonies, with the ATHOC representative arriving in the city while holding the Olympic Flame in a lantern each time always awaited Zeus' arrival.

The route

The IOFR route was: Sydney, Melbourne, Tokyo, Seoul, Beijing, New Delhi, Cairo, Cape Town, Rio de Janeiro, Mexico City, Los Angeles, Saint Louis, Atlanta, New York, Montreal, Antwerp, Brussels, Amsterdam, Geneva, Lausanne, Paris, London, Madrid, Barcelona, Rome, Munich, Berlin, Stockholm, Helsinki, Moscow, Kiev, Istanbul, and Sofia, Cyprus. Out of the 33 cities, 20[10] had organized Olympic Games. Four[11] had been included because they represented their broader geographical and cultural regions. Other cities[12] hosted international organizations like the United Nations in New York and the city of Brussels, where most of the European Union's offices are located. Finally Lausanne was included as the IOC's headquarters city. Also included on the itinerary were: Kiev, which had repeatedly asked ATHOC to be included; Sofia, as a neighbouring Balkan capital; Istanbul, to show the improvement of Greek–Turkish relations; and Beijing as the future host city of the 2008 Olympic Games. The city of Madrid was added at the last minute. I found out when we were in Brussels, almost a week before, that a small torch relay would take place in Madrid on the morning of June 28. The two airplanes arrived as planned at the Barcelona airport. Then, the crew was split; most remained at the airport, while about 10 of the crew flew on to Madrid to execute a small OFR there, with no more than 20 torchbearers. On their return from Madrid, the planned OFR started in Barcelona.[13] Madrid was added because the other cities that were candidates for the 2012 Olympic Games had been included in the IOFR because either they had organized Olympic Games before or they hosted international organizations (United Nations in New York, United Nations office in Geneva, European Union in Brussels).[14] Madrid, the fifth candidate city, complained about this, pushed hard, and was able to have a small torch relay in the city. In Cyprus, the torch relay was organized as an event throughout the island, not visiting just one city. However, it did not visit the sector that has been occupied by the Turkish army since 1974 and did not cross parts of the island where British military bases are located.

A day on the International Olympic Flame Relay

The IOFR daily journey usually started really early in the morning, sometimes just after midnight. We left the hotel – for example in Tokyo, the alarm clock rang at 1:30 in the morning to leave from the hotel at 2:00 – and headed to airport. We passed all normal security checks and boarded the planes. The only thing we did not go through was the baggage check-in, because our main luggage was always kept on the plane. We arrived on the plane, and went straight to our assigned seats. Although the food was excellent and plentiful, most of the time we fell asleep instantly. As we were arriving in the next city, and just before landing, we were given the directions for the day: who is going to be waiting for us at the airport,[15] where the starting point would be– most of the time somewhere within the city and not the airport – and some guidelines about the caravan vehicles. After landing, we passed through passport control – in most cases the procedure was collective, and we just waited in the VIP room – then we met the vehicles and headed to the starting point. There, we took our positions to form the caravan and awaited the start signal. The IOFR route in every city had some short breaks at significant city monuments lasting not more than 30 minutes. The breaks throughout the day were no more than three, and in most cities only two. During these breaks the personnel had the opportunity to eat and visit the restrooms. The day ended at the celebration site of every city, where the Olympic Flame was taken back into the lantern, to be transferred to the hotel. The celebration site was a significant one in every city. For example, in New York it was Times Square and in

Paris it was the Eiffel Tower. The last torchbearer was usually an important sports personality. For example, in Kiev it was the Olympic gold medallist and IOC member for Ukraine, Sergey Bubka, and in Rio de Janeiro, it was the famous football player Ronaldo.

Throughout the relay, the torchbearers were active athletes, former athletes, important figures in the society, 'community heroes', and ordinary citizens. The selection process in all cities was the same: 35% were appointed by Coca-Cola, 35% by Samsung, and 30% by the Municipality often with the cooperation of the NOC. The official policy was that if the torchbearers wished to keep the torch to commemorate the event they had to pay €360 euros towards its cost. However, if the torchbearer had been selected by a sponsor, the sponsor had already paid for the torch. Now this raises the question as to why the important figures in the society that were *chosen* to run had to pay for their torch, while 70% of the runners did not. This especially became an issue in countries where most people could never have afforded to buy the torch. It is perhaps no surprise that some torches 'got lost' during the IOFR.

After the end of the ceremony at the celebration sites, which included speeches by the ATHOC representative and city's representative, the caravan headed to the hotel. If the hotel was owned by Marriott, which was the official supplier, a small welcome was organized to receive the flame in a lantern. The organizers gave a commemorative torch to the hotel as a gift. The crew had dinner and went to sleep until the next morning's wake-up call. The schedule differed in four cities: Beijing, Rio de Janeiro, Brussels, and Moscow, where the majority of the crew rested a second day, while a short torch relay route was executed by a very small team.

We can certainly say that the IOFR was a project that was designed as a top-down global event. It operated under the so-called 'world's best practices model', and under Além International's management. It had the same characteristics in every city, the same selection process, the same torch, the same uniforms for the torchbearers, the same sponsors, and the same crew that planned, organized and finally executed the project.

The International Olympic Flame Relay on the road

First appeared the 'advance' caravan (a series largely of sponsor vehicles responsible for 'crowd building' before the arrival of the core caravan). The advance caravan consisted of: a local law enforcement vehicle; three Samsung crowd-building/advertising vehicles; and three Coca-Cola crowd-building/advertising vehicles. Then followed the 'core caravan'. The following is a description of these vehicles in the order in which they passed by a standing viewer.

- 'Pilot' vehicle: advanced the relay route, usually several minutes ahead of the core caravan. The Pilot's primary function was to check and establish pre-determined torchbearer exchange points as well as alert the Command vehicle of any route changes or operational dynamics.
- Two security motorcycles.
- 'Drop-Off Shuttle': the van that was dropping off the subsequent torchbearers in their respective positions, where they would wait for the flame to arrive.
- 'Media 1' vehicle: the van or truck that carried all the cameramen and the photographers on-board. They would film and take photos of each torchbearer. This vehicle would precede the torchbearer by only two metres (sometimes as little as one metre).
- Two security motorcycles.

- The torchbearer.
- Two security motorcycles.
- The 'Command' vehicle': it gave directions about the pace and style, and dealt with any problems that might arise. It ensured the efficiency of the caravan, and it had the overall command and control of the operation.
- The 'Caravan Services One' vehicle: it carried the lanterns with the back-up flames, extra torches in case the flame went out, and also served as a resting place for the escort runners. It also carried an extra torch that had more fuel, for adverse weather conditions.
- The 'Caravan Services Two' vehicle: it provided the same services as the previous vehicle and was only used in some cities. It was not used in cities that had requested elimination of the caravan, due to small streets or heavy traffic in the city.
- The 'VIP' vehicle: it carried the HOC and ATHOC representatives who were escorting the flame. In some cases, VIPs from the city were hosted in the same vehicle.
- The 'Media Two' vehicle': it did not operate in all cities. It gave the chance for local journalists to escort the torch relay.
- The 'Pick-Up Shuttle': it picked up the torchbearers after they had completed their part of the relay.
- The 'Broom' vehicle: it ensured that everything was fine in the back of the caravan.
- Two security motorcycles.

Therefore, there were at least nine vehicles to accompany a single person, not to mention the eight motorcycles that surrounded the torchbearer.

Security

I kept a journal throughout the trip, starting from the flight to Sydney for our first stop until our return to Greece, in Crete. The journal was kept on a daily basis, trying to highlight all the important moments of each day and in addition all the small details that I thought were interesting for further exploration.

I observed that one of the main concerns in the IOFR was security; security for the torchbearer, for the flame, and for the flame relay as an organization. This is underlined by the four, or in some cases eight escort runners who surrounded the torchbearer. They were all dedicated to protecting the torchbearer. Was security needed to protect the torchbearer? Or was it needed to protect the flame, to ensure its integrity? Or in the end to ensure that the torch relay as an organizational process was being executed with success?

This organization repeated the model used in 1996 and 2002 by Além, with employees who had participated in both of these torch relays. The 'protagonist' is the torchbearer. S/he is the principal actor in this ceremony. But it seems that s/he is also the main actor in a much bigger show. The whole scene of the torchbearer running, hearing the sirens of the motorcyclists, the number of the motorcyclists, the large number of the vehicles comprising the caravan, and the fact that the torchbearer is being treated in this model as a VIP gives more the impression of a show rather than that of a ceremony (see Figure 2).

MacAloon has argued that the Olympic Flame Relay is an event that everybody can see, you just have to place yourself where it is passing,[16] but this is now struggling to be the case. It is extremely hard to witness the torchbearer for more than a few seconds, as I observed trying to watch two of my good friends who were torchbearers in Cyprus and Rome. The goal of the 'world's best practices' model appears to be efficiency. If efficiency is the optimum method of getting from one point to the other, then the IOFR succeeded

Figure 2.   In Delhi, IOC member Randhir Singh carries the 2004 Olympic Flame through the Red Fort, an iconic site of Indian independence. Photo by the author (Pinelopi B. Amelidou).

in attaining this goal. But at what ritual cost? It certainly ensured the successful transportation of the flame from one point of the globe to the other, however, was this really the point? The predictability of the IOFR, that it used the same model, applied everywhere, in every city, in every country, in every continent did not recognize the culturally distinctive responses to as well as individual interactions with the flame. Instead, it seemed like the security, which is a major concern in our societies and certainly in the

Olympic environment, was brought very much to the fore. And in so doing it put in jeopardy a basic element of the torch relay, the spiritual element that verifies the relationship between the Olympics as a social movement and the relay.

Media van

The purpose of the Media van is to capture the moment for advertising reasons, either for the commercial sponsors or the OCOG. The media van was usually so close to the torchbearer (one to two metres) that s/he was not able to have visual contact with the audience. Similarly, the audience could not clearly see the torchbearer, since s/he was surrounded by motorcyclists and escort runners. It gave the impression that the whole organization was being executed for the sake of the media, for them to capture the torchbearer running and not for the actual moment of running itself. In this instance, the commercial side appeared to outweigh the spiritual, as the marketing dimension of the world's best practices model intruded on both the experience of running and of witnessing the passage of the flame.

The media van also caused practical as well as ethical concerns. In many cities the local authorities asked for the elimination of the caravan, usually for logistical reasons, due to traffic policy or very narrow streets. The biggest problem was faced in some European cities, especially when the organization had not taken into account the narrow streets of the European cities like Rome and Lausanne. A 'one-size fits all' approach proved a bad fit in more ways than one!

Personnel

The members of the crew were mostly US citizens, with the exception of the driver of the command car, the representatives of the ATHOC and the HOC, the torchbearer hostesses, and one VIP coordinator. We non-Americans accounted for only 10% of the crew. Most of the crew did not speak any languages besides English, which proved a problem when they had to cooperate with local staff. The native English speakers often failed to realize the challenges of language, even when working with those of us who did speak English. Some of the etiquette and courtesy required when conversing in a second language were unclear to the predominantly monolingual team. There were incidents where the vocabulary that was used was slang, which the local people could not understand. This created all kinds of miscommunication and anxiety. In other instances offence was caused by the perceived misuse of language. For example, a nickname was given to a local driver, because his name was too hard for the IOFR staff member to pronounce! Language became another point for potential conflict, and further highlighted the perceived lack of cultural sensitivity that the top-down system came to operate through.

Absence of volunteers in the International Olympic Flame Relay

Olympic volunteers have the opportunity to be a part of a unique international sports event, a global celebration; 'they have the chance to experience the "spirit of the Olympics"'[17] without being athletes themselves. They play a vital role in the actual organization of the Games, while saving enormous amounts of money for the OCOGs. It would be 'no exaggeration to say that the Olympics of today are as much a creation of volunteers as of anyone else'.[18] People have the chance to participate in something so unique and so different from what they do everyday. They feel important; they know they are the essence of the whole effort. They feel they offer something to their country by representing it through their own role, an essential social investment. As Ana Belen Moreno, invoking Durkheim, states, 'volunteerism represents the coming together of individuals to work on a particular project and it generates the feeling of solidarity among the group'.[19] The feeling of social effervescence, so essential to the spirit of the games, rests on the perceived selflessness of volunteerism.

However, there were no volunteers in the IOFR team. There were five people that were chosen from the pool of volunteers, but they were then enrolled among the paid staff. ATHOC officials knew about this, and seemed concerned by the potential public relations impact if it became public knowledge that some volunteers were paid, but they did not do anything to stop it or balance it with something else. I am not sure if this is something they knew before Colorado's test event, but I certainly remember a senior ATHOC official coming to me and underlying to me the importance of keeping this a secret. It seems to me that the concern was not the violation of the ethos of volunteerism, but the fear of the bad publicity should the media find out that ATHOC were paying for more than they needed to!

During my interview with Gillian Hamburger and Steven McCarthy in January, I asked them if I needed to pay for some of my expenses. It was then when they told me that I had to pay nothing – except for my extras in the hotels – and above all, I was going to get paid. I was so surprised I did not even ask how much I would get paid! While still in Colorado I later found out how much money I would receive. It was a huge amount for a month by Greek standards, and I was initially very shocked. However, once we divided it by 24 hours over the 33 days that we were offering our services to Além International, then the money was little. Nevertheless, I had expected to provide my services for free, simply for the honour of taking part. The business model that Além International operates under did not allow for this seemingly irrational response to what would prove to be hard and arduous labour.

Sponsor presence

The IOC forbids the presence of any sponsor within the venues where the Olympic competitions take place. This is referred to as the 'clean venue policy'. Conforming and similar banners outside the venues (stadiums, indoor halls, and so forth.) and in areas where the audience is moving towards or outwards from the competitions are permitted, but there is no advertisement within the venues visible to television cameras. When someone refers to Olympic advertising, this pertains to official, national, or international Olympic sponsors outside the field of play.

This is a rule that was not really applied to the IOFR. Sponsors' vehicles were part of the caravan, even at some distance. There were three promotional trucks from each major sponsor, Coca-Cola and Samsung. Their role was to attract a broader audience to the relay, to rouse up the audience, and to pass around souvenirs and paper flags of the sponsors. The music coming from the vehicles was different than the official song of the torch relay, and the flags and souvenirs did not always bear the logo of the Athens Torch Relay.[20] In most cases the sponsors flags and little banners were more evident in the audience than anything else. ATHOC did not pass out any little flags with the official Athens emblem[21] or the Olympic symbol.[22] ATHOC, as every other organizing committee, had very strict policies regarding the marketing rules for other Olympic sponsors, but their attitude during the IOFR was more lax with respect to Coke and Samsung. This appears to be a contradiction occurring within the same organizing committee.

As I mentioned previously, the HOC is responsible for the torch relay within Greece, until they pass the flame to the respective OCOGs. Never before had they accepted the presence of sponsors within Greece. The HOC does not usually cooperate with sponsors. They are used to receiving funds from the Hellenic Ministry of Culture and the national lottery, and thus they do not seek sponsorship. ATHOC, closely following the IOC practices, accepted the presence of sponsors in the torch relay in all three parts and treated them with extreme tolerance as opposed to the national sponsors in other events. Having worked for a national sponsor myself and knowing ATHOC's rules, I witnessed many of the activities the sponsors did during the IOFR which were against the guidelines that the ATHOC has given to the national/international sponsors of the Games.

An example is the issue of flags. During the IOFR, little flags were distributed to the public but surprisingly enough, were not the ATHOC ones. They were Samsung's flags, size 20 cm × 50 cm with a single logo on: SAMSUNG. There was no ATHOC logo on these flags, nor any IOFR logo! Coca-Cola was more IOFR-oriented in this and was giving little flags with Coca-Cola on them, and the name of the city as well as the IOFR logo on. I remember that we had already reached Tokyo (our third city) and George Bolos was trying to solve the issue. I imagine that Coca-Cola was furious with the photos of a public with big blue flags! I don't think that the issue was ever solved. It is simple to prove, just by looking at the photos of the IOFR: Samsung and Coca-Cola flags! As to my question of why there were no ATHOC or Greek flags given to the public, I got the response that ATHOC had no budget. The only exception was Tokyo; the audience was full of Greek flags that had been distributed by the Greek Office of Tourism in Japan. I would have much preferred to see ATHOC flags in the hands of the people around the world, but I cannot lie: it was a moral satisfaction to witness the Japanese leaving behind the flags of the sponsors and taking the Greek ones home after the Torch Relay was over that day.

Conclusion

Whether this huge scale project was successful in achieving its goals is too complex to be answered in this paper. There were elements that detracted from the impact that it had on people, and these were heavy security around the torchbearer, the media van preceding him/her, the absence of volunteers, the lack of employees with some multicultural background and understanding, and finally the absence of firm regulations for the sponsors.

Overall, the IOFR did not lose its essence completely, which is the human contact with the flame. The flame is like a mirror that can be interpreted for different reasons by each person. It has subjectivity and that is its power. Unfortunately, the model ATHOC and its partner Além International used gave too much weight to the security, and that almost lost the important attribute which was the flame. If the flame cannot be seen, if the torchbearer is visible only by the media people in the media van for promotional purposes, then the Olympic Flame Relay is being transformed from a special ritual to just another television event. But the goal is not to televise the event, it is primarily to make people participate and to make them emotionally moved. The aim should be to have as many participants as possible in these public events. By participating and feeling emotions during the IOFR, people engage themselves with what is called the 'Olympic Movement'.[23] It is an experience no one forgets and no one stays untouched by it.

The different treatment that the sponsors of the IOFR had in comparison with the national and international sponsors of the Olympic Games shows us that the IOC needs to be present in efforts like this. This was the first global torch relay. It reached places where the Olympic Games had never been held, and may never be held in the future. But the

Olympic Flame Relay was there, and so should the IOC be as the governing body of the Olympic Movement. To understand the importance, the IOC needs to experience the Olympic Flame Relay as a part of the Olympic Movement and to realize what a great tool the IOFR is in spreading the Olympic Movement around the world.

I hope that in the future, the elements of participation and emotions will not be neglected in subsequent Olympic Flame Relays. I also hope, that these efforts in bringing the Olympic Movement closer to people, to all sorts of people, will continue and that the IOFR, focusing more on the human interaction, will become a tradition to follow. For the moment, the IOC has banned international relays in reaction to Beijing, but the future for this global ritual remains open.

Notes

1   I would like to thank my brother Panos, who was then working for ATHOC designing the route of the domestic relay. He called me one day at my office where I worked full-time for the official bank of the Athens Olympic Games on its sponsorship. My brother asked: 'Would you like to go around the world in a month?' In response, I asked if I seemed like Phileas Fogg to him? He suggested that I should send my resume to Além International, the company that was undertaking the execution of the project, and due to my past Olympic experiences and language skills I should volunteer.

2   'The IOA is like the Olympic Village without the anxiety of competition'. Bruce Kidd, personal communication, April 2005.

3   The Archaeological site is situated one kilometre away from the village of Ancient Olympia. The lighting ceremony for the Olympic Games takes place near the ruins of the Temple of Hera. The lighting ceremony for the Winter Olympic Games has evolved over the years but now has two parts: the lighting of the flame at the ruins of the Temple of Hera, and the chorus performance which takes place at the monument where Pierre de Coubertin's heart was buried. The first torchbearer makes his first stop at the monument in the case of the Olympic Games, and starts from the monument in the case of the Winter Olympic Games.

4   The National Olympic Committee (NOC) of Greece.

5   The idea of keeping the flame lit outside the Panathenaic Stadium for two months was received with reservation by the Greek public. The HOC board members were affiliated with PASOK, the Socialist party that was then in power. The coming parliamentary elections were scheduled for the beginning of April, so the HOC wanted to give an opportunity to the Socialists for a public appearance with 'Olympic' significance. Unfortunately for them, the Parliament decided that the elections would instead take place on March 7, one month before, giving the opportunity to the newly elected Conservative party (NEA) to preside at the first Olympic ritual event.

6   Nikolaou means the date of the opening ceremonies of the 1896 Olympic Games, not the lighting of any flame.

7   The first modern Olympic Games were held in this stadium in 1896. For the internal debates on this programme, see MacAloon, 'A Conversation With Athanassios Kritsinelis', in this volume.

8   George Bolos was the marketing chief of ACOG who acquired control over the flame relay as part of his portfolio (for details, see MacAloon, 'A Conversation With Athanassios Kritsinelis', this volume). When Mr. Bolas was present on the relay, he was the one to step down the airplane's steps with the lantern and deliver the speech on behalf of ATHOC during the evening celebration.

9   According to Greek mythology, Zeus was the 'father figure' and leader of all 12 Greek gods and Hera was the wife of Zeus. The Olympic Games of Antiquity were held to honour him and the whole site of Olympia was dedicated to him.

10 Sydney, Melbourne, Tokyo, Seoul, Mexico City, Los Angeles, Saint Louis, Atlanta, Montreal, Antwerp, Amsterdam, Paris, London, Barcelona, Rome, Munich, Berlin, Stockholm, Helsinki, Moscow.

11 New Delhi, Cairo, Cape Town, Rio de Janeiro.

12 New York and Geneva.

13 The IOFR in Barcelona started around 02:00 in the afternoon. It is well known that around that time the 'siesta' starts throughout Spain, that is the 2–3 hours in the afternoon while everything is

closed and people rest at their homes. A small but important detail that was not taken proper notice of and had as a result empty streets for the first two hours of the IOFR.

[14] The candidate cities for the 2012 Olympic Games were: London, Madrid, Moscow, New York, Paris.

[15] An advance team with a manager was already there to take care of all details.

[16] See MacAloon, 'Introduction' and 'A Conversation With Steven McCarthy', in this volume.

[17] Karlis, 'Volunteerism and Multiculturalism'.

[18] MacAloon, 'Volunteers, Global Society, and the Olympic Movement'.

[19] Moreno and de Moragas, 'The Evolution of Volunteers at the Olympic Games'.

[20] The logo of the International Olympic Flame Relay included the brand names of the two sponsors, Coca-Cola and Samsung.

[21] The Emblem of the Athens 2004 Olympic Games was the olive tree wreath in circle.

[22] The Olympic symbol is the interlocked five rings.

[23] On emotions and social movements, see Turner, 'Liminality and the Performative Genres'; Katz, *How Emotions Work*; Jasper, 'The Emotions of Protest'.

References

Katz, J. *How Emotions Work*. Chicago, IL: University of Chicago Press, 1999.

Karlis, G. 'Volunteerism and Multiculturalism: A Linkage for Future Olympics'. *The Sport Journal* 6 (2003): 11–22.

Jasper, J.M. 'The Emotions of Protest: Affective and Reactive Emotions in Social Movements'. *Sociological Forum* 13 (1998): 397–424.

MacAloon, J.J. 'Volunteers, Global Society, and the Olympic Movement'. In *Volunteers, Global Society and the Olympic Movement*, edited by M. de Moragas, A. Moreno, and N. Puig, 17–28. Lausanne: IOC Olympic Museum, 2000.

Moreno, A., and M. de Moragas. 'The Evolution of Volunteers at the Olympic Games'. In *Volunteers, Global Society and the Olympic Movement*, edited by M. de Moragas, A. Moreno, and N. Puig, 133–54. Lausanne: IOC Olympic Museum, 2000.

International Olympic Committee. *Olympic Charter*. Lausanne: International Olympic Committee.

Turner, V. 'Liminality and the Performative Genres'. In *Rite, Drama, Festival, Spectacle: Rehearsals Toward a Theory of Cultural Performance*, edited by J.J. MacAloon, 19–41. Philadelphia, PA: University of Pennsylvania Press, 1984.

Struggling to celebrate: management of the 2004 Olympic Flame Relay segment in Greece

Spiros Spiropoulos

The University of Technology, Sydney, Australia

This article offers a first-hand account of the experiences of an advance manager of the flame relay team of the Athens Olympic Games Organizing Committee (ATHOC). It covers the first and third segments of this relay within Greece and offers a focused description of the standard celebration events that punctuated the passage of the Olympic Flame. Organizational and managerial successes and failures shape the public experience of the Olympic Flame Relay (OFR), and the celebrations join the local and the global into performances of special demographic and symbolic power. In the model adopted for the 2004 OFR, these celebrations offered particular targets of attention for the various stakeholders (ATHOC departments, commercial sponsors, national government cultural officials, local authorities, and police). Power struggles among the various stakeholders are analysed, and the tactics deployed by sponsors to win these struggles are particularly revealed in a case study of the battle over the relay anthem. This article provides a rare published account of the experience of being a flame relay staff organizer under the emergent 'world's best practices' model.

Introduction

My involvement with the Olympic Movement began a few months before Athens won the bid for the 2004 Games on 5 September 1997. My undergraduate mentor hoped to develop a programme in Sydney that would allow Greek sports science graduates to study for a postgraduate degree in sport management, while carrying out an internship with the Sydney Organizing Committee of the Olympic Games (SOCOG). After Athens won the bid, my mentor travelled to Sydney and started implementing his vision. Meanwhile, I completed my military service and, a few months before the staging of the 2000 Olympic Games, I met him in Sydney and became a student in the art management postgraduate programme of the University of Technology, Sydney. Once I got involved with SOCOG's Olympic preparation, I knew straight away that my next goal would be to become a manager for the 2004 Athens Games.

In May 2002, I returned to Greece with the intention of applying for a position with Athens Olympic Games Organizing Committee (ATHOC). Through the daily press I learned that the Torch Relay Department was looking to recruit. I applied for a job and on 2 January 2003, I was invited to sign a contract. I was very happy to have my goal fulfilled, but I had no idea what the next two years of my life as an event manager would be like. I quickly met with the other members of the team and started reading the 'Transfer of Knowledge' documents from the 2000 Torch Relay. As the sixth person hired by the Torch Relay Department, I was one of the few who experienced the Athens OFR from vision through implementation.

The head of the department and the person who hired me was Athanassios Kristinelis, a passionate 'old-school' lover and expert of the torch relay and a former executive member of the Hellenic Olympic Committee (HOC). He had been responsible for the planning and implementation of many flame-lighting ceremonies in Olympia. Moreover, he had been present in all Greek Olympic torch relays since 1976, including, most recently, being the project manager for the 1996 relay in Greece. Although not a professionally trained events manager, Kritsinelis' experience, along with his strong commitment to the ideals that the Olympic Flame represents, gave him a thorough understanding of the event. Kritsinelis was unconditionally passionate about the flame relay, and he transferred his passion to all the team members. After my orientation week, I was assigned as an Advance Team Coordinator, responsible for the planning and implementation of the ceremonies that would be organized along the flame route all over Greece. In practice, this meant that I was the lead contact person for all the municipalities and other stakeholders hosting the organized celebrations along the OFR route.

Torch relay preparation

In June 2003, a new manager Penny Mikelopoulos came from the ATHOC marketing department to the torch relay. She brought fundamental changes to our department. While we sorely missed the passion and spirituality of Mr Kristinelis, in retrospect it is clear that the preparations to date had not met the deadlines set out by both ATHOC and the IOC, and the only way to get the job done was to adopt the more rigorous corporate culture of ATHOC. Unfortunately, it would turn out that the new manager had no idea about event management, let alone anything about the OFR. However, she had the support of senior management and knew how to get the job done at any cost and by any means. Understanding the nature of both national and global corporate culture would turn out to be essential in ensuring the success, commercially and politically, of the Athens 2004 OFR. During August 2003, the department started to recruit new members from other divisions and by September 2003, the Advance Team was fully staffed.

The 2004 OFR relay comprised of three legs. The first one started with the flame-lighting ceremony at Olympia on March 25 and lasted five days. After arrival in Athens and the handover ceremony between the HOC and ATHOC, the flame remained in the Panathenaic Stadium until its departure on the second, international leg of the relay. The third leg commenced on July 9 in Heraklio, Crete, and lasted until August 13, when the cauldron in the Athens Olympic Stadium was lit during the Olympic Opening Ceremony.

The official explanation for the relay start date was that the national day of March 25 had to be celebrated, along with the opening date of the first modern Olympic Games in 1896.[1] The unofficial explanation was that the ruling party wished to use the OFR as a promotional vehicle for the upcoming national elections, then scheduled for April. Both the official and unofficial explanations must be seen as equally important, in my opinion. Its power to mark a historically important event, as well as its perceived potential to influence a national election result further demonstrate the magnitude of the OFR and the Olympic Games for Greece.

The route, the sites, and the protocol for every celebration had been created by the former manager, Mr Kritsinelis. I was tasked with re-grouping the celebrations in a more functional and time-manageable manner. The spiritual had to be made practical in a model that could be repeated across Greece. So my first priority was to organize the celebrations into set categories and to try to figure out a typical format for each category.

Originally, there were 10, 20, 30, 40, 50, and 60-minute celebrations scheduled, together with the end-of-the-day celebrations. The practical necessity of having fewer celebration categories was clear to me. In harmony with the international 'best practices' OFR model carried into ATHOC by Além International Inc., our subcontractor, I proposed four categories of celebration halts. These were: (1) the 15-minute stops that were also operational stops to facilitate crew needs; (2) the 30-minute stops that facilitated the lunch needs of the crew and/or paid tribute to important places, archaeological sites, for example; (3) the 60-minute stops, to honour the capital cities of the areas that were not chosen to host an overnight stop; and (4) the end-of-the-day celebrations. The 174 total ceremonies were divided by the 41 days of the relay's first and third stages, producing an average of four to five stops per day.

Content of the celebrations

At this point, a brief description of the relay celebrations in Greece should help the reader comprehend the size and the organizational complexity of the OFR. All ceremonies included a standard protocol for the arrival of the flame, scheduled for 23 minutes, but generally stretched to 30 minutes for safety and practical reasons. The content of the standard protocol for the arrival of the flame in these 30-minute celebrations was as follows:

- ATHENS 2004 flag is flown at full mast.
- The Ceremony starts as the final torchbearer arrives and lights the altar cauldron (3 minutes).
- The Olympic flag is hoisted, to the playing of the Olympic anthem (5 minutes).
- The Greek flag is hoisted, to the playing of the Greek national anthem (3 minutes).
- Address by a representative of the Municipality (3–4 minutes).
- Reply by a representative of ATHENS 2004 (3–4 minutes).
- Exchange of gifts (3 minutes).
- Torchbearer ignites the torch from the cauldron and departs on the next relay segment.

To suit the requirements of the 15-minute ceremonies, some adjustments had to be made. Hence, the performance of the Olympic anthem and the address of the ATHOC representative were excluded from the protocol at these stops. The 60-minute ceremony included all the elements of the 30-minute protocol above, together with a cultural programme of 30 minutes, organized by the local municipalities for showcasing local identity.

End-of-the-day celebrations: programme and venues

The end-of-the-day celebrations were the most important, the most well-attended, and the most managerially complicated of all of the celebrations. A typical programme is presented below:

- Soundcheck for the music concert: 2 hours.
- Activation programme/music presentation by Sponsor A (30–50 minutes depending on the time of the flame arrival).
- Activation programme/music presentation by Sponsor B (30–50 minutes depending on the time of the flame arrival).
- ATHOC torch relay show reel and official relay song (30 minutes).
- Arrival of the torchbearer and protocol ceremony (30 minutes).

- Local cultural programme (30 minutes).
- ATHOC music concert (75–120 minutes).
- Sponsors' activation after-party (30–90 minutes).

A main challenge that had to be faced was the selection of the actual celebration site in every stop. It needed to be: (1) accessible by the main relay convoy; (2) a major highlight of the city or the prefecture; and (3) of certain dimensions. However, the effort to combine these specifications often led to the selection of unconventional venues that were poorly equipped with certain necessary amenities. ATHOC could do very little about this, because the main purpose of the celebrations was not to just organize protocol ceremonies and concerts in typical venues such as football stadiums, but to also showcase the host city and its heritage. Hence, places such as main squares and main crossroads in small towns were often used as venues.

Five out of the forty-one end-of-the-day venues were archaeological sites, where strict governmental regulations applied. Sometimes even robots had to be used to transfer the musical instruments (including a piano) to these venues, because the paths leading to the site were small and difficult to access. In the case of the island of Samothraki (Samothrace), the celebration took place in the highest part of the main archaeological site that had never been used before, for any reason.

The division of authority: ATHOC and the HOC

When the Olympic Games are not held in Greece, the organizational jurisdiction for the relay is clear. The Greek leg is organized by the HOC, while the relay in the host country is organized by its Organizing Committee for the Olympic Games (OCOG). With Greece as host for 2004, the boundaries were blurred, and the separation of powers in Greece between the HOC and ATHOC was always in tension. The agreement between the HOC and ATHOC made the HOC responsible for implementing the first leg of the OFR, while ATHOC was in charge of the second and third legs. However, while the HOC was in charge for the protocol ceremonies of the first leg, ATHOC was responsible for providing extra staff for the end-of-the-day celebrations as well as sponsor arrangements and services according to ATHOC's contractual agreements. Since the HOC had historically been opposed to sponsor presence during Greek flame relays, this led to some complicated negotiations. Moreover, ATHOC's Culture Division was in charge of implementing the large outdoor music concerts for each end-of-the-day celebration and for insuring that IOC rules and regulations were respected during these performances. This added another dimension of organizational challenge and sometimes struggle.

As the date for the lighting ceremony approached, our anxiety rose as ATHOC employees were expected to cooperate both with the HOC and with the sponsors. In the beginning, the HOC was completely against having sponsors at all, saying that they commercialize the true spirit of the relay. However, the HOC already had a backstage contract with the Hellenic Postal Service (ELTA) that allowed it to be present at every end-of-the-day celebration venue, without being one of ATHOC's official national or international torch relay sponsors. By this stage ELTA took for granted that the position of its kiosks in the venues would be of its own choosing. So, wherever the advance team went to check the end-of-the-day celebration locations, we found ELTA kiosks already set up in the most desirable spots, leading to conflict with official relay sponsors. The presence of ELTA continued on the third leg of the relay as well, but in a more discreet manner, because by this point they had received clearer instructions for their presence in these venues.

Poor planning for the concert stages at the end-of-the-day celebrations also left the main sponsors unhappy with the placement of their kiosks.[2] Furthermore, the official sponsors had subcontracted the celebration sites to private production companies, which created an additional level of competitiveness and tension for everybody because of the high motivation level of the subcontractors – mainly to over-deliver to their clients and thereby get the contract for the third relay segment – and the inaccurate initial site plans. This happened because the Torch Relay Department had decided to fully trust the Advance Team sent by the Culture Division, while the Culture Division was very inflexible regarding the subject of the distance of kiosks from the main stage, thus making things more difficult. So even *within* ATHOC, tension over the separation of powers between divisions caused conflict and resulted in administrative and organizational oversights. In two cities the kiosks had to be relocated because they did not meet ATHOC's regulations, and in one of them, the relocation of the kiosks had to actually be enforced by public order officials of the local municipality.

Another difficult situation arose when ATHOC signed the contract with the company that supplied the necessary technical equipment for the music stages two days *after* the relay started. Hence, the stakeholders who were involved in the first segment celebrations did not have enough time to prepare themselves accordingly as to what was really going to happen.

However, the Torch Relay Department eventually managed to overcome these difficulties, and through closer cooperation with the Culture Division, they did not reoccur during the third leg of the relay. Along with a representative of the Culture Division, I was sent to inspect all the celebration venues for the third segment, and detailed site plans were produced that exactly specified not just the locations but even the distances of the sponsors' kiosks from one another and from the stage.

However, additional problems arose during the third leg related to last-minute elements added in the site plans through the failure of the sponsors' production companies to comply with the Olympic regulations, sometimes on purpose.[3] No incident better exemplifies the difficult balancing act between ATHOC and the sponsors than the case of the official anthem.

The torch relay official anthem

ATHOC had come to an agreement with EMI record label to produce the official anthem of the torch relay, and Yiannis Kotsiras was selected to perform the song titled *Pass the Flame, Unite the World*.[4] By choosing to work with an international record label and producer, ATHOC recognized the significance of joining the local and the global. The song was released as a maxi single in April 2004, in Greek, English, and dub versions, and it was officially launched during the open-air concert on the last day of the first leg of the relay.

However, the official anthem was to prove a relative failure. The 'presenting partner' Coca-Cola – a company highly practiced at embodying the intersection between local and global – took advantage of the situation and announced its intention to produce its own torch relay song. Coke asked ATHOC for permission and was refused. But the company persisted anyway and proceeded to record a song by a famous female Greek pop artist. Although they did not launch it as an 'official' torch relay song, it made its way to the public in a more efficient manner and soon overshadowed the official ATHOC anthem. The Coke song was more pop and trendy, and it was heavily promoted both by the record company and Coca-Cola's marketing department. Both on the relay route and at the celebration sites, the song was heavily performed during all Coke's activation activities. The whole situation caused disappointment, anxiety, and panic among EMI's people, who, instead of redoubling their efforts in the promotion game, chose just to complain instead. After the launch of their official song at the end of the first leg, EMI withdrew the official artist from the celebrations, and he did not perform at any other concert. This decision left the way open for Coke to promote its song more easily and to make it appear affiliated with the torch relay. While ATHOC understood what needed to be done to create an official anthem that both acknowledged the international dimension of the games and did so with a distinctly Greek flavour, it fell down in implementation and especially in marketing. Not only was ATHOC in frequent battle with the HOC over the organization of the relay, but we also found ourselves in a struggle with the sponsors over control of the performative dimensions of the relay celebrations.

Popular celebrations on the first leg

Despite all of these conflicts and difficulties, the overall outcome of the celebrations on the first leg of the relay was more than satisfactory for the public. All of the end-of-the-day celebrations on this leg drew large and enthusiastic crowds.

There were six major stops on the first leg of the route across the Peloponnesus: Andritsaina, Pylos, Kalamata, Gythio, Tripolis, and Nafplio. Andritsaina, a small, beautiful, mountain village, hosted its celebration in the main crossroad. The happy vibe in the village was spread to all visitors from the citizens who were very proud to have been chosen to host the first overnight stop on the relay (see Figure 1). About 2000 people

Figure 1.   Expectant crowds awaiting the flame arrival celebration in Tripolis. Photo by the author (Spiros Spiropoulos).

participated in the celebration, making it a great start for the tour. Production-wise, as the venue was a crossroads, traffic was not so easy to manage and there were almost no parking places.

In Pylos, a small seaside town, the ceremony took place in the central square. Everything went as planned and about 3000 people showed up to attend the ceremony. The next stop was Kalamata, a city full of life. On that day, the good mood regarding the sponsors changed and right up until the flame arrived, a silent war unfolded over the issue of the sponsors' kiosks. It was the first of the cities for which the site plan was inaccurate and the allocation had to be made on the spot. Unfortunately, a change of the concert stage position along with the ad hoc presence of ELTA kiosks made things difficult. Moreover, the Culture Division made things more difficult by asking for the relocation of the kiosks once again, after they had been set up. The issue was escalated to upper management level, and it took a lot of patience and diplomacy to be resolved. But most of this was invisible to the public, and this celebration was the biggest success of the first leg. Some 25,000–30,000 people showed up for the event and the downtown area was paralysed. The moments we experienced there were more than emotional. Demographically speaking, the people who attended the ceremonies included all ages, and their impatience to see the flame convoy coming turned to real enthusiasm when it arrived. Older people stood for nearly two to three hours without complaining, feeling very proud to be there and to experience that moment.

The incident over the kiosks' placement forced me to travel right after that celebration to the next overnight stop, Gythio, a very beautiful small seaside town. Almost everything there went as planned. The local fishermen created an extraordinary atmosphere by placing their boats near the port and making cycles with special effects. Only minor problems arouse.[5]

The next stop was Tripolis, a city of 25,000 people, in the middle of Peloponnesus, surrounded by mountains. The venue of the celebration was its main square, the biggest in the Balkan territory (see Figure 2). In Tripolis, as I have already noted, renewed conflict over the placement of the sponsors' kiosks escalated to the point where the municipal authorities had to intervene. Apart from this, the celebration was as successful as it had been in Kalamata. About 20,000 people from all nearby areas of the prefecture showed up to participate in the celebration of the Olympic Flame.

The final stop of the relay's first leg was Nafplio, a historical city with many restored houses. As previously noted, EMI chose Nafplio to launch the official torch relay song. After the soundcheck was finished and everything seemed okay, to our surprise we saw five cars parked on the site. The local representative of the Hyundai company – an Olympic sponsor, but not a torch relay one – had misunderstood the situation. We explained to him what we had to ask him to do, and he apologized and removed the cars right away. Although there was an open-air music concert, the ceremony at Nafplio was not a typical end-of-the-day celebration. After Nafplio, the flame travelled by helicopter to three islands in the Argosaronikos bay, and ended up in the Panathenaic Stadium of Athens, where the first modern Olympic Games were held in 1896. Here, a special ceremony was organized by the HOC to handover the flame, along with the responsibility of the relay, to ATHOC's president Mrs. Gianna Angelopoulou.

For this ceremony a special protocol was designed, because it carried very important symbolism for all Greek people. It was 108 years since the modern Olympics Games were revived in Athens, and for the first time in history, the HOC handed the flame over to Greek hands. About 40,000 people gathered to express their respect for the return of the

Figure 2.   An Andritsaina man expressing his feelings about the novel flame relay celebrations of 2004. Photo by the author (Spiros Spiropoulos).

Games to their birthplace. For ATHOC, this ceremony represented the beginning of the operational period of the ATHENS 2004 Olympic Games.

The relay's final leg to the Olympic Stadium

The third leg of the ATHENS 2004 relay was to us the official pre-Games event and the major publicity vehicle for the Games. All ATHOC, media, and public attention was concentrated on our team and on the flame arrival ceremony in Heraklio, Crete, that would open the main segment of the Greek relay. The time invested in the negotiations for this ceremony was more than one-third of the overall negotiations for the celebrations through the rest of the relay.

The municipality of Heraklio did a very good job and prepared many events along the way from the airport to the celebration venue. The protocol ceremony was very officious, and it was attended by national and international media, the president and senior management of ATHOC, parliament members, and government representatives. After the protocol ceremony, came the first concert of the final relay segment. The famous Charoula Alexiou performed, supported by local artists. Alexiou was the only artist to receive a fee for her performance; all other artists who participated in the relay celebrations did so on voluntary basis.

The next stop of the relay was Sitia, a small seaside town on the east side of Crete. The last torchbearer of the day was a local 85-year-old veteran athlete, whose presence created a very emotional atmosphere. A funny thing happened during the municipality's cultural programme that followed the ceremony. According to the celebration running sheet, the local artists were supposed to perform for 30 minutes. To our surprise, when the time was over they refused to stop. Their continued playing put pressure on our team. They insisted that if anyone tried to stop their performance, they would make an announcement complaining to the public, so they were given an additional 15 minutes. My guess is that they had never performed in front of 3000 people before, especially in their own city, and they wanted to enjoy the moment as long as they could.

The next stop of the relay was in Chania. The venue selected for the ceremony was the square in front of the city's main church. For this occasion a special lighting plan was implemented, as the church provided such a good backdrop. A bit of a headache was caused when the stage manager of the concert provided all of the musicians and artists with water of a different brand than the official sponsor's. Unfortunately, the national media broadcasted the lead performer consuming it, making the official sponsor and ATHOC's marketing division very upset. To avoid a similar incident, the company provided upfront all necessary refreshments for the ensuing concerts.

Our next stop was the island of Rhodes, capital of the Dodecanese. A few minutes before the programmed arrival of the flame, I was informed that the convoy had lost its way in the narrow Rhodian streets. To keep the audience occupied, I tried to find stories about the relay to feed to the master of ceremonies who had no idea what was happening. Three minutes before the arrival of the flame, one of the sponsors took the initiative to play its relay jingle, thus breaking the agreed-upon rules for ritual silence. The flame arrived 15 minutes behind schedule. It has to be mentioned that this was the only time the convoy was delayed during this phase of the relay. The municipality of the island had prepared a unique display by a special forces climbing team. Ropes had been stretched between the two main buildings of the venue, and as soon as the protocol ceremony finished, three flags – one with the peace logo, one with the municipality logo, and one with the Olympic logo – were dropped down by this climbing team. At the same time, white pigeons were released in a symbolic call for peace among all nations.

The next day's celebrations in Syros and Mytilini went as planned and no notable incidents occurred. After that, we went to Samothraki, a beautiful island in the northern Aegean Sea. My personal opinion is that the ceremony that took place there was one of the two most spiritual of all the relay ceremonies. It took place in the highest part of the ancient 'Temple of the Great Gods'. The stage was set up just a few metres away from the original location of the statue of 'Nike of Samothraki'.[6] In ancient times mystical ceremonies, the *Kaveria*, took place there. For the piano to reach the highest point of the temple, a small robot carrier had to be used. The artistic programme that followed the ceremony was a duet by a soprano and a piano soloist, together with local traditional musicians. The last torchbearer of the relay was a local physical education teacher, who had to run through the entire ancient site. I told him that the relay, combined with the atmosphere of the site would make him feel very special. He appeared not to understand what I was trying to tell him. After the ceremony, he came to me almost crying and told me that when he was carrying the flame through the site, he began feeling very strange, despite his frequent prior visits there. As he was approaching the celebration stage, he started to comprehend the magnitude of the assignment that he had been called upon to accomplish. Once he lit the altar cauldron, he went through the most emotional moment of his life.

Our next stop was the city of Alexandroupolis, a prefecture capital city. By that time one thing had become clear. The longer the flame was on the road, the more enthusiastic the reception it received from the people in the cities, especially for the end-of-the-day celebrations. This could be attributed partly to the fact that the date of the Olympic

Opening Ceremony was dramatically approaching and partly to the fact that this relay was organized by Greeks and was offered to Greeks.

Xanthi, one of the most active cities in Thrace, was the next major celebration stop, and the venue was the central square. Production-wise this proved a challenging moment, as the crew had great difficulty in communicating with the local coffee shop owners, who were occupying part of the venue with tables and chairs to expand their shops and cater to more clients. Although many days before the municipality had asked them to remove their equipment from the venue, they had not done so. When the crew arrived, they had to negotiate with the shopkeepers to make the venue passable for the torchbearer. Finally, a compromise was reached, and only half of the restaurant equipment was removed.

Our next stop for a major celebration was another archaeological site, the ancient theatre of Fillipoi (Philippi). There, although all sponsors had been informed in advance that no promotional activities would be permitted in the site, the local representative of ELTA showed no intention of removing the kiosk he had set up for the celebration. It took some time, lots of negotiations, and communication with the upper management of ELTA to get the kiosk removed. I was also informed that one of the two artists scheduled to perform there had been involved in a car accident on his way to the venue. Despite such short notice, that artist's agent managed to arrange for Domna Samiou, a famous Greek traditional singer, to replace him. Although this was a last-minute choice, the vibe created by Ms. Samiou was perfect for the venue and the occasion. During the concert many people were dancing along with the traditional rhythms, transforming it to an interactive celebration with the public that lasted longer than programmed.

Our next three overnight stops were in Serres, Kilkis, and Polygyros. Everything went as planned and we had no unexpected events. The next city to host the flame was Thessaloniki, the second-biggest city in the country. The preparations for the ceremony took a lot of effort and everything was organized to welcome the flame. To give the celebration a higher profile, the national men's basketball team was chosen to be the last torchbearer(s). About 20,000 people attended the ceremony along with one Coca-Cola VIP guest, Tsaki Tsan (international martial arts film star Jackie Chan), who had earlier participated in the relay as well. When Tsaki Tsan arrived at the celebration venue, a few minutes after he carried the torch, he seemed thrilled and unable to believe this was happening to him. He asked for nothing special and did not mind where he would be seated or even if he would be seated at all. In a Chinese traditional manner, he thanked anyone and everyone wearing an ATHENS 2004 uniform for allowing him to participate in the relay, and he did not stop applauding during the whole ceremony.

The next major celebration stops were the ancient theatre of Dion and then Vergina, the royal cemetery containing the grave of King Phillip II.[7] In Vergina, the protocol ceremony was performed, however the concert was cancelled due to unexpected rain. The cities of Florina, Kozani, Kastoria, Ioannina, Kalabaka, Volos, Skiathos, and Chalkida followed before the flame reached the archaeological site of Delphi, on August 3.

In ancient Greece, Delphi was considered to be the centre of the world, and it was famous as the sacred place where the Pythia, the high priestess of the temple, had the power to see the future and advise people on what to do. Today there is a very interesting archaeological site there, as well as a museum with distinctive pieces of ancient art from area excavations. The celebration in Delphi had two very distinctive highlights and one lost opportunity. Starting with the lost opportunity, ATHOC missed the chance to host the celebration in the ancient theatre of Delphi by a foolish administrative mistake. The theatre of Delphi is one of a kind and along with the theatre of Epidavros (Epidauros) is the most important theatre in Greece. Due to the theatre's fragile condition, the archaeological council had stopped issuing permission to stage events there. Only a very few highly significant events have been staged under an exemption status in the last 30 years, the last being some 12 years prior. I was aware of the theatre's background and its importance, and I also knew that when I would meet the local archaeologist responsible for the site, she would deny us access for the celebration, as she did. She recommended that we address ourselves to Delphi's ancient stadium, site of the Pythian Games so an important venue too, but not as significant as the theatre. However, I knew that ATHENS 2004 had the 'green light' from the Ministry of Culture to obtain permission to use the theatre for this once in a lifetime opportunity. So I emphatically insisted to the torch relay manager that she should be very specific when approaching the Ministry of Culture about the particular setting where the celebrations of the flame arrival would take place.

Unfortunately, at that time she did not grasp the importance of these words, and when she prepared the request, she just mentioned the site of Delphi in general, and not the theatre in particular. I was informed about this when the signed permission was faxed to our department by the Ministry of Culture, and by then nothing could be changed. The local archaeological council stepped in on this decision and sent us to the ancient stadium instead of the theatre, arguing that deciding the place of the celebration was under their authority, since the permission from the Ministry of Culture was generic and did not indicate the theatre specifically for the celebration. So, the relay missed the opportunity to stage its celebration in the theatre, and the theatre to host the Olympic Flame once in its lifetime of two and a half thousand years of existence. In this moment we also see an interesting parallel with the jurisdictional struggles between local and national government, as we ourselves had experienced between ATHOC and the HOC in the earlier stages of the relay.

Delphi also had two very distinctive highlights. The first one concerned the last torchbearer of that day, Maria Hors, a lovely 91-year-old lady, who is herself a symbol of the Olympic Movement. Since the 1960s, Mrs. Hors has been the choreographer of all of the flame-lighting ceremonies in the ancient stadium at Olympia. She has shaped the artistic part of these ceremonies as nobody else has done since the torch relay concept was conceived and implemented for the first time in 1936, when she took part as a young girl in the very first flame-lighting ceremony at Olympia. Having the privilege of accommodating this great lady was a thrill for me, and the moment when I most truly understood the importance of the task I had been assigned to deliver.

The second highlight was an initiative of the Mayor of Delphi. He was a very passionate gentleman, a true lover of the history of his town and with deep knowledge of the Olympic Movement and the torch relay symbolism. Apart from the pre-ceremony local dances and the after-ceremony concert of ATHOC, the Mayor had organized a cultural programme to honour the presence of the flame in Delphi that lasted all night long. The few people who stayed all night and followed the complete programme, including the Mayor himself, witnessed a magical night that cannot be forgotten, with choirs, psalms and the playing of ancient musical instruments. The next morning, we all felt very tired but also very blessed to have witnessed this special celebration.

Trying very hard, the team managed to get organized and move to the next destination, which was the island of Zakynthos. Personally, I did not go there but continued to the next stop which was the island of Corfu, because they were preparing a big celebration in the heart of the city, and I had to make sure that everything went according to plan. Corfu is one of the seven islands of the Ionian Sea to the west of mainland Greece. Its natural beauty, along with an infrastructure that can cater to many people, make it a famous holiday destination that attracts many tourists. The celebration venue was a former cricket field in the heart of the city, and the municipality tried its best to prepare for the event. The arrival of the flame encouraged most of the local travel agents to organize daily tours from other parts of the island to make it possible for as many people as possible to attend the celebration. The municipality arranged for eight traditional dance groups to perform before the ceremony, accompanied by a local band. The plan was to form circles and dance among the crowd, showcasing the local traditional dances. Unfortunately, the band arrived just 10 minutes before the torchbearer entered the venue. By that time, about 25,000 people had gathered to attend the celebration, and it was clear that there was no time left for the traditional dances.

A further challenge was created by the fact that the boy-scout team that was supposed to form a human chain and create a corridor for the last torchbearer to pass through the crowd never showed up. Later we found out that people from the municipality had instructed them to stay behind the stage! Because of the large crowd, I was greatly concerned about the corridor for the torchbearer. Having no other recourse, I asked the dancers dressed in their traditional outfits to create the corridor, and they arranged it just before the torchbearer entered the venue.

During the music concert that followed, the three singers just could not stop singing. They got more and more excited and kept performing for much longer than they were supposed to. The Mayor of Corfu got a bit nervous about that, because he had programmed a spectacular fireworks show at the end of the concert for which he wanted everybody to remain present. Also, the travel agents had specific time schedules for the departures for their groups and were complaining about the programme delay. Half an hour after the concert was supposed to finish, and without any warning, the Mayor ordered the pyrotechnics show to start. The artists stopped until the end of the show, and then they kept on performing for another hour, giving the best they had to the audience, who encouraged them to continue.

The next day, the flame moved on towards Preveza, next to Agrinio, and then on to the city of Patras, the third-biggest city of Greece, and one of the four Olympic cities. (A number of preliminary football games took place there.) The arrival of the last torchbearer and the cultural programme after the protocol ceremony were two of the celebration highlights. Five different bands of some 70 members each came from all over Greece to participate in the programme. The planning for the bands was quite complex, but that is what made the ceremony special. Each band had a starting point in a different central location of the city and followed a different route until they all reached the celebration venue, one after the other, performing live all along the way. A few minutes after the last band reached the venue, the torchbearer arrived, stepping down 178 stairs before he reached the stage. After the protocol ceremony, the cultural part included, along with the five bands, an additional choir of 300 people and Patras's best classical orchestra. About 750 artists comprised the artistic programme of that day and transformed the venue, the central square of the city, into an extraordinary music hall with an audience of 25,000 people.

After Patras, the flame moved on to Korinthos, and the next day it reached the prefecture of Attica. Only three days were left until the Opening Ceremony of the Games and everybody could feel the excitement. The first overnight stop was in the municipality of Marathon. The celebration there did not go as well as others in the third leg of the relay. While the celebration in Patras was going on, it was suggested that the upcoming music concert in Marathon be staged at a nearby beach, since the original venue was a big parking lot near the start of the Marathon race. Everybody liked the idea, except for the people in ATHOC's Culture Division, who were informed last and tried hard to prevent the plan from proceeding. Things got more complicated when the manager of the leading scheduled artist was informed about the change of venue. Somehow, he had got the idea that the concert would take place outside the Marathon Tomb. First he got confused (what parking lot? What beach?), and then he got mad. After hard negotiations that lasted all night and until noon the next day, the beach idea was abandoned and the concert returned to the parking lot. However, there were only 5 hours left before the beginning of the performance, and nothing was set up at the venue. There was confusion and panic, because the concert stage had already been set up at the beach. After huge efforts and exhausting negotiations, extra technical equipment was found, brought to the parking space and set up. According to the technical crew, a record was broken that day. Normally it takes eight to nine hours to set up such a stage. The one at Marathon was put up in five hours by eight people, most of whom were not technicians. Once again administrative power struggles tarnished the celebration of the passage of the flame.

The following day the convoy moved on to Piraeus. The celebrations staged during the day, as well as the end-of-the-day ones seemed more impersonal. No meetings were held, and the tension was high. The celebrations in Marathon, Piraeus, and on the Acropolis the following day were dominated by mayors, government representatives, ATHENS 2004 officials, and other powerful people, whose presence made the situation stressful for everyone. Two buses with police SWAT team personnel now accompanied the convoy increasing the tensions, although they remained undercover.

Some members of the sponsors' production companies met their psychological limits as well. After the cultural programme in Piraeus, one of these sponsors organized a DJ party in and around its kiosk for about 1 hour. Our team helped arrange for a company to provide barriers around the kiosk party. When the party ended, the head of the barrier company asked the head of the production company to return the barriers. For some reason, the sponsor's production manager got mad and began shouting at him. The barrier provider's crew – 15 stressed and psychologically exhausted men, who were setting up and dismantling barriers all day long – and the production company's crew – 18 people, who had been on the road for 35 days – very nearly came to blows in downtown Piraeus. Credit needs to be given to the activation manager of that particular sponsor who worked with me to avoid a fight and a real mess.

The final end-of-the-day celebration was staged at the sacred rock of Acropolis. Many VIPs and some 200 invited guests were present on the site, including Greece's Prime Minister, the Mayor of Athens, and the president of ATHOC. The ceremony was humble in nature and included only the protocol section. The second to last torchbearer was the Olympic champion Carl Lewis, who gave the ceremony extra acclaim, and the last torchbearer was Niki Bakigianni, who had won the silver medal in women's high jump in Atlanta 1996. On that night, my mission officially ended.

The next day, the relay officially ended its route at 5:30 pm at the Olympic Stadium. Immediately thereafter, a spontaneous party took place that released the incredible stress, anxiety, and fatigue that engulfed all the relay crew members. After 30 minutes of screaming, crying, and celebrating, photos were taken, hands were shaken, hugs were given, and the ATHENS 2004 Olympic Games Torch Relay became a part of the Modern Games history, as did we.

Some final observations and puzzlements

There can be no question that the great majority of people who attended the end-of-the-day celebrations wanted primarily to welcome the flame and to express their satisfaction for the return of the Olympic Games to their birthplace. I would estimate that, on average, about 70% of the audience remained for the concerts that followed the protocol section of these end-of-the-day celebrations. Each evening, after the end of the performances, people waited from 30 minutes to 2 hours to get a commemorative photo of themselves and their families in front of the cauldron burning with the Olympic Flame. In some cities, this kept on throughout the night and until the caravan's departure the next morning.

The HOC's historical resistance to torch relay sponsors now seems to be a thing of the past. Perhaps this is more than just a further indication of the increasingly corporate, bottom-line nature of the whole Olympic Movement. It has been observed that while many of those who came together for the end-of-the-day celebrations were there simply to experience the flame, I was frankly very surprised by the reaction of some parts of the audience to the sponsors' self-promotion activities. No matter what type of sponsor-branded memorabilia was being given away, some portion of the audience was always queuing up at the kiosks to get what was offered. When t-shirts were being given away, audience behaviour could even get a bit scary. Some people even missed the arrival of the torchbearer, preferring to stay in line trying to get a free pencil or a baseball cap from the sponsor kiosk.

This sort of enthusiasm for the sponsors' activation tactics raises difficult and uncomfortable questions as to exactly what their role has now become under the 'world's best practices' torch relays of today. Is it possible that the sponsors' presence was for some people as significant a part of the celebration as witnessing the passage of the Olympic Flame? These end-of-the-day celebrations were full of historically significant Greek cultural expressions of spiritual and symbolic power tied to the universal values of Olympism. Did the presence and performances of local and global sponsors allow in this space for a segment of the public to engage with the complex internationalism of the Olympic Games through a medium that is altogether familiar and even banal, that is to say, commercial advertising and sponsor-branded souvenirs? Perhaps even more so than in the prior, sponsor-free relays, the Greek imagery and cultural performances of these celebrations had a deep national resonance. In this case Greece was finally at the centre of the global world, delivering *its* flame not to a foreign OCOG but to itself. Did the sponsors get a one-time free ride in Greece in spite of Greek nationalism? My experiences as an event manager lead me to suggest that we need to think from multiple perspectives about the role of sponsorship within the torch relay context.

The self-interested actions of the sponsors must also be taken into account in facing these questions. I have documented how Coca-Cola took advantage of ATHOC with their torch relay anthem, and I've analysed repeated struggles among the sponsors' production companies themselves and with the relay organizers over the distance of their kiosks from the main stage. Such struggles distract OFR managers from their core duties, while, at the same time, such marketing and sponsor servicing is understood to go hand in hand with the rest of the event under the 'best practices' model. However, these conflicts can be partially attributed to the pressure activation teams felt from their upper management to maximize sponsorship benefits. In any case, the crowd was always big enough for each sponsor to get the desired exposure to the people attending the ceremonies. Last but not least, it must be reiterated that whatever difficulties sponsor presence occasioned for the OFR operational framework, without the sponsors the flame and its symbolism would never have been able to reach 27 countries and 33 cities all over the world.

Exposing these backstage arrangements and struggles to public view and debate should not distract from or diminish the fact that the flame created feelings of enthusiasm and unforgettable moments for the relay crew members and managers, as well as for the spectators in every city and every village it visited. It was a distinctive experience, and it made us feel that we were doing something very important for ourselves, for the public, for our country, and for the whole world.

Notes

[1] 25 March 1821 was the day that the Greeks started their revolution against the Ottoman Empire.

[2] These kiosks formed the bases for all of the 'activation', that is to say promotion activities of the sponsors: handing out or selling merchandise, playing music and videos, arranging contests for the spectators, etc. The reader should not imagine small newspaper kiosks, but rather more or less elaborate temporary stages and awnings (see Figure 1).

[3] For example, playing a jingle during the mandatory silent period.

[4] *Pass the Flame, Unite the World* was produced and composed by Trevor Horn.

[5] The promotional balloons a sponsor had given to the crowd made the job of the TV crew difficult, as they disturbed the live national broadcast of the protocol ceremony.

[6] The original statue of Nike of Samothraki is currently exhibited in the main lobby of The Louvre in Paris.

[7] The father of Alexander the Great.

American media, intercultural stories and the 2004 Olympic flame ceremonies

Marianthi Bumbaris Thanopoulos

Social Sciences Division, University of Chicago, Chicago, USA

This paper explores backstage conventions and conditions for national and local broadcasting of the Olympic Games. While the Olympic Movement sees sport as a means to the larger end of intercultural understanding, American media largely frame the Games as a competition among nations for the glory of athletic victory and superiority. 'Covering' the Olympics within this dominant framework leads the American broadcaster National Broadcasting Corporation (NBC) to a studied disinterest in intercultural stories, becoming itself a roadblock to understanding foreign cultures and the Olympic ethos, rituals and symbols. The author, a Greek-American and local NBC employee at the time of the Athens 2004 Olympics, describes her struggles to generate intercultural programming and interprets NBC's refusal to allow American audiences to view the 2004 flame-lighting ceremonies at Ancient Olympia and the relay through Greece as lost opportunities to temper the stereotyping of host cultures for the American public.

The Olympics ignite a global passion, and fans travel great lengths to celebrate the Olympic ideals of sport, culture, peace and humanity. The 2004 Athens Olympic Games were initiated by the Olympic flame-lighting ceremony, held as ever at Ancient Olympia, but given special meaning in this instance as Greeks for the first time were lighting the flame for their own Games. Tens of thousands of Greek people, together with officials, pilgrims and tourists from other countries, flocked to Olympia, Greece, for this significant world event. However, the message that the American Olympic broadcaster, the National Broadcasting Corporation (NBC), sent to its millions of viewers back home is that Athens 2004 officially began with the Olympic Opening Ceremonies, not the lighting of the Olympic flame. NBC barely mentioned these Olympic flame rituals and certainly did not 'cover' them, thus completely downplaying this intercultural story.[1] In news terms, NBC treats the flame lighting and Greek relay as 'non-events'. How can this be?[2]

In this paper, I will argue that Athens 2004 represents an important example of how the tensions and limitations found within the field of American television production marginalize intercultural stories and limit the American public's understanding of global events.[3] To show how such marginalization develops, I will analyse the struggles among those who package the news – reporters, videographers, producers, news directors and executives – and show how news stories are determined to be newsworthy.[4] On the basis of his cultural performance theory, John MacAloon asserts that 'the chief reason that American news media do not want to cover the flame-lighting ceremony is due to their discomfort with rituals'.[5] An analysis of my experiences with Athens 2004 suggests that this is only part of the problem. A number of other forces within the field of television production must be considered, including television news formats, the value of cultural capital and professional experience, and the space (or non-space) for culture exhibits. To reveal these tensions, I will use my insider experience of producing programming on Greek culture in the context of the 2004 Athens Olympic Games. Throughout this paper, I will provide an ethnographic account of how news media institutions function while simultaneously providing a window into a mass-mediated American cultural perception of sport.

I will examine the hoops I needed to jump through to get the story, detailed 'out-in-the-field' experiences, and how I was received by the national NBC Network.[6] In addition, I will indicate how my identity as a Greek-American reporter overcame some of the normal status hierarchies of experience in local and national television news, thus convincing 14 local broadcast stations to sponsor sending me to Greece. In Greece, my liminal status, in particular my language competence (with an American accent), allowed me to gain access to people and stories that NBC Network, the rights-holding broadcaster, with its reluctance to employ Greek-speaking journalists, could not so easily find.[7] Yet, in crucial instances, organizational hierarchies, status conventions and ethnic stereotypes led NBC to disregard what I was giving them on the spot. Thus, the portrayal of the Games and Greek culture constantly reinforced a dominant American – rather than a global, intercultural – understanding of the Games.

Social science scholars have analysed such struggles for decades, but rarely have they actually worked within the field themselves. For instance, Pierre Bourdieu[8] and Edward S. Herman and Noam Chomsky[9] analyse the field of television production from an outsider perspective. While one can still be an anthropologist and be an insider, a division exists between the executive and the academic that conceals crucial information. At stake, therefore, is a professional insider's perspective that offers a distinct analysis hidden from those outside of media.

Throughout my analysis, I try to suggest the potential significance of intercultural stories as a key passageway towards global acceptance and cultural enlightenment. Intercultural communication breaks down and reveals parts of a culture that go unnoticed, dispels or attempts to dispel stereotypical definitions of that culture, and provides a more complicated understanding and acceptance for different cultures. While intercultural communication has these strengths, it also has its limitations. In the process of defining a culture, one selectively chooses what parts of the culture are worthy of interpretation. Also, the problem of subjectivity comes into play because of the nature of interpretations themselves. Despite these limitations, interpreting common observations can shed light on foreign cultures and offers people of those cultures an opportunity to at least attempt to share their beliefs, experiences and stories.[10] But achieving these effects on the scale imagined by the Olympic Movement requires mass media. Building on my direct experience of American Olympic television production, I will show aspects of how this production marginalizes intercultural stories and by so doing severely restricts its audiences' understanding of the true nature of this global event.

Ethnography and journalism

This paper is based on subjecting my experiences as a reporter to a retrospective social-scientific analysis.[11] As an ethnographer, I observed, conducted interviews, kept detailed notes and interpreted culture through social practices and sacred rituals.[12] However, as a television news reporter, the majority of my data could not be included in my news reports due to traditional story time limits, a practice that leaves little room for sufficient description and analysis.[13] In reference to how producers view longer stories, a friend and former colleague of mine, Stacy Daily, has said: 'We like to call them show killers. A normal package is a minute – at most a minute-and-a-half – quick and concise. Leave that other stuff for [cable channels] CNN and MSNBC.'[14] I challenged this genre limitation because I felt the Olympic Games lacked adequate intercultural coverage, and I convinced the news executives to allow me to double, even triple, my story time slots, in order to present to American audiences' Greek perceptions of time, entertainment habits, dining practices, religious customs and, of course, attitudes towards the Olympics.[15]

As settings, I included the capital city of Athens, the northern city of Thessaloniki, the religious site of the Meteora, the village of Ancient Olympia and several other towns, villages and ancient sites along the way.[16] Olympia, the birthplace of the Olympic Games in 776 B.C., is a historic village that lies between two rivers, the Alpheios and Kladeos, in the district of Ilia, located within the western region of the Peloponnese in the southern part of Greece. Olympia's only main street is only a few hundred metres long and is lined with tourist shops. In the winter months, Olympia is a quiet, remote village, but from May through September, tourists saturate the streets. On the eve of the 2004 flame-lighting ceremony, the village square was filled with Greek traditional dancers from nearby towns and villages, who entertained thousands of spectators. After witnessing the spectators' solemn silence during the flame-lighting ceremony and through subsequent interviews,[17] I came to realize that most were not mere spectators or tourists, but rather people who travelled great distances to pay homage to the Olympic ideology and ritual practice.[18] The majority had travelled to Olympia as one would travel to Mecca or other centres of pilgrimage for an experience that would surely move and might even transform them. Therefore, by ignoring the flame celebrations and treating the Olympics as mere games, NBC loses the ritual significance, the connection to a broader Olympic ideology and the intercultural stories of the Olympic Movement.[19]

Intercultural narrativity and the Olympic ethos

As a television news reporter for a mid-market local NBC affiliate, I wanted to show my audience of American Midwest and 'Bible Belt' viewers a version of Greek culture that would be missing from national NBC's Olympic coverage. While pitching my idea of sending a crew to Greece, Nexstar's[20] corporate news director Susana Schuler[21] advised me to first present my idea to my station's general manager, Bob Sulley,[22] and then to proceed up the corporate ladder. I approached Bob in January 2004, and as I began to share my idea with him he closed his eyes, raised his hand and gestured for me to stop talking. He informed me that there was no money for that 'sort of thing'. I told him that I realized our station could never afford to send a crew to Greece, but if additional Nexstar stations were interested, then it would be feasible. Bob said, 'I know your culture is important to you and all. But, people down here [in Indiana] just don't care. They care about *local* sports, *local* news and weather. That's it.' I thanked him for his time and told him that I would be writing a proposal to the corporate offices, which greatly upset him because I was challenging his authority and professional viewpoint.

As Bourdieu points out, executives and journalists often disagree on what product the public desire to see covered on the news.[23] Following the lead of television executives, producers tend to treat the public as pre-existent and non-participatory; they give a product that they think people want and often nothing more. In contrast to Bourdieu's conception of the public as a mutual agreement between producers and consumers, I prefer Warner's understanding that the public does not pre-exist, but rather is generated in the moment of address.

> A public sets its boundaries and its organization by its own discourse rather than by external frameworks only if it openly addresses people who are identified *primarily* through their participation in the discourse and who therefore cannot be known in advance.[24]

Therefore, there are multiple publics within any potential audience and a reporter can never predict exactly which public is watching. The public unites strangers who set up their own boundaries designed by a common ideology. In this sense, the public resembles a distinctly circular formation consisting of active participants. I attempted in my proposal to convince Nexstar executives that my stories would appeal to (that is, would constitute) a wide audience, and that I had access to stories national NBC would not carry.

I proposed a 12-day trip to Greece gathering stories on the Olympic Flame Relay, Greek Orthodox Christianity, Greek culture, cuisine and entertainment, and daily life. With Susana's additions, the total budget came to 10,000 dollars or less than 1000 dollars per station, a remarkably low cost for such an endeavour.[25] During a conference call made in a sales-pitch tone-of-voice, Susana informed station news directors that if one of Nexstar's stations wanted to cover the Super Bowl they could not do it for as little money. During the same conference call, Bob suggested sending someone with more experience, which was a valid concern on his part because I had merely two years of combined reporting and field-producing experience.[26] Nexstar had hundreds of more experienced journalists, however not one could speak Greek, embodied Greek cultural knowledge and held valuable Greek contacts.[27] Therefore, Bob's suggestion was dismissed, and I was sent to Greece.

The 'un-newsworthy' flame-lighting ceremony

In the process of framing and marketing the Olympics almost exclusively as athletic games, NBC misses much of the cultural significance of the Olympic Movement, thereby doing its part in leaving most Americans ignorant of Olympism and the Olympic Movement.[28] This Olympic ethos or spirit can be defined, following MacAloon, as a sense of solidarity and common humanity that acknowledges and celebrates cultural differences while recontextualizing them in shared cultural performance forms.[29] As MacAloon argues, Olympic rituals, such as the flame-lighting ceremony, set the Olympic Games apart from other sports competitions. In this 'complex and ramified performance system', rituals serve to reframe the competitive and hierarchizing sports results into representations of international peace, collaboration and solidarity while also celebrating human diversity.[30] Therefore, to selectively ignore key Olympic rituals, as NBC does with the flame lighting ceremony, is necessarily to distort the entire Olympic phenomenon.

While isolated images from the flame-lighting ceremony did appear on *The Today Show*, NBC's morning news and entertainment programme, the attention was minimal and NBC blatantly and consciously avoided anything that could be said to resemble 'coverage'. Instead, Katie Couric, the show's co-anchor at the time, merely read a thirty-second voice-over.[31] There was no interview shown – or to my knowledge even conducted – with any of the ritual personnel or dignitaries present in Olympia, and the NBC producers made no attempt to 'unpack' the ceremony for the audience, thus further downplaying the significance of the event.[32] NBC did send a producer to the 2004 flame-lighting ceremony; however, they chose to rent only one Greek freelance camera crew for this event – a striking fact considering that during Athens 2004 NBC hired hundreds of freelancers.

Yet, the flame-lighting ceremony merited only four people, none of whom was a reporter and, in notable contrast with its practices in covering sports and the opening ceremonies, NBC drew nearly all the images in its scant presentation of the flame ceremonies from the 'world feed', footage generated by the host broadcaster ERT, the Greek public channel.[33]

During the ritual at Olympia, I positioned myself inside the media zone of the ceremonial venue at Olympia with a tripod and a Sony mini-DV camera, alongside the national NBC 'crew' and ERT's several crews. Mark Fuller, my videographer,[34] was positioned on the slopes of the Kronos hill outside of the arena, about 150 metres from the media zone, in order for him to capture an overview shot of the chief priestess lighting the flame. While I was shooting video of the crowd, the band and the Olympic flag, I noticed that the NBC rental crew was shooting formal speeches by various leaders. For Greeks, the media practice of covering official speeches is absolutely customary; however, this video would never appear in America, as it would be judged uninteresting since these leaders were not previously known. Ironically, the video necessary to make a suitable American media story was never shot. This convinced me that the presence of an NBC crew in Olympia was merely to 'save face'. But to save face for whom?[35] Was it in order not to insult the Athens Olympic Committee (ATHOC)? Or did NBC decide to go after being informed that an NBC-affiliated corporation, Nexstar, was sending a crew? I can only speculate, based on a bit of prior knowledge.

In February 2004, I discovered from one of my NBC sources that the network was not planning on going to the flame-lighting ceremony. This information was later confirmed to me by an NBC Sports & Olympics executive. Nexstar executives were sceptical of my claim, so Susana called the NBC offices in New York to ascertain the location of NBC headquarters in Greece. To her amazement, she was told nothing would be set up by the March ceremony date, and that NBC was not sending a crew to cover it. The on-site producer in Olympia later told me that an NBC Sports & Olympics executive producer did not want to send a crew either. These facts reconfirm NBC's low estimation of Olympic ritual values and further suggest that eventual dispatch of a token freelance crew may indeed have been in response to my presence for Nexstar.

Unpacking an Olympic ritual

The ancient stadium at Olympia consists of a packed dirt field surrounded by grassy banks where the spectators sit today, as they did in ancient times. The flame-lighting ceremony begins with flag-raisings, anthems and speeches on the stadium floor, after which an official delegation enters the sanctuary through the ancient passage to witness the actual flame lighting from the rays of the sun in a mirror placed on the ruins of an altar outside the Temple of Hera. Spectators seated within the stadium cannot see the lighting ritual, though those standing on the road above the ruins can do so. Although I could not see the initial lighting from where I was positioned, I experienced a mystical connection with those present. No one spoke; it was as if time stood still. I felt a sense of pride and humility towards my Greek ancestors, who conceived the Olympic Games. According to Turner's definition of ritual[36] and MacAloon's model of ramified performance types,[37] I was pulled into a ritual frame and enjoyed an experience of something much bigger than myself. Overall, I felt a sense of comfort and peace and a great deal of energy and reverence in the air.

Within my television series, I attempted to reveal that the flame was not a mere light. As MacAloon argues, the opening ceremonies, including the lighting of the sacred flame at Archaia Olympia and the relay to the 'New Olympia', are rites of separation from 'ordinary life,' initiating a period of public liminality.[38] This 'New Olympia' is the host city of the Olympic Games, in this case Athens, creating an especially intense linkage of the old with the new. One person who passionately understood this symbol is Enriqueta Basileo, the athlete who lit the cauldron during the opening ceremony of the 1968 Mexico City Olympics, becoming the first woman to do so. In Olympia, she described to me the compelling power of the flame:

> 'To know the magic of the flame is something I wish everyone could experience. I hope the light not only fills the hearts of the children and young people but over all humanity to promote peace and tranquility.'[39]

By presenting the flame as magical and a symbol of peace, this Olympic ritual seeks to regenerate the sense of common humanity. The similarities between the flame-lighting ceremony and explicitly religious rituals cannot be ignored. During an interview following the ceremony, an Olympic sculptor Petros Lambidetzis[40] spoke of the 'reverence' of the site of Olympia:

> It's a sacred place. I feel the energy, the feeling, the light, the smell of the place. It's fantastic, magic. The flame symbolizes the freedom, the love for knowledge, the human dignity.[41]

The Olympic flame represents something alive and powerful, yet simple and delicate. The Olympic flame is obviously a symbol worthy of analysis. However, comparative studies of television commentaries on the stadium arrival of the final torchbearer and the cauldron lighting in Barcelona 1992 show a certain superficiality in how commentators interpreted the ritual:

> It is also during the torch entrance where television commentary seemed most lacking in its attempt to link television audiences to some shared meaning for the ritual. While it's tempting to say that 'words can't describe' such dramatic moments, few commentators fall to silence … Possibly because of the familiarity of the ritual steps, most broadcasters choose to ignore the media script provided to them and simply describe what is happening on screen.[42]

By treating the performance more as a live show, commentators miss the significance of the flame symbols by taking them out of a ritual frame and placing them into a spectacle frame.[43] Flame performances are narrated as 'entertaining' rather than as moments of reverence and deep meaning. In an attempt to overcome this in my stories, I relied on those who have directly 'experienced' the flame to provide comment on the symbols. While the descriptions differed, everyone I interviewed agreed that the Olympic flame was more than a mere light.

Cultural knowledge and television news

I also wanted to introduce my audience to experts on Olympic rituals like John MacAloon, who has ethnographically studied and participated in flame relays around the world for nearly three decades and has been awarded the Olympic Order by the International Olympic Committee for his scholarship and intercultural diplomacy.[44] Ironically, while he is very well known to senior NBC Sports & Olympics executives, he has never been interviewed by NBC field producers or reporters about Olympic Flame Relay history and meaning. The same does not hold true for American print journalists. While I was again working for NBC Olympics in August 2004, I overheard a conversation on this very matter, between two journalists – one broadcast, the other print. On the way to Olympia for the shot put competition, MacAloon's name came up as I was discussing the Olympic Movement with Alan Abrahamson, a *Los Angeles Times* reporter who was also freelancing for NBC. Jimmy Roberts, the veteran NBC broadcast reporter along on the trip, had never heard of the scholar and had to be informed by Abrahamson that 'If you need to know anything about prior Olympics, MacAloon is your man. He knows everything'. This conversation illustrates how differently print and broadcast journalists can evaluate sources of information, which directly impacts what kind of news their respective audiences receive.

In television, reporters write as they speak and try not to alienate the viewers with speech that might be 'over their heads'.[45] Newspaper writers are likelier to welcome more elaborate arguments from experts, because newspapers have more space than a television news story and target a more articulate audience. The experts sought out by television news producers are ones comfortable speaking in ten-to-fifteen second sound bites leaving no room for analysis. Even within my own extended reports, this restrictive framework created obstacles. Moreover, providing educational and historical information that might seem controversial to some within the US television field created tensions among my peers and superiors, further illustrating how culture comes to be marginalized.

During the editing process in June 2004, Mark, my videographer, questioned a report I produced on the history of Greece, a piece that focused partly on Greek mythology. While Mark and I were at the Acropolis in March 2004 shooting video, I interviewed Robin Mueller,[46] a second-grader from Texas, who was visiting Greece with her family during her spring break holiday. She was posing for a photograph as an ancient Greek goddess. I asked Robin what she had learned in school about the Greek gods, and she told me, 'Zeus is the god of the Heavens.' Following the statement, I voiced-over these comments:

> The ancient Greeks had gods for just about everything – from love, to the arts, to wine. According to mythology, the city of Athens is named after Athena, the Goddess of War and Wisdom, who won the people's admiration when she gave Greeks the olive tree. But, even the Gods couldn't save Greece as it fell to the hands of invaders.[47]

Because of my reference to the ancient Greek gods, Mark refused to edit my piece, because, he said, it went against his Christian morals. He told me that the way the story was written, it could be inferred that Nexstar believed in multiple gods. Clearly, my intention was to provide the audience with the Greek historical background and not to present a theological position. Nevertheless, he regarded these statements as both controversial and offensive. I reminded Mark that I was also a practising Christian and that it was my plan to feature two stories on Christianity, accounting for 20% of the series. In a religious key, Marks' attitude reproduces a customary media practice in the general treatment of intercultural stories as too complex and controversial to cover. As Bourdieu argues, television news producers not only seek to report on topics that would attract the most people, they also strive to avoid offending anyone in the process.[48] Intercultural stories publicly introduce important issues whose existence some people may find difficult to accept. While producers broadcast news stories with just enough sensationalism to attract attention, they tend to avoid stories that generate too much intercultural challenge or exchange. Mark's opposition to my story speaks of a certain reading practice in play within the field that mishandles this complexity and reduces everything to one meaning. This practice is deeply problematic when it places the duty of editing into the hands of those predisposed to misinterpret intercultural stories. Mark's refusal offers further evidence in favour of MacAloon's observation that Olympic ritual content can offend conservative American Christians. MacAloon argues that a chief reason NBC does not cover the Olympic flame-lighting ceremony is to avoid offending American Christian sentiments.

> By the time we left for Greece to pick up the Olympic flame in 1996, ACOG [the Atlanta organizing committee] had received an inch-thick stack of letters from Christians urging the committee not to participate in this 'pagan' ceremony. Priestesses bringing fire down from heaven in ancient temples is evidently too much for many of our fellow citizens. Some of

these letters were sufficiently threatening that the FBI took an interest. [NBC Sports & Olympics chief] Dick Ebersol has denied to me that religious considerations have anything to do with NBC decision-making. Instead, he's told me, he doesn't cover the ritual because he thinks it's 'boring'. But the mere fact that 'ritual' is a taboo word in NBC Olympics coverage tells a deeper story.[49]

With respect to my story, the problem could have easily been solved if I agreed to leave out the 'controversial' comments about ancient polytheism, but I did not view them as problematic and did not think that I was in any position to rewrite Greek history so as not to offend the sensibilities of Bible Belt America. Instead, I told Mark, 'Kathy, my news director, already approved all my stories. If there's a problem, then perhaps I should talk to Susana and get her feedback.' Within the field of television production, executives and producers fact-check reporters' stories. By questioning and interfering with my work, Mark was indirectly attacking my news director's discretion and judgement. He backed down when I put it to him this way. In this case, corporate hierarchy trumped religious distortion and rejection of intercultural encounter.

Habitus – silent yet noticeable

The television broadcasting hierarchy includes network executives at the top, followed by executive producers, consultants, anchors, reporters, producers, videographers, technical staff, cameras-for-hire, production assistants and interns.[50] A network producer holds higher status than an affiliated reporter within the field, a fact brought home to me when I encountered an NBC network producer in March 2004 while preparing my report on the Olympic flame-lighting ceremony. In Olympia, I noticed a familiar sort of figure. Although I was not acquainted with this tall, medium-built man in front of me, I immediately knew he worked for NBC. He was dressed in khakis and a white polo, casual sports attire similar to what one might wear on a golf course. His posture was stiff and his head was raised up, as if dismissing others 'beneath' him. He was standing with two Greek videographers asking them about the scenery, when I walked up to him and asked, 'Are you with NBC?'

'Yes', he replied in a short, matter-of-fact way.

'So are we', I said with a big smile. 'Well, actually NBC affiliates. I'm with WTWO from Terre Haute, and Mark Fuller[51] (pointing to my videographer) is from KARK in Little Rock. Oh, and I'm Marianthi Bumbaris. And you are?' I said kindly offering my hand. He reluctantly shook my hand and told me his name was Chad Baker.[52]

Looking straight ahead and avoiding eye contact, he said, 'I'm surprised they sent you.'

I instantly replied, 'Why?'

He was not expecting a response to his comment. 'Well, it's just that we had a lot of red tape to cross to get here.'

'Well, when you know the rules and can speak the language it's a lot easier,' I responded, indirectly pointing out that NBC's disinterest in hiring people with local cultural capital would continue to be problematic for those out in the field attempting to gather stories.

Then, he refocused his attention on his videographers and the upcoming ceremony. Observing his demeanour and the way he carried himself, I realized that he perfectly embodied and performed the habitus, in Bourdieu's sense, of the NBC professional. One can think of habitus as embodied cultural knowledge that is consciously experienced and physically learned and is often only recognized by others within the same group because it has become implicit and 'naturalized'. This embodied knowledge provides 'meaningful practices and meaning-giving perceptions'.[53] The fact that I also belonged to this group enabled me to recognize a characteristic concern on Chad's part to remind Mark and I that as affiliates, we were not in his league, and that this fact was more important to him than our being NBC colleagues in a foreign land. However, his demeanour changed dramatically when he met me again in Athens, the International Broadcasting Center (IBC), during August 2004. Suddenly, he and I were on the same team because he realized he needed my greater cultural capital to cut through local 'red tape' and get stories more efficiently.[54]

Liminality, cultural capital and professional experience

In the process of crossing cultural registers, I felt pulled in opposing directions. Greece, of course, cannot be easily defined or packaged, but this was the task my news directors expected me to fulfil within the confines of American broadcast news and its particular unfriendliness to intercultural stories. I myself had stepped into a liminal space, in Victor Turner's sense,[55] of being neither Greek nor quite American. While covering the flame-lighting ceremony in Olympia, an art gallery, the famous Galerie Orphée became my home base and temporary newsroom, where the cameraman and I charged batteries, changed tapes and stored equipment. After a long day at work, the owner Apostolos Kosmopoulos – son of a former mayor and an Olympic torchbearer himself in 1964 – would greet me by playing a song, written by Manos Hadjidakis, a famous Greek composer, called *Marianthi of the Winds* which bears my name,[56] while he handed me a glass of local red wine telling me, 'Sit down. Relax'. The melody and Apostolos' hypnotic voice urged me to forget my American news deadlines and to enjoy Greece and even my liminal condition.

Liminality offers access and knowledge of two cultures, shedding light on cultural rules, rituals and behaviours that otherwise go unnoticed. Throughout my 12 days of reporting in Greece, I figuratively bounced from one culture to another.[57] On my journey to the 'homeland', I planted one foot in American broadcasting soil and my other foot on the land of my ancestors, crossing cultural barriers and discovering the complexity of intercultural stories. This approach influenced the construction of the 'news' events that I was sent to cover by challenging me to see my own culture through a different lens.

In August 2004, I returned to Olympia on two separate occasions with NBC Network to assist in covering Olympic history and the shot put competition. During this period, my professional status became extremely blurred. I was officially hired and paid as a production assistant, an entry-level role that I also previously held at the 2002 Salt Lake City Olympics. However, to my immediate supervisor, I was an assignment desk editor, a title that was included in NBC's official Olympic directory. Out in the field, I served various roles – as a field producer, translator and road navigator. My cultural capital forced me to serve different professional roles simultaneously. Unlike other genres of television reporting, intercultural stories can create an intense struggle between experienced and inexperienced reporters because, suddenly, cultural knowledge can translate into greater access, recognition and power.[58] Usually, the amount of professional experience one has within the field determines the right to cover a high-profile news assignment. However, the intercultural setting of the Olympics contradicted this regular structuring of the field. This point was brought vividly to life within my production fieldwork during Athens 2004.

Just days before the Opening Ceremony, a doping scandal involving two prominent Greek track and field athletes broke,[59] and international television crews hastened to the Hellenic Olympic Committee (HOC). My boss sent me to the HOC to bring lunch to the NBC crew staked out there with a hundred other reporters, photographers and audio technicians.[60] Within moments, my job as a production assistant quickly changed into that of a field producer (a position usually reserved for a person with 6–10 years of professional experience) when the 'Dateline NBC' producer and NBC Sports & Olympics field producer, Sam Struthers,[61] handed me the microphone and said, 'Here you go, you speak Greek. They're doing everything in Greek, so I can't do much.'

This response greatly intrigued me because three years before the Games, when I was applying for a field producing position with NBC Sports & Olympics, my language skills had been dismissed. An executive producer told me, 'Marianthi, we're doing business in English. We are not dealing in Greek.' At that time, the NBC Sports & Olympics executive producer did offer me an in-house position as a tape producer for Athens 2004, which would lead to a promotion for the 2006 Torino Winter Games. However, I felt my Greek language skills would be poorly used in this way, so I passed up this opportunity. Although, NBC had disregarded my cultural capital then, suddenly my bi-cultural qualities served as a bridge of access to valuable information.

After patiently waiting for about an hour, a gentleman holding a cleanly pressed suit coat over his shoulder emerged from the front doors of the HOC headquarters. After observing his demeanour,[62] I assumed he was an important person and informed the NBC videographer and audio technician to 'get ready'. When Greek reporters asked him about the scandal, he curtly responded. Then, I asked him a question in English, he responded in Greek, 'I do not speak English.' Immediately, I redirected my question in Greek using formal-tense as a sign of respect, 'Have you decided what action will be taken in the case of Kenteris and Thanou [the two Greek athletes suspected of doping]?' With a smirk, he told everyone in Greek, 'I have nothing to say at this point,' and walked off with four police officers by his side.

Half a dozen reporters turned to me, realizing I spoke English and Greek, and asked me what he said, and I informed them he did not say much of anything, but I told them, 'Let's follow him. He may say something.' Amidst the other international reporters' questions, I politely asked him in Greek, once again addressing him in formal register, 'What kind of message do you feel this sends about Greece to the rest of the world that is watching?' He stopped walking, looked me straight in the eyes and said with a sign of contempt in his voice and body language, 'You have a lot of *thrasos*.'

The word *thrasos* means audacity or shameless boldness, which translates into 'having a lot of nerve'. I later discovered that he was Vassilis Sevastis, the president of the Greek Athletic Federation. He is considered rude by some who know him personally. Also, speculation exists that he may have had some involvement or prior knowledge of the doping scandal.

In retrospect, this encounter revealed cultural differences within the field of television production. Although I was in Greece, American media practices governed me and directed my choices, but I also consciously obeyed and represented Greek cultural norms, such as showing signs of respect for one's elders. In the process of crossing cultural registers, this intercultural story becomes accessible while exposing the tensions involved when separate cultures governed by different social rules collide.

This encounter intrigued a Greek news reporter Vaggelis Pihas, who caught this cultural exchange on camera for Mega, a top, privately owned Greek television station. After I left the NBC crew and returned to the IBC, Vaggelis informed an NBC associate producer that they wanted to interview me live on their set about the encounter. However, Sam, overheard and refused. While I was field producing, Sam had noticed the Greek cameras catching the action on tape, which I was not aware of, and tapped me on the shoulder telling me, 'Stop. I don't want to become someone else's story.' This objection pointed to the media practice of avoiding professional controversy. My appearance on Greek television would have exposed NBC's decision in placing a production assistant in the role of the interviewer with NBC's image at stake, a decision that would have undermined NBC's Olympic broadcasting authority. NBC refused to have its media practices scrutinized under a foreign cultural lens.

Greek culture – stereotyped, edited and redefined

In the process of covering an unfamiliar culture, NBC repeatedly stereotyped Greek culture in its quest to illustrate social practices. This point was exemplified in an incident during my fieldwork during 2004 Athens. NBC Sports & Olympics chief Dick Ebersol suggested to Jimmy Roberts, an NBC sports reporter, that he write a story on Greek culture in the Plaka neighbourhood. Lying directly underneath the Acropolis, the Plaka is home to the Roman Agora, many tourist shops and restaurants, and tiny, curvy streets designed for strolling. Jimmy and his producer selected me to field-produce the story, but I informed Jimmy that one does not go to Plaka to find Greek culture, or what Jimmy called 'the Greek way'. As most local Athenians agree, Plaka is the place tourists go to shop, eat and dance Greek 'traditional' dances. Despite the fact that during the Olympics Greeks from distant villages and towns visited Plaka as foreigners do, it served as more of tourist attraction than a local gathering place. Jimmy dismissed my advice, obeyed the boss and travelled to Plaka in search of Greece. He described Plaka to the American public not as place constructed to feed the fantasy of tourists but as a place one could live as the Greeks live:

> The Plaka – it isn't only a place to gather, it's an attitude, and a window in which a country reveals itself in a most naked way. Time here is meaningless. Nothing could be more Greek.[63]

By reducing foreign culture to the symbol of Plaka, the story romanticizes Greek culture into something exotic and 'timeless'. Within the NBC perspective, the Greek way is the opposite of the time-conscious American way.

In a further attempt to construct an example of Greek cultural ways, Jimmy used the Olympic Stadium as an extension of how Greeks operate. In the process of constructing the Olympic Stadium, Greeks were behind schedule. As a result, the IOC and especially the American media questioned whether Greece would be ready. Jimmy told his audience that the Greeks responded to these concerns calmly by saying, 'Don't worry. We'll be ready. It's just the Greek way.'[64] Thus, the 'Greek way' becomes a comic representation of Greeks as relaxed, carefree Mediterranean people.

By innocently stereotyping Greeks, NBC portrays them in a favourable light and reinforces a sense of security, which was an important news media story before and during the Olympics. NBC's entertainment stories attempted to convince the American public that Greeks are not people America should be worried about, especially important during the American government's war on terrorism. However, despite the 'safety' of Greece, NBC hired an outside firm of security guards, many of whom were former FBI agents and military personnel, to protect some of their reporters, including Jimmy Roberts, who admitted he felt more safe with their protection. The guards wore identical khaki pants, black polo shirts and walkie-talkies, which revealed their 'undercover' identities. They attempted to navigate the small, crowded streets of Plaka, but in the process attracted negative attention. Instead of NBC blending in with the locals and experiencing 'Greek' life, people made room for NBC's entourage of 12 – 4 bodyguards, 5 NBC crew members and a Greek family whom Jimmy was interviewing – to pass. This points to how the field of television production separates itself from and elevates itself above a culture while claiming to offer an insider's perspective, a contradiction impossible to overcome under these circumstances.

Conclusion

'Beyond the Olympic Flame', my series of regional television reports, challenged the traditional news story by making culture into an area worthy of analysis.[65] Reactions to my effort at legitimating culture as newsworthy demonstrated once again that there is not one truth but many truths in the way of representing culture. Although complex events and structures require time to unpack, producers of intercultural stories nevertheless attempt to expose cultural symbols and practices within professional media constraints. My intercultural stories challenged the traditional news format by providing a space, no matter how small, for otherwise marginalized stories. Broadcasting and unpacking ceremonies and rituals, such as religion and the Olympic flame, exposed small American towns and cities to stories that would have otherwise remained hidden. In these ways, intercultural stories expose the limitations of the field of television production, but they also reveal the possibility for change. I did manage to convince a major media corporation Nexstar that intercultural stories could be interesting, affordable and profitable.[66] I have analysed how the tensions found between the different positions within the organizational hierarchy pose challenges in producing intercultural stories. For instance, while the corporation recognized and showcased my ethnic roots, it simultaneously misunderstood my mission, a fact apparent in the ways the stations marketed my stories. Instead of highlighting interculturality, they portrayed me as simply 'returning to my homeland'. By allowing Nexstar executives to label me as a 'Greek', I reinforced the normal media routines of transforming what I intended to be educational programming into light entertaining stories.

While the Olympics represent just one setting in which the field of television production marginalizes intercultural communication, in particular by misplacing and mistranslating ritual symbols and values into an entertainment spectacle frame, it is an important example because of its global reach. In the case of the American television field, moreover, this process is not restricted to NBC. In July 2005, I was watching *Good Morning America*, the ABC network's morning news and entertainment show, when the co-anchor Charles Gibson announced they were 'cutting' to an IOC 'news conference', where the host city for the 2012 Olympic Games would be announced. At the moment the directors cut into the IOC Session, the Olympic anthem was being sung, and Gibson apologized to his audience several times and openly shared his annoyance by saying it was 'typical' of the IOC to 'take their time' and 'put on a show'. As Bourdieu asserts, 'time, on television is an extremely rare commodity',[67] and for ABC television, the IOC was wasting precious television time with 'mere ritual'. What the IOC considers essential symbolic elements communicating the Olympic ethos, in this case the Olympic anthem, American television broadcasters collectively treat as frippery. ABC's commentary is just another representation of how the Olympic Movement does not currently 'fit' within American mainstream media's cultural perception of Olympic sport and its definition of news.

Notes

[1] An 'intercultural story' reveals aspects of a group of people who share a common heritage, nationality, customs and ethos from the specific vantage point of those occupying a space constituted between cultures.

[2] According to Melvin Mencher: 'Most news stories are about events that (1) have an impact on many people, (2) describe unusual or exceptional situations or events, or (3) are about widely known or prominent people.' Cited in Block, *Writing Broadcast News Shorter, Sharper, Stronger*, 34.

[3] The field of television production includes the planning, producing, executing and marketing dimensions that exist in covering news stories. It is also a space of tensions that remain largely hidden from the public.

4 The 'field of cultural production' can be understood as 'the site of struggles in which what is at stake is the power to impose the dominant definition of the writer and therefore to delimit the population of those entitled to take part in the struggle to define'. Bourdieu, *Field of Cultural Production*, 42.

5 John J. MacAloon, interview with author, Chicago, May 2005.

6 NBC Network signifies the media conglomerate, the National Broadcasting Corporation, whose main headquarters are in New York. NBC has affiliated stations throughout the USA. In discussing NBC Network, I will refer to the entity simply as NBC.

7 'Liminal entities are neither here nor there; they are betwixt and between the positions assigned and arrayed by law, custom, convention, and ceremonial.' Turner, *Forest of Symbols*, 95.

8 Bourdieu, *On Television*.

9 Herman and Chomsky, *Manufacturing Consent*.

10 While some scholars, such as Adorno and Horkheimer, consider 'the fusion of culture and entertainment' as a 'depravation of culture', I am asserting that the fusion, if executed in an educational way, can shed light on the intricacies of culture and preserve culture not destroy it. Adorno and Horkheimer, *Dialectic of Enlightment*, 143.

11 Within the field of television production, I have learned how media practices form and get performed on a daily basis. As a college senior, I interned for an investigative reporter and producer at WMAQ-TV, or NBC5, the local NBC owned and operated station in Chicago, Illinois. After college, NBC5 hired me as a production assistant and field producer. In 2002, I held a production assistant position with NBC Olympics in Salt Lake City, Utah. Later that year, I served as a reporter for WTWO, an NBC affiliate owned by Nexstar Broadcasting Group, in Terre Haute, Indiana, for nearly two years. During my time as a reporter, in the spring of 2004, Nexstar sent me with a videographer from another NBC-affiliated station to Greece to gather stories on Greek culture and the Olympic Movement. In August 2004, I travelled back to Greece, at my own expense, and served as a news assignment desk editor, on-site translator and field producer for NBC Sports & Olympics.

12 'By "ritual" I mean prescribed formal behavior for occasions not given over to technological routine, having reference to beliefs in mystical beings or powers.' Turner, *Forest of Symbols*, 19.

13 A 'traditional' American news story includes short, eight-to-ten second sound bites and about three-to-five short paragraphs of reporter voice-over. Overall, a story totals less than about 20 sentences. A 'sound bite' is the interviewee's reaction to a reporter's question. It usually is one or two sentences and typically no longer than 15 seconds long.

14 Stacy Daily, phone interview with author, 30 December 2006.

15 My stories averaged two-and-a-half minutes, which took up a whole segment between news and weather, a practice extremely uncommon in local newscasts nationwide.

16 Ancient Olympia is a small village with few hundred permanent inhabitants. The Greek Ministry of Internal Affairs recognizes Ancient Olympia as an honorary municipality (demos), but usually a location with such a small population is officially designated as a village.

17 In this essay, all names are pseudonyms except for public persons such as former Olympians, politicians, television news anchors, some television executives and professors.

18 The term 'Olympic Movement' will be defined subsequently.

19 In my perspective, a story impacts people, offers new information and attempts to explain 'why' something happened by revealing hidden aspects. News stories take on a different meaning as a result of field experience. For instance, a news story is determined by its availability and the crew's availability, whether it is an event that the competing stations will attend, and if it is a story that can be packaged quickly, or 'punched out', with as little controversy surrounding it as possible. Of course, there are exceptions, but the majority of the stories closely ascribe to this framework.

20 At the time of my proposal in January 2004, Nexstar Broadcasting Group owned 44 television stations, which included ABC, NBC, CBS and Fox affiliates. Nexstar's place within media ownership continues to grow to include small-to-middle-sized television stations throughout America. In 2004, Nexstar served 7% of the American public.

21 Throughout my broadcast journalism career, my superiors have asked me to address them by a first-name basis. This presents the facade that everyone within the organization is equal. However, no employee can escape the hierarchy that gets performed in different contexts such as making the final decision on story selection, length and content. In this paper, I will honour this convention and speak of my colleagues by their first names.

22 Pseudonym.

23 'The executives who worship at the altar of audience ratings have a feeling of "obviousness" which is not necessarily shared by the freelancer who proposes a topic only to be told that it's "not interesting."' Bourdieu, *On Television*, 26.

24 Warner, 'Publics and Counterpublics', 50.

25 The list of proposed expenses included hotel accommodations, rental car, car fuel, airfare for two, ferry boat tickets, ground transportation and food, for a total of US$5500. Ten stations showed initial interest. By March 2004, 14 stations wanted to broadcast the series, which further lowered the cost to about US$750 per station. My series eventually aired on 10 NBC-affiliated stations, 1 ABC station, 1 CBS station and 2 FOX stations.

26 Within journalism, experience constitutes achievement within the field. Experience determines respect from colleagues, the possibility of mobility to bigger cities and monetary success. Thus, a reporter 'moves-up' the corporate ladder only after putting time into the field.

27 Following Clifford Geertz's approach, I treated culture as a discovery of relationships and interpretations. Thus, intercultural stories require producers to identify, define and attribute significance to social and ceremonial practices. 'Believing, with Max Weber, that man is an animal suspended in webs of significance he himself has spun, I take culture to be those webs, and the analysis of it to be therefore not an experimental science in search of law but an interpretative one in search of meaning.' Geertz, *Interpretation of Cultures*, 5.

28 According to the *Olympic Charter*, 'The goal of the Olympic Movement is to contribute to building a peaceful and better world by educating youth through sport, practiced without discrimination of any kind in the Olympic spirit, which requires mutual understanding with a spirit of friendship, solidarity, and fair play.'

29 'In Olympic rituals, the symbols of generic, individual, and national identities are assembled and arrayed in such a way as to model, or to attempt to model, the shared humanity that is both the ground of the structural divisions the symbols condense and portray as well as the ultimate goal of Olympic ideology and practice.' MacAloon, 'Olympic Games and the Theory of Spectacle in Modern Societies', 251.

30 MacAloon stresses that 'from the earliest years of the movement', Coubertin, the renovator of the modern Olympics, emphasized the importance of Olympic ritual. 'In 1910, he wrote: "It is primarily through the ceremonies that the Olympiad must distinguish itself from a mere series of world championships."' MacAloon, *Great Symbol*.

31 A voice-over is when an anchor or reporter reads a few sentences while the video simultaneously plays on the television screen. In this instance, the video was a romanticized moment of the ceremony, the priestess holding the flame in a ceremonial bowl.

32 By unpacking, I mean assigning meaning to culturally significant events. In other words, producers should break down the event and reveal the importance of cultural beliefs and practices condensed in its symbols. According to Victor Turner, a symbol is 'the smallest unit of ritual which still retains the ritual behavior; it is the ultimate unit of specific structure in a ritual context'. Turner, *Forest of Symbols*, 19. When it comes to other performance genres, such as a basketball game, television has less need to unpack the symbols of the game because such events are common within American culture. If one knows the rules of the game, then one can understand the game. However, when producers introduce a ceremonial ritual that belongs to an unfamiliar culture or to a transnational and intercultural formation like the Olympic Games, even the master symbols require some explication.

33 The 'world feed' is the video distributed to the rights-holding broadcasters from around the world providing an exhaustive and 'neutral' coverage shot entirely by the official host broadcast agency. ERT, the Greek government channel, was one partner among others in forming the 2004 host broadcast agency, but ERT held sole broadcasting rights of the flame-lighting ceremony at Olympia. ERT offered international cameras an open-air shooting platform in the stadium.

34 Pseudonym.

35 By 'saving face' I mean avoiding embarrassment. As Goffman states, 'A person's performance of face-work ... represents his willingness to abide by the ground rules of social interaction. Here is the hallmark of his socialization as an interactant.' Goffman, *Interaction Ritual*, 31.

36 Turner, *Forest of Symbols*, 19.

37 MacAloon, 'Olympic Games and the Theory of Spectacle', 260.

38 MacAloon, *Great Symbol*, 252.

39 Enriqueta Basileo, interviewed in Bumbaris, 'Beyond the Olympic Flame' [BOF], 17 August 2004.

40 Pseudonym.

41 Petros Lambidetzis, interviewed in Bumbaris, *BOF*, 17 August 2004.

42 de Moragas et al., *Television in the Olympics*, 133–4.

43 As MacAloon argues the spectacle's grand qualities serve to delight the audience while also providing a 'metamessage', a message about how to take the message that says 'admire but do not be fooled'. MacAloon, 'Olympic Games and the Theory of Spectacle', 265.

44 MacAloon, 1981, 1984.

45 When I first started reporting, I was told to 'dumb it down' because my writing included too many 'big words'. Essentially, my superiors wanted me to sound 'conversational', but ironically this meant using words that everyone, from ages 5 to 95, could understand.

46 Pseudonym.

47 Bumbaris, *BOF*, 20 August 2004.

48 'Sensationalism attracts notice, and it also diverts it, like magicians whose basic operating principle is to direct attention to something other than what they're doing. Part of the symbolic functioning of television, in the case of news, for example, is to call attention to those elements that will offer something for everyone. These are things that won't shock anyone, where nothing is at stake, that don't divide, are generally agreed on, and interest everybody without touching on anything important.' Bourdieu, *On Television*, 17–18.

49 Interview with John MacAloon, Chicago, November 2002. See MacAloon, 2002. 'Greek/American/IOC Relations' in this volume for his more detailed argument.

50 This organizational hierarchy complements Bourdieu's theory of domination apparent within any field. Bourdieu, *On Television*, 37.

51 Pseudonym.

52 For some reason, he gave me a name that he does not use in the professional world. When I told some of my former NBC Olympics colleagues from the 2002 Salt Lake City Games that I met Chad Baker, they did not know who he was. That is because he goes by his middle name, Chris, which I found out when I met him again in Athens during the 2004 Games. In Olympia, he did not want me to know who he was and kept his real identity hidden. Again, I am using a pseudonym here.

53 Bourdieu, *Distinction*, 170.

54 I am using the term 'cultural capital' as cultural knowledge that translates into greater power, recognition and accessibility to intercultural stories.

55 Turner, *Ritual Process*

56 Manos, 'Marianthi of the Winds'. *The Ballads of Athenas Streets.*

57 Greeks in the diaspora have a saying, 'Ehoume ena podi edo, kai ena podi ekei', which literally translates into, 'We have one foot here, and one foot there.' 'Here' refers to America, and 'there' refers to Greece. In essence, it means 'we are neither here nor there', which expresses liminality and a sense of being pulled between two cultures.

58 The distinctive features of professional experience are the number of years one puts into the field learning the media practices, rules and expertise.

59 The scandal 'broke', or came to the public's attention, a couple of days before the Opening Ceremony. Journalists speculated that Kenteris, one of the athletes who missed a mandatory drug test, was meant to be the last torchbearer in the stadium, a very high honour. ATHOC to this day has not revealed whether Kenteris had indeed been scheduled as the last torchbearer until he was brought down in the doping scandal.

60 Media crews create temporary 'camps' when waiting for something big to happen, such as an announcement or news conference.

61 Pseudonym.

62 I am using Goffman's definition of demeanour: '[That] element of the individual's ceremonial behavior typically conveyed through deportment, dress, and bearing, which serves to express to those in his immediate presence that he is a person of desirable or undesirable qualities.' Goffman, *Interaction Ritual*, 77.

63 Roberts, *Chevrolet Olympic Moments on NBC*, 25 August 2004.

64 Roberts, *COM on NBC*, 25 August 2004.

65 Nexstar's Marketing Director urged me to develop a more 'catchy' title, such as 'My Big Fat Greek Adventure'. By placing an entertaining title to describe my stories, I felt this would minimize the importance of a cultural series. Therefore, my title was left unchanged.

66 The series was produced for US$10,000. Since I knew the importance for television corporations of turning a profit, I recommended selling each story to a sponsor. As a result of my suggested

marketing strategy, Nexstar ended up making a considerable profit, revealing that intercultural stories can be educationally and economically valuable.

[67] Bourdieu, *On Television*, 18.

References

Adorno, T., and M. Horkheimer. *Dialectic of Enlightment*. New York: Continuum, 1989.

Block, M. *Writing Broadcast News Shorter, Sharper, Stronger: A Professional Handbook*. Chicago, IL: Bonus Books, 1997.

Bourdieu, P. *Distinction: A Social Critique of the Judgment of Taste*. Cambridge, MA: Harvard University Press, 1984.

Bourdieu, P. *The Field of Cultural Production*. New York: Columbia University Press, 1993.

Bourdieu, P. *On Television*. New York: New York University Press, 1996.

de Moragas, M., N. Rivenburgh, and J. Larson. *Television in the Olympics*. London: John Libbey, 1995.

Geertz, C. *The Interpretation of Cultures*. New York: Basic Books, 1973.

Goffman, E. *Interaction Ritual: Essays on Face-to-Face Behavior*. New York: Pantheon Books, 1982.

Herman, E.S., and N. Chomsky. *Manufacturing Consent: The Political Economy of the Mass Media*. New York: Pantheon Books, 1988.

MacAloon, J.J. *This Great Symbol: Pierre de Coubertin and the Origins of the Modern Olympic Games*. Chicago, IL: University of Chicago Press, 1981 (Second revised edition. London: Routledge, 2008).

MacAloon, J.J. 'Olympic Games and the Theory of Spectacle in Modern Societies'. In *Rite, Drama, Festival, Spectacle: Rehearsals Toward a Theory of Cultural Performance*, edited by J. MacAloon. Philadelphia, PA: Institute for the Study of Human Issues Press, 260 (1984): 251.

Manos, H. 'Marianthi of the Winds'. *The Ballads of Athenas Streets*. Athens: K. Papageorgoriou-Ch. Nakas Music Publishing House, 1983.

Turner, V. *The Forest of Symbols: Aspects of Ndembu Ritual*. Ithaca, NY: Cornell University Press, 1967.

Turner, V. *The Ritual Process: Structure and Anti-Structure*. Chicago, IL: Aldine, 1995.

Warner, M. 'Publics and Counterpublics'. *Public Culture* 14, no. 1 (2002): 50.

Hybridity and subversion: the Olympic flame in India

Boria Majumdar[a,b] and Nalin Mehta[c]

[a]*University of Central Lancashire, Lancashire, UK;* [b]*Monash University, Melbourne, Australia;*
[c]*Institute of South Asian Studies, National University of Singapore, Singapore*

This article presents the results of a field study of the 2008 Olympic Flame Relay in
Delhi, India, where Tibetan and pro-Tibetan protests against the Chinese Olympic
hosts generated a state security transformation of Olympic ritual and a parallel Tibetan
counter-performance. These events are placed in the context of earlier Indian practices
of indigenization of the Olympic Flame Relay in 1960, 1964, and 2004. If Delhi 2004
represented a further hybridization of indigenous and international 'best practices'
models for flame relays, Delhi 2008 demonstrated the failure of the standard model to
cope with the political and moral forces unleashed when the host nation is as
challenged as China in the field of human rights. This article concludes with an analysis
of the Queen's Baton Relay for the 2010 Delhi Commonwealth Games, showing the
chaotic caricature that results when transnational standard practices for relays of sports
festival icons are completely set aside.

The 1960 and 1964 precedents

On its first visit to the subcontinent, an Olympic-style flame was literally worshipped by a
million Indians. Though the Olympic flame itself first appeared in Delhi on the occasion of
the 1964 Tokyo Olympics, the first Indian exposure to the idea of the sporting flame can
be traced back further to 1960, when the key precedent for Indian indigenization was set.
Hidden in the International Olympic Committee (IOC) archives at Lausanne is the
intriguing story of an attempt to create an Indian equivalent of the torch relay in the town
of Jwalamukhi. Just as an Olympic torch is carried from Olympia to each Olympic Games
host city every four years, so Indian sport administrators emulated this practice for the XIX
National Games of 1960, creating a relay from the Jogmaya temple in the holy town of
Jwalamukhi near Hoshiarpur in Punjab. With officials trying to create a national sporting
culture, the Greek-IOC ceremony took an Indian form in Jwalamukhi with high priests
chanting Sanskrit *shlokas* and lighting the relay flame from the temple's sacrificial fire.
This was a deliberate strategy by the organizers to build local interest. Such was the
popular interest in the 1960 event that the Indian Olympic Association's chronicler noted:
'As the torch emerged from the temple, there was a tremendous ovation from the crowd of
10,000 that had collected outside the temple'.[1]

About 1500 torchbearers carried the flame for 350 km from Jwalamukhi to Delhi over
10 days, and it is significant that as many as a 'million people' turned up to see them en
route. The Jogmaya connection seems to have given the Indian equivalent of the Olympic
flame a kind of religious sanctity. At Jullunder, for instance, the Town Hall, where the
torch was kept for the night, became a 'virtual *mandir*' and thousands filed past the flame

and 'made their offering'. At Ludhiana, on February 18, as many as 50,000 lined up on both sides of the Grand Trunk Road as the torchbearers made their way into the city. Such was the rush that policemen and soldiers 'found it difficult to control the rush of people who wanted to pay their homage to the flame'.[2]

> When the torch reached Patiala, the Indian Olympic Association's (IOA) effusive chronicler noted:
>
> Almost the entire population of Patiala came out to give an unprecedented reception to the torch on February 20. The main bazaars wore a festive appearance unknown in the recorded history of that city ... at various corners in the city people distributed sweets. Milk, fruits and flowers were offered to the runners. Thousands of men and women filed past the torch at Yadavindra Stadium where it was kept for the night.[3]

Similarly at Ambala city and cantonment, 'all arrangements to control the crowds broke down' as thousands gathered far exceeding the expectations of the organizers. From Panipat to Delhi, the Grand Trunk Road was lined up with thousands as they came to get their glimpse of this holy fire that was to start the National Games.[4] Part of the fervour was certainly attributable to the sanctity attached to the Jogmaya temple of Jwalamukhi, but no one doubted the sporting nature of the event. The distant rituals of Olympia and the Olympic movement had been Indianized, and the breathtaking popular response was the strong measure of the support that the National Games and Olympic-style sport had at the time, at least in north India. The 1960 Jogmaya relay was a fascinating example of how similar ritual forms surrounding the lighting of a flame could provide such deep resonance in two very different cultural contexts within the modern Olympic movement.

The success of the 1960 Jogmaya relay set the grounds in India for the highly successful Olympic Flame Relay of 1964. The Tokyo Games organizers had designed an international relay along the southern Silk Road. After being lit at Olympia in Greece, the flame travelled by plane to various capitals of South and Southeast Asia, where it was relayed around these cities. The relay was managed by the Japanese organizers with input from local authorities on matters of routing and crowd control. In Delhi, as *The Times of India* described it:

> Shoppers in Connaught Place and Janpath stopped whatever they were doing and rushed to cheer the relay, managed by smart Japanese in dark suits and neat white gloves. The flame rested for the night at New Delhi's Town Hall before being given a ceremonial send-off the following day on its flight to Tokyo. No security problems those days, no fears of protests and demonstrations.[5]

Memorable images of the Olympic flame's passage through Delhi were circulated internationally in Kon Ichikawa's famous film *Tokyo Olympiad*.

The retrospective question to ask in the light of the events of 2008 is why Tibetan protesters did not try to use the 1964 event as a vehicle for publicizing their cause in India, like they did in Delhi 44 years later. In 1964, after all, the Tibetan refugees were still fresh in India and India had just suffered a humiliating military defeat at the hands of the People's Army. Even though, publicly, at least, China was still firmly in the Communist camp in the cold war, the Soviet Union had refused to support its military foray into India. Indian public opinion would arguably have been ripe to support anything that could diplomatically embarrass the Chinese. The obvious answer is that in 1964, the host nation in charge of and benefiting from the Olympic flame in Delhi was Japan not China, as would be the case in 2008. This shows that on international relays, the relationship between the transnational humanistic meanings of the Olympic flame and the country through which the flame is passing will always be critically mediated by the identity of the Olympic host nation for which the flame is bound on its journey.

The Athens 2004 flame in Delhi

Forty years after India's experience with the 1964 Olympic flame, it returned to Delhi on 11 June 2004, as a stop on the global relay for the Olympic Games of Athens. In the interim, a particular operations model for flame relays had been developed and endorsed by the IOC as 'world's best practice'.[6] In Delhi and the other cities visited in 2004, this model was deployed by the Athens Olympic Organizing Committee (ATHOC) through its contractor, the Além International Management firm. Not only the massive and fervent crowds, but also and most importantly India's indigenous tradition of receiving the Olympic flame as if it were a temple deity in ritual procession through the streets overwhelmed the globally 'standard' model in its crowd control preferences, biased as they were towards Western conceptions of policing and public order.[7] In India, ritual devotion and personal empowerment not only permit but also require pushing as close to the sacred object as possible. In other respects, however, the standard operations model held its own, and the 2004 relay through Delhi could be viewed as a successful moment of intercultural hybridization.

But from the standpoint of Indian public culture, a certain elite hybridization on the part of the IOA and its government partners generated real controversy, with many asserting after the relay that the symbolism of the Olympic flame had been subverted and that the whole occasion was trivialized. For their own political and economic reasons, the Indian authorities chose to feature Bollywood celebrities and cricket stars as torchbearers instead of Indian Olympic athletes. The shoddy treatment meted out to Indian Olympic legends like P.T. Usha, who refused a last-minute invitation to run with the flame, provoked a significant backlash in the media once the flame had left Indian shores.

The flame arrived in a special 747 Boeing aircraft named 'Zeus' on the morning of 10 June, and Suresh Kalmadi, then President of the IOA (and currently in jail for alleged misappropriation of 2010 Commonwealth Games funds), received the flame at New Delhi's Indira Gandhi International Airport. Thereafter the flame was taken to the historic Qutab Minar from where it started its formal journey through select streets of the national capital. At Qutub Minar, Delhi Chief Minister Sheila Dikshit handed over the flame to Kalmadi as the first of a hundred runners, and the IOA president then handed it over to former Indian field hockey captain Ajit Pal Singh. Singh together with his compatriot Milkha were among the few Indian Olympic legends present and the flame was soon passed on to Indian cricket stars like Virender Sehwag, Anil Kumble, and Rahul Dravid. With thousands lining up on the streets to catch a glimpse of the flame and with the security present looking distinctly unprepared to control such a huge crowd, people soon decided to intervene in the day's proceedings.[8] The ATHOC operations and security team guarding the flame found themselves helpless in the middle of thousands of Indians and it was only a miracle that saved the flame from being snatched away. Virender Sehwag, a proud torchbearer, recounted later:

> It was chaotic. There were thousands of people on both sides of the street and they were constantly trying to come into the inner cordon. I was doing my best to guard the flame but it was very difficult under the circumstances. No doubt it was a proud moment but things could have been much better organized.[9]

Only Doordarshan, India's national broadcaster, was allowed to beam the relay live from start to finish. Other channels were allotted select spots to 'shoot' causing further confusion and multiple parleys with the security personnel manning the flame. The relay ended with a cultural programme at the National Stadium late in the evening.

Bollywood stars Aishwarya Rai, Rani Mukherjee, and Aamir Khan were also part of the relay in Delhi. Their presence resulted in serious criticism in the aftermath of the relay and *The Hindu*, one of the country's most respected newspapers, published a series of letters to the editor questioning the IOA's decision to leave out leading Indian athletes in favour of such celebrities.[10] Here are a few samples:

Sir, — The photographs of film stars carrying the Olympic flame through the streets of Delhi saddened me. More saddening is the fact that newspapers tend to focus on these actors, not athletes. Are these film stars going to represent India at Athens?

Vivek Bhaskar, Chicago, US

Sir, — It was heart-breaking to listen to the golden girl P.T. Usha lamenting the fact that she could not carry the Olympic flame. She may not be as glamorous as Aishwarya Rai or Aamir Khan, but she has brought glory to the nation.

Saju C. Mannarath, Bangalore

Sir, — Will the film industry allow a sportsman to inaugurate a film festival? Sponsors should not be allowed to dictate terms during an event as prestigious as this.

E. Muralidharan, Chennai

Sir, — In India, cine stars may even speak in science congresses. No wonder our Olympic record is so poor.

Srinivasan, Chennai

V. Srinivas, speaking on behalf of his wife P.T. Usha[11] a day before the relay, best summed up the organizational chaos and controversial decision-making in New Delhi:

I do confirm that Usha has received a written invitation on behalf of the Indian Olympic Association but it came only last night. Two days ago Suresh Kalmadi, president of the IOA and Lalit Bhanot, secretary, Amateur Athletics Association of India spoke to Usha and invited her to join the relay. This invitation came only after Usha told the media that she had not been called. She is naturally disappointed and feels hurt.[12]

Reacting to Usha's omission, Ajit Pal Singh was scathing in his criticism of the IOA:

They should have prepared the list of top 30 athletes and sportspersons and then sent them the invitations instead of accommodating people who live in and around Delhi. How can they forget a name like P.T.Usha? I feel that even cricketers should not have been invited for the event leave alone inviting film stars and people from the cultural field. When there is a film awards function, have you ever heard of an Arjuna awardee being invited there.[13]

Embarrassing China: Tibetan protests and the 2008 Flame Relay

The 2008 Olympic Flame Relay in Delhi was completely taken over by security personnel and closed to the public. This outcome was the result of massive and spontaneous Tibetan protests that emerged in India as an important link in the global chain of pro-Tibetan protests that the hosting of the Olympics by the Peoples Republic of China ignited after the Chinese crackdown on the Tibetan uprising in March of the Olympic year. This section studies the local manifestations of the Delhi protests, the organization and mechanism of the agitation, the countermeasures adopted by the state, the national and international implications of the protests, and finally their broader meaning for the institution of the flame relay itself. This is an attempt to analyse the impact of the political tightrope walked by the Government of India, as it sought to balance its diplomatic priority to pursue the recent thaw in Sino-Indian relations with the imperatives of a democratic public culture. India has been host to the Dalai Lama since the 1950s, and the Beijing Olympics provided the trigger for a renewed focus on the Tibetan question in a newly sensitive diplomatic environment.

16–18 April 2008: Delhi in turmoil

The Olympic Flame Relay during the third week of April 2008 brought the city of Delhi to a standstill. Seven security checkpoints on the way to India Gate were manned by 21,000 security officers. An attempt was made by protesters to storm the Le Meridian, a hotel turned into a fortress and the site where the Olympic flame was sequestered after its arrival from Islamabad at 1:10 am on 17 April. A series of peaceful, synchronized democratic protests were mounted by Tibetans and human rights groups from 8:00 am in the morning not only in Delhi, but throughout the country. The Olympic flame was relayed along a truncated route behind massive security, a performance closed entirely to the Indian and international public, and therefore severed completely from the indigenous Indian forms developed to culturally handle the Olympic master symbol. Delhi 2008 was indeed an ensemble of extraordinary developments.

The Olympic Flame Relay was never only about sportspeople. The relay is not restricted to countries that win the most medals or those that have the best sports facilities for their athletes. International relays like those of 1964, 2004, and 2008 have been promoted as bringing 'Olympism' to some of the poorest of countries whose men and women will hardly ever make it to an Olympic sports contest. Moreover, attending the flame relay is free and unticketed, in contrast to Olympic sports events that are prohibitively expensive for most people. The torch relay is a public event both seeking and generating mass support. The visits of the Olympic flame, a world peace symbol, have played a considerable role in making the world's biggest sports spectacle relevant and real for many in India. The flame has emerged as an enduring symbol of global harmony and mobilization, a fact evident on the streets of Delhi on 17 April 2008.

The Olympics have long provided a forum for issues of international concern, the dispossessed, marginalized, and aggrieved using the glare of public spotlight to focus world attention on their causes. Seoul highlighted the Korean national division. Barcelona focused on ethnic differences within Spanish society. Atlanta drew world attention to the race issue in the US while Sydney highlighted the Aboriginal crisis Down Under. When Cathy Freeman lit the flame at the Sydney Games in 2000, much more than a sporting ritual was performed. It had immense symbolism for the tensions at the heart of modern Australian society, all the more so when she later wrapped herself in the Aboriginal flag in full view of the world's cameras. Similarly, when the Tibetans organized a parallel relay in Delhi on 17 April 2008, the Tibet crisis became the cynosure of international attention. In a country which has hosted the Dalai Lama since the 1950s, and which has remained embroiled in a border dispute with China for over five decades, the Olympic Flame Relay provided the trigger to focus attention on the Tibetan question as never before. In trying to fully understand the complexities of the Delhi relay we had to become ethnographers, and our journey into the heart of the Tibetan agitation on the streets of Delhi further extended our research into the Olympic movement in the subcontinent, while offering some important pointers towards the social meanings of the Olympic Flame Relay itself.

The Government's double bind: diplomacy or democracy

Before the Indian leg of the torch relay, there was considerable debate on whether New Delhi would allow Tibetan protesters to carry on with their demonstrations. With the Left Front governments in West Bengal and Kerala governments adopting a hard-line approach towards such protests, the issue had assumed added significance. The Left Front government in West Bengal went so far as to ban Tibetan protests ahead of the torch's arrival in India.[14] At one level, this was simply a case of the Left's repeated support for positions taken by the Chinese Communist Party. With the Left also a crucial partner, at the time, in the Congress-led coalition government in Delhi, such an approach by a powerful partner in the alliance reduced the manoeuvring space for the central government. But, at another level, the prospect of widely publicized Tibetan protests also created apprehensions in New Delhi about their diplomatic impact on the ongoing boundary disputes with China. At the same time, the world's largest democracy could not be seen to be muffling dissent, even if this dissent was opposed by those who were advocating a closer strategic engagement with China.

Caught in a double bind, the Congress, therefore, hedged its bets. What added to the anxiety of the government was the news that some Tibetan protesters had managed to break the heavy security cordon outside the Chinese embassy in New Delhi's diplomatic enclave of Chanakyapuri, and had managed to scaled its walls to register their concerns. Two widely differing concerns played on the minds of national political leaders: What message would banning protests in the national capital playing host to the Olympic flame send out to the international community? Second, the government was acutely aware of the strategic conclusions that Beijing would draw from New Delhi's handling of the Tibetan protests.[15] So Government decided on a two-pronged approach. The protests would go on elsewhere in India – in any case it would have been impossible to police a wider ban – but the protesters would not be allowed anywhere near the Olympic torch in Delhi. Everyone, therefore, could save face.

It was a delicate balancing act: allow the Tibetans their fundamental right to protest in full public view but guard against a diplomatic incident by ensuring that the torch relay itself, guarded by massive Indian security accompanied by Chinese military police, is not disrupted. The diplomatic impact of New Delhi's double-edged response to the flame relay is open to debate, but the clear price was excessive security and a huge inconvenience caused to Delhi's residents on the day of the ritual, leaving a bitter taste in many mouths.

Once the decision was taken to quarantine the Olympic flame away from the Tibetan protestors, the Union Home Ministry swung into action. It announced an unprecedented security clampdown for the torch relay, of the kind that Delhi witnesses once every year on Republic Day, when the central parts of the city are sealed off completely to all traffic to facilitate the annual military parade to celebrate the Indian Republic. The Chinese Ambassador to India personally met the city police chief Y.S. Dadwal at the police headquarters, and as mentioned earlier, a total of 21,000 security personnel were specially deployed across the city. Central paramilitary forces and commandoes were requisitioned and the relay route was severely reduced from the planned 9 km to 2.7 km. *The Times of India* summed up the massive security build-up in a telling full-page banner headline: 'It's a fortress out there'.[16]

Despite this huge presence, on April 15, before the torch arrived in Delhi, Tibetan protestors demonstrated their organizational skills by lighting a replica of the Olympic torch at an under-construction Metro station just a kilometre away from the Rashtrapati Bhawan (President's House) in central Delhi. They called it the 'Tibetan Independence Torch Relay'. In the heart of Delhi's most secure zone, a short walk away from Parliament and the Central Secretariat, they came in quietly in auto-rickshaws, hiding their banners and flags under their clothes before suddenly unfurling them before thousands of armed policemen deployed for just such an eventuality. They wanted to walk towards India Gate – the memorial to Indian war-dead – to hold a protest vigil but as the policemen tried to snuff out the Tibetan flame, the flames caught the clothes of a woman protestor. They were quickly put out and the protestors were led away in police trucks but it had been a powerful demonstration of what could happen when the Olympic flame actually came to town.

Jittery at the prospects, the Union Home Ministry convened a high-level meeting that same day to review the security arrangements. This was monitored at the highest levels of the government. At the meeting were IOA officials, representatives from the Intelligence Bureau, the Delhi Police, and the Union Home Minister of State, Shakeel Ahmad who told reporters, 'It is our responsibility [to ensure safe passage for the torch]'.[17] One measure of how seriously the government was taking the relay was the fact that even the Delhi Metro was asked to close services to all stations in the vicinity of the torch relay for the day. The Olympic torch relay had now turned into an issue of national importance, diplomatic gamesmanship, and civic inconvenience. Even the UN advised all staff in Delhi to avoid any movement in the relay route due to safety reasons and to reschedule or postpone planned meetings in the area.[18]

Following the agitators

For us, the experience of the relay had begun on the night of 16 April when we watched Tenzing Tsundue, a noted activist and leader of the Free Tibet movement, on the 24-hour satellite news network *Times Now*.[19] Soon after the show, Tsundue, we were later informed, was dropped of at an unknown location with the police desperate to detain him. The *Times Now* driver, Amjad, who ferried him to his hideout and who was with us the following day, took us to the secret location at the stroke of dawn. At the hideout, a group of senior Tibetan leaders were in attendance and were keen to ensure that 17 April 2008 turned into a day of international impact for their cause. Knowing full well that the police would outnumber them, they were planning guerrilla attacks on the flame on its way out of the Meridian on Janpath Road and on its way to India Gate. While these Tibetans were determined to make a mark and were not averse to violence, others, who had already made Jantar Mantar their home were single-minded in their determination in trying to keep things peaceful. For them non-violent protest was the way to capture world attention and hence life-size cut-outs of Mahatma Gandhi were juxtaposed with those of the Dalai Lama at the forefront of most protest rallies.

For these and thousands of other Tibetans who had arrived in Delhi the night before, things got underway in the wee hours of the morning of 17 April with an assembly at Rajghat. This venture needed planning and coordination on national scale, from the strategic to the mundane. When we arrived at 7:30 am, we saw groups of men and women bracing themselves for the day's events by writing out posters or painting placards. Some were busy packing pouches of water and food, while others, who had travelled thousands of miles to be a part of the movement, were busy catching up on a quick hour's sleep. Members of the Tibetan Parliament-in-Exile, key organizers of the rally, were busy putting final touches to preparations for the protest march. 'We wanted the Dalai Lama to be visible alongside Mahatma Gandhi for both are messiahs for global peace',[20] was their reasoned answer to our query on why most posters had the Tibetan leader sharing stage with the man who the Indian state calls the father of the nation.

Just as the clock struck 10:00 am, there arrived at Rajghat a slew of Hindu, Muslim, and Sikh religious preachers for joint prayers in solidarity with Tibetans at Gandhi's Samadhi. It was surreal, a motley mix of preachers from varied religious backgrounds coming together to pray for a cause of real global significance. It was good event management to be sure but none but the most cold-hearted cynic could afford not to be moved by the solemnity of it all and fail to observe the fact that the global appeal of contemporary sport had made it possible.

With the prayers over, the Tibetans lit their own parallel flame. This was different in shape from the Olympic torch and was more in the nature of a *diya* [traditional earthen lamp] that was subsequently placed inside a round frame. They had been told that only a 'non-official' torch of this kind would pass official muster. As chants of '*Karuna ki jyoti amar rahe*' [May the torch of tenderness live forever] and '*Shanti ki jyoti Amar Rahe*' [May the torch of peace live forever], shattered the silence, assembled leaders from all major religious groupings joined in carrying the flame out of Rajghat. This was the point at which the huge police contingent, men and women who did everything possible to cooperate till now, began to visibly look a tad jittery until the rally leaders assured them that the march would be kept peaceful. So powerful was the group dynamic that some security men too were caught up in the emotionalism of the moment, a couple of those standing nearest to the protestors with tears in their eyes.

Once out of Rajghat, the rally began its 4 kilometre march to Jantar Mantar, the site which the Tibetans had made home for the day. Thousands of Tibetans from Varanasi, Mcleodganj, Bangalore, and Dharamshala had already assembled at Jantar Mantar the night before, carrying with them bare minimum supplies. The location was not unsurprising. Jantar Mantar after all is the permanent protestors' corner in Delhi. For years it has been the site where the dispossessed and the marginalized of India come to present their woes before the national media, hoping for higher visibility with the powers that be. And so the Tibetans came, jostling for space in this parliament of the oppressed, alongside stalls set up by the Bhopal gas tragedy victims, the Vishwa Dalit Parishad [World Council of Dalits], the Foundation for Common Man: Justice for Natihari, and even the Group 4-Securicor Mazdoor Union, asking for better wages.

As hundreds of specially deployed policemen watched from the sidelines and scores of reporters took notes, the entire panoply of anti-Chinese dissent was on display in a tent city that had come up virtually overnight on one of the sidelines leading up to Jantar Mantar. At its entry point, someone had prominently placed a huge poster on the windshield of a parked car: 'Just raped in Tibet'. It summed up the mood, and to enter the tent city was to enter a virtual marketplace of oppression. The centrepiece was a day-long funeral service to those who died at the hands of the Chinese conducted by specially brought in monks. As their chants and gongs filled the air, the observer could see a whole range of stalls, including representatives of the banned Falung Gong, posters showcasing the pictures of those dead and missing, and pictures of torture and death at the hands of Chinese troops. The posters were saying: 'Shame on you China', 'Where are you UNO', and even included one depicting the Chinese President as an incarnation of Dracula. Policemen and intelligence sleuths in plainclothes mingled with the protestors, although none tried to intervene.

With hundreds of local students joining hands, Jantar Mantar was turned into a mini-Tibet, the adjoining alleyways and streets leading up to the now virtually deserted Janpath Road. Cannaught Place was now choc-a-block with activists sporting 'Free Tibet' t-shirts and head-bands. Their one point demand: China open its doors to envoys of the Dalai Lama. Their slogans shouted out in Hindi, mixed their animosity with China to chants of friendship with India: '*Gali-gali mei shor hai, Hu Jintao hatyara hai*' [Every street rings, Hu Jintao is a killer], '*Azadi sab ko pyara hai*' [Freedom is beloved by all], 'North Pole South Pole, *Bharat hamara saath do*' [India, support us].

How spontaneous was this agitation and what had gone into its planning? Our interviews with nearly hundred of the protestors provide a clear picture. One of the agitators had been arrested two weeks earlier for breaking into the Chinese embassy. His story summed up the story of this gathering. Born of Tibetan refugee parents in Mysore, Karnataka, he was a farmer who had been camping in Delhi for 45 days. He was a member of the Tibetan Youth

Congress but he said that initially 'it all happened suddenly' once the Tibetans realized that they could use the Olympic torch relay to showcase their cause. He had come down to Delhi because 'it was the national capital' and it was important to magnify protests here.[21] The Tibetan protestors saw this is as an unparalleled opportunity to put pressure on the Chinese government, using the oxygen of publicity, because for the national and international media, their story now had immediacy. This was also the argument given by Dhondup Dorji, Vice President, Tibetan Youth Congress. Appearing on a special half-an-hour live programme called 'Torch of Protest' on *Times Now*, he argued that this was the first time that the electronic media had given support to their cause. 'Normally we have support from the print media only', he opined.[22] He had a point. On the same programme, television viewers saw two young Tibetan college students from Mumbai breaking from their prepared speeches to suddenly question Dorji on how he would motivate the Tibetan youth after this event. The young questioners had been rustled to the live satellite link by the channel's reporters to show their national coverage of the protests, but this was a spontaneous question, one that reflected the internal dilemmas of the Tibetan movement on how to sustain momentum. Sitting in the Delhi studio, Dorji answered on the live satellite link: 'Tibetan youth have a moral responsibility to keep up the struggle. We must dedicate our lives to Tibet'.[23] It was an extraordinary moment; it was like listening to an intra-party discussion forum. The Tibetan Youth Congress on that day had a national platform to reach out to its own cadres on national television and disseminate internal messages that would normally have passed through the usual hierarchies of leadership. This was direct communication and it came at a time when protests had also simultaneously broken out in Bangalore, Mumbai, McLeodganj, and Dharamshala.

The official relay: a damp squib

By the time the Tibetans resumed their rally in the afternoon, the action had shifted to India Gate, and we followed it there. It was an ordeal getting through, with frisking going on at every roundabout. Because we were late, the police were determined to stop us, despite possessing all the necessary official invitations from the IOA. Finally, only we, the official invitees, were allowed inside.[24] At exactly 4:40 pm, Kunjarani Devi, India's legendary female weightlifter, started running with the flame. This time, however, emotions were not running as high. There was a lot of tension in the air and the challenge was to get the events done with as soon as possible. With no spectators to cheer the athletes on, the flame travelled its destined distance within 50 minutes. Finally, when Leander Paes and Mahesh Bhupathi lit the cauldron, Suresh Kalmadi, then President of the IOA, looked justly relieved. As one NDTV reporter on the spot summed up in a live report: 'Who saw it [the flame]? Certainly not the people of Delhi'.[25]

In summary, the 2008 relay represented a catalysis of the hybrid form established in India over the previous 48 years: the spiritual frames and ritual practices and experiences pioneered at Jwalamuki in 1960 were displaced entirely onto the Tibetan counter-ritual; while the official flame relay was an austere simulacrum, an extreme caricature of the world's best practice model.

The flame relay as inter-cultural communication

The global pro-Tibet people's protests in 2008, of which Delhi formed only a part, were a product of geopolitics as they were of new communication technologies, being fuelled by the oxygen of the Internet and the power of global satellite television imagery. Back in 1964, China was relatively closed off from the pushes and pulls of international public opinion. The military clashes with the Soviets on the Ussuri River were still five years away and Kissinger's path-breaking trip to Beijing even further in the future. China remained firmly isolated from the international stage, and Tibetan protests against China during the Olympic Flame Relay in New Delhi would have received little traction. By 2008, though, the world had changed, and so had China. The high-velocity protests in 2008 were a reflection of the changed international power balance, of the new weight of international opinion against the Chinese leadership after the Tibetan suppression in the year of the Beijing Games, and of the organizing capacities of Tibetan groups. As the troubled flame left Indian shores for Bangkok and then on to Canberra, Osaka and Seoul, a stocktaking of the tumultuous events surrounding the flame in Delhi helped drive home the truth that the Olympic movement is not simply a sports movement. It is a complex vehicle that, by virtue of its global and public nature, provides a high-stakes playing field for the competitive interplay of various kinds of competing interests, agendas, and power plays. The IOC officially champions sport as a medium for inter-cultural communication and peaceful democratic exchange. It has been argued by many that the Tibetan protests were an illustration of the fact that meaning of Olympism has now expanded to embrace human rights as well. The unfolding of the Delhi protests, however point to a much more complex reading.

The imperatives of international politics and security concerns meant that Delhi was turned into an armed camp, the relay was shortened and the dialogue between competing groups was reduced to shouting over barricades. It could legitimately be argued that 'peaceful inter-cultural communication and exchange' could not happen under such circumstances. Further, if one listened closely to the Tibetan protesters, they argued that the very fact of the Games being held in Beijing constituted a backwards step for the human rights movement and a global act of solidarity with the Chinese regime. (Though the Dalai Lama himself supported the Beijing Games.) In their eyes, the Games symbolized support for repression, not human rights. Simultaneously, the IOC itself was deeply embarrassed by the worldwide protests that engulfed the Olympic torch relay, even as it talked the talk on human rights.

On balance, it seems that the moral promise of the Olympic movement is such that it cannot publicly be seen to repudiate human rights causes. Even if it compromises the marketing and political alliances that the IOC makes, it cannot allow itself to be seen to be supporting what are seen as unjust causes. This explains the acute discomfiture of the IOC when it was confronted by the Tibetan challenge. It could not publicly denounce their cause and at the same time it was placed in the unenviable task of keeping Beijing in good humour. Stung by the worldwide negative publicity, IOC President Jacques Rogge repeatedly dismissed calls for a boycott of the Beijing Games saying that it would mean 'penalizing innocent athletes and ... stopping the organization from something that definitely is worthwhile organizing'.[26] Even though the IOC insisted that it would speak to the Chinese government on human rights issues and that 'every use of violence is a step backwards',[27] it firmly stood by the idea of the Games. There was simply too much at stake for the IOC: money, organization, sport, politics. The IOC after all, since the mid-1980s, is a commercial venture as well as a social movement, sustaining itself on the successful marketing of the Olympic Games. This is why its response seemed to reflect a certain ambivalence, a tightrope performance to balance the avowed idealism of Olympism with the hard-headed practicalities of *realpolitik*. At the same time, the accessibility and the publicity around the international relay was such that it became an ideal site for legitimate protest against the denial of human rights by those involved with hosting the Olympic Games. In a sense, the relay, in real terms, became what it was always intended to be: a people's movement.

It was organized by officials, no doubt, but it was no more in their control. The flame relay became a flashpoint for the human rights movement and the Tibetan cause, *despite* the IOC. Herein lies the real success of the Olympic movement as a moral cause and one that will always be a tempting site to be used by the dispossessed of the world to their benefit.

The experience of the 2010 CWG baton relay

We conclude with an ethnographic account of the 2010 Delhi Commonwealth Games baton relay to show what happens when the sports icon to be relayed is very different from the Olympic flame, having little or no spiritual power and meaning, and therefore unable to activate the indigenous ritual forms developed for the first time with Jwalamukhi in 1960. As solely a secular prestige object, the baton would prove largely at the mercy of those seeking prestige for themselves. Having no best practices model for baton relays and no transnational supervisory body available to discipline the organizers, the result was largely a farce.

The Queen's Baton relay originated at the 1958 British Empire and Commonwealth Games at Cardiff. This multinational, multi-sport festival only changed its name to the Commonwealth Games at Edmonton in 1978. The baton relay was a frank emulation of the Olympic Flame Relay. It attempted to forge a symbolic unity among commonwealth nations in the period of decolonization, when the very existence of the Commonwealth Games was being debated. Hence, the significance of the iconic object, the Queen's baton, was politico-cultural and highly ambiguous from the very beginning, and remains so today. Until 1994, the baton relay was restricted to England and the host nation. Malaysia, the first Islamic state to host the Games, broke this tradition in 1998, hosting a wider international relay. The baton relay for the Delhi CWG of 2010 began at Buckingham Palace, where the Queen handed the baton to Indian President Pratibha Devisingh Patil. The baton reached India on 25 June 2010 after covering a distance of 170,000 kilometres, having travelled through all of the Commonwealth member countries across the world.

The baton was received with much fanfare at the Wagah border, the contentious boundary separating India and Pakistan at India's north-western frontier. Soon after, it embarked on its 25,000 kilometre journey across India to reach Delhi on 30 September 2010 in time for the opening ceremony on 3 October. While the CWG organizers made much of the fact that it was the longest baton relay in Games history and had touched all the 71 participating countries/commonwealth principalities, their neglect of the symbolic dignity of the baton resulted in serious questions being asked of their understanding of the significance of the relay. We were fortunate to be asked to carry the baton in Kolkata when it reached Eastern India's biggest metropolis on 1 August 2010. In hindsight, however, we regret the decision to be baton bearers. It ended up being a farce, and certainly not an act to remember and cherish.

The arrival of the baton: 1:00 pm at Salt Lake on 1 August 2010

The day before the baton reached Kolkata we were called by a senior member of the Organizing Committee and were asked to reach a destination at Salt Lake in north Kolkata by lunchtime. The group carrying the baton was led by Colonel Banstu of the Indian Army, we were told. The group would meet us at 1:00 pm and we would proceed together to Victoria Memorial, the venue for the relay. As advised we were at our destination by 12.30 pm waiting for the entourage.

It was at Salt Lake that we encountered our first shock of the day. At approximately 1:00 pm, we received a telephone call from a frantic Colonel Banstu asking for directions to the meeting point. Only after we had spoken to him did we realize that the IOA had not arranged for a pick up at the airport, despite knowing full well that Colonel Bantsu's group were carrying the CWG baton with them. When they finally did reach the meeting point at Salt Lake, the five-member team appeared exhausted, hungry and frustrated from the morning ordeal. To make matters worse there was no lunch for anyone, though the Bengal Chapter of the IOA had been advised to arrange for food.

As natives of Kolkata, we thought it best to take the delegation to a nearby restaurant for a quick buffet lunch, a hasty affair as little time remained before the start of the relay. Having grabbed a bite, we started for Victoria Memorial, the site of the day's festivities.

En route to the venue, it was time for the second shock of the day. A huge security presence stopped us in front of Birla Planetarium, some 200 metres from Victoria Memorial, declaring rather tersely that all roads to the venue had been sealed off to ensure smooth conduct of the baton relay. Despite Colonel Banstu's fervent pleas explaining that the relay could not start without him for he was the one in possession of the baton, the security personnel in charge remained unmoved.

Here's a transcript of the conversation:

Colonel Banstu: Inspector I need to get there immediately for without me there is no relay. I have the baton with me and have been taking it all round the country.

Inspector: I can't allow you to go through this checkpoint for I have instructions from my seniors that no one should be allowed.

Colonel Banstu: May I then please speak to your superiors and explain the situation and the importance of me getting there for as I said without me there is no relay!

Inspector: All my superiors are busy at Victoria and it impossible for me to connect to them at this point.

An exasperated Colonel Banstu next called one of the senior members of the Organizing Committee and explained in detail his rather sorry plight. We, on our part, called the Kolkata police chief, a close friend and one who is much respected all over the state. Within minutes, Gautam Chakraborty, Police Commissioner of Kolkata, had arrived at Birla planetarium to escort us all to Victoria Memorial. A spate of apologies followed from his juniors and it seemed for the time being that our troubles were finally over.

Running with the baton

At the Victoria Memorial, a sea of humanity was dressed up in Games t-shirts and dancing to the music being played from a loudspeaker. Cultural performances by the state's leading musicians were on, and the temporary stage set up in front of one of Kolkata's biggest tourist attractions was a site of frenzied activity. On seeing the Games baton the frenzy reached fever pitch. There was an unseemly scramble among the local politicians, administrators and others present to hold the baton, and Colonel Banstu and his team were soon pushed to the side. Some volunteers, embarrassed at these scenes, came up to us and suggested that we board a bus reserved for baton bearers. The plan, they told us, was that the bus would drop us at 200-metre intervals and that once we had finished our drill, we would board another pick up bus stationed behind. Since this echoed today's standard practice in Olympic Flame Relays, it appeared sensible to begin with.

Just as we were boarding the bus, we heard a chorus of voices coming from close to the stage at Victoria Memorial. On enquiring what had happened, we were told that Saurav Ganguly, former Indian cricket captain and Bengal's biggest sporting icon, had been pushed by someone and the baton had been snatched from him. The charade had started again.

Saurav, the first baton bearer for the day, had not even carried it for 10 metres.[28] He soon left the venue trying to avoid further controversy. In the bus were some 30 baton bearers, with no one having a clear idea on what the final plan was. The two volunteers directing the bus driver were clueless as well. From our seats in the bus, we could see the baton being carried around amidst much confusion and were left wondering when, if ever, our turn would come. When the bus finally reached Eden Gardens, 3 kilometres from Victoria Memorial, we decided to get off and to try to take our turns. It was our own decision to get off, because we had realized by then that there was no plan in place. When the flame reached Eden Gardens, guarded by 50 or so security personnel, we decided on entering the inner cordon to take our turns as baton bearers. After some initial resistance, the security guards being unsure if we were actually baton bearers, we were allowed into the inner cordon.

Running with the baton was fascinating. The symbolism that MacAloon talks about was finally a reality for us.[29] The very realization that the baton had travelled 180,000 kilometres before coming to Kolkata made us feel part of a privileged few. This feeling, however, was short-lived as we were soon pushed aside and the baton was snatched away from us by the security guards to be handed over to the many other baton bearers waiting in the wings. There was no orderly handover, no process of moving the baton from one bearer to another or no pre-determined order of bearers. Many, it was later revealed to us, had not even managed to touch the baton in the course of the relay.

'Don't worry, you can run again': an ordeal of apathy

After our stints as baton bearers had ended prematurely, we could do little but wait for the designated bus to get back to Victoria Memorial. Our vehicle was parked there and we needed to get back to the point of origin to make our way home. It was soon evident to us that there was no bus coming to pick us up. Either it had already gone past or had been re-routed. And with all roads sealed off for the relay, the only way we could go back to Victoria was walk back the 3-kilometre stretch in the sweltering Kolkata heat. With no options left we walked back to the parking bay to conclude what had been a rather bizarre day.

Smarting under the experience and frustrated with the mismanagement we decided to call Suresh Kalmadi, the Chairman of the 2010 CWG Organizing Committee to report our ordeal. Kalmadi, now in jail for alleged mismanagement of Games funds, seemed unperturbed after hearing the whole story. What to us was an unacceptable farce, a complete subversion of the world's best practices model, appeared routine for him. This is what he had to say, *'Achha aisa hua hai. Koi problem nahi. Delhi mein fir se bhag lena'* (Is this what happened? Don't worry for you can once again run with the torch once it reaches Delhi).[30]

That the Kolkata leg was not an aberration was borne out by the events in Lucknow on 15 July 2010. On this occasion there was much confusion based on a rumour that the Games baton had gone missing. This is how the event was reported in the *Times of India*. It was only a prototype, but officials thought that the original CWG baton had been hijacked. Because of the confusion, the celebrations organized by the Lucknow administration to welcome the Queen's baton ended with an avoidable controversy. The prototype baton was taken to the office-cum-residence (Sahara Shaher) of Subrata Roy Sahara on Saturday morning when the relay baton was on its way to Rae Bareli from the KD Singh Babu Stadium at 9:30 am. As five cars out of a cavalcade of 30 went off the planned route, an impression was created that the original baton had been hijacked. The vehicles were trailed by a group of additional district magistrates (ADMs) and intercepted. Two women and a man — identified as head of Queen's Baton Relay Lt. General (Retd.) Raj Kadyan, project officer Shruti Menon, and advisor and convenor Alka Lamba — were questioned by the ADMs who asked them where they were going and why. 'Without answering the questions, they all got down from the official car and shifted to a private vehicle and reached Sahara Shaher where a programme was organised to mark the occasion', claimed an ADM. 'Simultaneously, the status of the original baton was also checked. Since we found that the original one was in place, we let the cavalcade go', he said. District magistrate Anil Sagar in particular was fuming over the 'dramatic course of events' that created the misimpression that the original baton was 'hijacked'. Though DM and DIG Rajeev Krishna initially contemplated legal action against representatives from the Commonwealth Games Federation, the idea was dropped after written apologies from three CWG officials. The Lucknow fiasco had failed to create a stir among the organizers, and Kalmadi later laughed off the debacle saying 'these things happen when you have to cover a distance of 180,000 kilometres. Don't make a mountain of a molehill'.[31]

Kalmadi's reaction had summed it up well. It was once again evident to us that CWG 2010 belonged to the Organizing Committee and the Government of India and not to the Indian people at large. It was evident why little was done to give Delhites the feeling that it was their event and that it was being organized to benefit them in the long run. While Delhi inhabitants did not raise the slogan, 'We want bread not circuses', raised by Toronto's citizens in the 1990s and one which had derailed the city's Olympic bid in 1996, the average Delhite, smarting under the impact of the entire city being turned upside down, was opposed to the biggest event in India's sporting history. Ethnography around Kolkata and the state of West Bengal in the aftermath of the baton relay helped demonstrate that the ordinary taxpayer on the street, whose money was being used to fund the Games, was in the dark about most things pertaining to the event. Most did not even know that the games baton was coming to Kolkata on 1 August. For the average Kolkatan, the baton relay and also the Games spectacle were an exercise in opulence with little or no benefit in the long term. Most believed that the sports facilities created for the Games were destined to be white elephants, never to be within the reach of ordinary citizens.

The baton relay experience made it obvious to us that there remained a sizeable section of India that had chosen to remain beyond the realm of the Games, for whom the Commonwealth Games did not signify much more than opulent spending with little tangible gain in the long run. For slum dwellers in Kolkata or Kerala, people ravaged by incessant cyclones along the Andhra coast or the thousands who were forcibly resettled owing to the construction of the Games village, the torch relay amounted to an unwarranted spend. As Ashis Nandy argued:

> Anybody who spent a few weeks in Delhi before the Games would have known that there was another India which was rebelling against the version of the official India, the ultra modern India being hammered home by the government. The slums of Delhi for example were in a different kind of dialogue with the mainstream discourse on the Commonwealth Games.[32]

For Nandy, the contradiction between the official rhetoric on India championed by the government and the 'dissent' that was so easily noticeable in the slums of Delhi was too obvious to not to be taken note of by global commentators and policy makers interested in studying the legacy of the Games. Such comments gained in strength as the clock ticked on, once again drawing attention to the issue of sustainable legacy of the games.

Conclusion

Thus, as demonstrated by the farce of the 2010 CWG baton relay, contempt for ritual – or as John MacAloon puts it, the slide of ritual into spectacle – is associated with public doubts about the entire sports festival project. Beginning with Jawalamukhi in 1960, a rich indigenous tradition for relaying the icons of mega sporting events was developed in India. In 1964 and again in 2004, that tradition was more or less successfully hybridized with the international flame relay 'best practices' of the respective eras. In 2008, geopolitical and Indian diplomatic circumstances drove the practices and expressive styles of Jawalamukhi out of the Olympic Flame Relay in Delhi, but they reappeared in full force in the procession and celebration of the Tibetan counter-flame. The Queen's baton is manifestly not the Olympic flame, but the effect of the actions of the 2010 CWG organizers was to cut India off entirely from its own half-century of built tradition. With the IOC having banned international flame relays in response to Beijing 2008,[33] and the project of a future Delhi Olympic Games placed on hold by the scandals and ineptitudes surrounding the 2010 CWGs, it is not clear when, if ever, that India will get another chance to reconnect.

Notes

[1] Butalia, 'Jwalamukhi: The Olympia of India'.
[2] Ibid., 36–7.
[3] Ibid., 38.
[4] Ibid.
[5] Datta, 'Keep Politics Away From Sports: Protests, Boycotts Only Affect the Athletes'. *The Times of India* [New Delhi], April 16, 2008.
[6] See MacAloon, 'Introduction' and 'Flame Relay Operations under a "World's Best Practices" Regime', in this volume.
[7] See Amelidou, 'The 2004 International Relay', in this volume.
[8] Interview with Virender Sehwag on the flame relay, 20 June 2004.
[9] Ibid.
[10] All of these letters were published in *The Hindu*, 14 June 2004.
[11] P.T. Usha, 'the Queen of Indian athletics', won five gold medals in a single Asian Track and Field Championships (1985), was five times named best woman Asian Athlete of the Year, and won the top female athlete award at the 1986 Seoul Asian Games.
[12] For details, see http://www.rediff.com/sports/2004/jun/10usha.htm (accessed September 11, 2011).
[13] Ibid. The Arjuna Award is India's top honor in Olympic-style sport. Cricket is not, of course, an Olympic sport though it today reigns supreme in Indian sporting and popular culture. On the place of Olympic sport in the overall Indian 'space of sports', see Majumdar and Mehta, *India and the Olympics*.
[14] Thakur, 'Tibetan Protests Banned in Arunachal', *The Times of India* [New Delhi], April 16, 2008.
[15] The protest ban in Arunachal and the heavy security was scathingly critiqued as a sign of Indian weakness before Beijing by many media publications. See, for instance, Anonymous, 'Torching the Lines', *The Indian Express* [New Delhi], April 18, 2008.
[16] Ibid.
[17] 'Foolproof Security for the Torch Relay', *The Hindu* [New Delhi], April 16, 2008.
[18] This advisory was issued by UN security officers on 11 April 2008.
[19] *Times Now* is India's most popular 24-hour English news channel. It is owned by Bennett and Coleman company which also runs *The Times of India*.
[20] Personal interview at Rajghat on 17 April 2008.
[21] Interview with Pasang Tsering, Tibetan protestor, New Delhi, 18 April 2008.
[22] Dhondup, Dorji, Vice President, Tibetan Youth Congress, 'Torch of Protest', *Times Now*, special broadcast, 17 April 2008.
[23] Ibid.
[24] For further ethnographic details of the day, see Majumdar and Mehta, *India and the Olympics*, 306–14.
[25] Anusuya Mathur, report on NDTV 24x7, broadcast on 17 April 2008.
[26] Jacque Rogges quoted in Associated Press (AP), 'IOC: Don't Boycott Olympic Over Tibet'. 15 March 2008. http://www.breitbart.com/article.php?id=D8VE054O1&show_article=1 (accessed March 31, 2009].

[27] IOC Vice President Thomas Bach quoted in Associated Press (AP), 'IOC: Don't Boycott Olympic Over Tibet'. 15 March 2008. http://www.breitbart.com/article.php?id=D8VE054O1&show_article=1 (accessed March 31, 2009].

[28] Saurav Ganguly later confirmed this to us in a personal interview on 4 May 2011.

[29] See MacAloon, 'Introduction', this volume.

[30] Telephone conversation with Suresh Kalmadi, then Chairman, Delhi 2010 Organising Committee, on the evening of 1 August 2010.

[31] Interview with Suresh Kalmadi, then Chairman, Delhi 2010 Organising Committee, 13 August 2010.

[32] http://www.bbc.co.uk/iplayer/episode/p007qdkn/The_Monday_Documentary_Soft_Power_India/ (accessed June 3, 2010).

[33] See MacAloon, 'Introduction', this volume.

References

Butalia, J. 'Jwalamukhi: The Olympia of India'. *Indian Olympic Association Official Bulletin* 2 January–March (1960).

Majumdar, Boria, and Nalin Mehta. *India and the Olympics*. London: Routledge, 2009.

Index

Page numbers in **bold** type refer to figures
Page numbers followed by 'n' refer to notes

Leisure Studies Journals from Routledge

Visit the journal homepages to:
- Read a free online sample copy
- Learn more about the journal and how to submit your paper
- Register for Table of Contents Alerts

Leisure Sciences
www.tandfonline.com/ulsc

Leisure Studies
www.tandfonline.com/rlst

World Leisure Journal
www.tandfonline.com/rwle

Leisure/Loisir
www.tandfonline.com/rloi

Annals of Leisure Research
www.tandfonline.com/ranz

Managing Leisure
www.tandfonline.com/rmle

 www.facebook.com
/tandfsport

 @tandfsport

 Routledge
Taylor & Francis Group